W9-ABI-527

U.S. NATIONAL SECURITY

A Reference Handbook

Other Titles in ABC-CLIO's
CONTEMPORARY
WORLD ISSUES
Series

Books in the Contemporary World Issues series address vital issues in today's society such as genetic engineering, pollution, and biodiversity. Written by professional writers, scholars, and nonacademic experts, these books are authoritative, clearly written, up-to-date, and objective. They provide a good starting point for research by high school and college students, scholars, and general readers as well as by legislators, businesspeople, activists, and others.

Each book, carefully organized and easy to use, contains an overview of the subject, a detailed chronology, biographical sketches, facts and data and/or documents and other primary-source material, a directory of organizations and agencies, annotated lists of print and nonprint resources, and an index.

Readers of books in the Contemporary World Issues series will find the information they need in order to have a better understanding of the social, political, environmental, and economic issues facing the world today.

U.S. NATIONAL SECURITY

A Reference Handbook

WITHDRAWN
L. R. COLLEGE LIBRARY

Cynthia A. Watson

**CONTEMPORARY
WORLD ISSUES**

ABC-CLIO

Santa Barbara, California
Denver, Colorado
Oxford, England

Library of Congress Cataloging-in-Publication Data

Watson, Cynthia Ann.
  U.S. national security : a reference handbook / Cynthia A. Watson.
     p. cm.—(Contemporary world issues)
  Includes index.
  ISBN 1-57607-598-2 (hardcover : alk. paper); 1-57606-609-1
(e-book)
1. National security--United States. 2. United States--Military
policy. 3. World politics--1945- . 4. United States--Foreign
relations--1945-1989. 5. United States--Foreign relations--1989- I.
Title. II. Series
  UA23 .W36397 2002
  355'.033073—dc21

                                                              2002006366

08 07 06 05 04 03 02 10 9 8 7 6 5 4 3 2 1

This book is also available on the World Wide Web as an e-book.
Visit abc-clio.com for details.

ABC-CLIO, Inc.
130 Cremona Drive, P.O. Box 1911
Santa Barbara, California 93116-1911

This book is printed on acid-free paper ∞.

Manufactured in the United States of America

"To scream and not be heard, yet whisper and stun the world"

To Bonnie and Scott

Contents

ix

Preface

The concept* of U.S. national security has grown to encompass far more than simple territorial integrity, although the relative isolation of the United States is always a component in the national security calculation. Traditionally, the United States has never had to fear the type of aggression that has characterized Poland's history, for example. Two oceans separate the nation from much of the world except two relatively peaceful neighbors. Canada is a relatively similar socioeconomic state constituted from an ethnic and historical mix similar to our own. Although Mexico has had a different and sometimes frustrating historical, political, and economic experience, it has not posed a serious military threat to the United States since the Mexican War in 1846. Indeed, the United States probably represents the larger threat, as Mexicans sometimes note that their country lost fully half of its national territory in the mid–nineteenth century to the northern colossus. Today, the U.S. economy and society are closely tied to those of Mexico.

The geographical imperative of relative isolation has given the United States the luxury of physical security, which cannot be forgotten in examining our foreign affairs. However, during the twentieth century and particularly during the last fifty years, successive presidents of both parties have been concerned not only with the physical security of the territorial United States but also with the security of U.S. citizens living or working overseas and the sanctity of U.S. industries operating in an increasingly globalized world. Americans have expanded the definition of national security as the U.S. role in the world has changed. With international trade an increasing goal for the United States and the

---

*The views expressed in this volume are entirely personal and do not represent those of any agency of the U.S. government.

importation of cheap products an ever-growing trend, U.S. interests outside national boundaries will continue to develop, and
hence the ability to provide security for those interests will
become more important as time goes on.

While I was completing this book, the luxury of relative isolation collapsed with the twin towers of the World Trade Center
in New York and several corridors of the west wing of the Pentagon, the result of an unprecedented terrorist attack. National
security has evolved dramatically over the course of the past half
century; it has now taken on a renewed sense of urgency at home.
Other parts of the world have long suffered the vagaries and
unpredictable nature of zealots aiming to disrupt daily life, but the
United States did not believe it would be subjected to such irra-
tional actions: The terrible death of thousands of average citizens
on their way to work or flying across the country proved how
erroneously we had viewed the world and our own security.

This volume examines U.S. national security, looking not just
at specific events but at the reasons behind those events. It is
intended to be a starting point for study rather than to lay out a
comprehensive theory or to provide an exhaustive history. I hope
this book helps readers to begin considering, debating, and
studying national security so that we may finally have a genuine
national debate rather than merely taking our security and our
ability to defend ourselves, at a relatively low cost, for granted.
For many reasons, those days are gone.

One note on names throughout this volume. I have used
more formal names than many other sources, particularly in the
chapter on personalities; hence Fidel Castro Ruz is used rather
than Fidel Castro, for example. This is to be more inclusive, rather
than less so. Additionally, I have tried to use the pinyin versions
of Chinese names, although the documents, in chapter 5, often
use the old Wade-Giles system and cannot be altered for copyright reasons.

Many people have supported me throughout the preparation
of this volume. At the risk of disappointing some, I will mention
only a few in detail. Mildred "Mim" Vasan, long my friend and
editor, remembered me for this book, having been involved in
two of my earlier projects. Alicia Merritt and the staff at ABC-
CLIO, along with Deborah Lynes and Patricia Heinicke Jr., have
been just terrific, helping me identify what specialists need to
explain to nonspecialists for this book. Dr. Carla Klausner is only
beginning to understand what a profound role model she has

been in so many aspects of my life. The only female professor in my history department when I was an undergraduate, she proved to me that a professional woman can be elegant, funny, engaging, challenging, and supportive. Dr. Sharon Murphy of Nazareth College has earned the epithet of true friend, colleague, and critic in the more than two decades since that initial Sunday afternoon in Notre Dame's O'Shaughnessy Hall with a congressman and a Wall Street lawyer. Mary Clyde Bettge is both an inspiration and a gentle support. Scott and Bonnie Nordstrom have proven to be stronger, more patient, and more resilient than I could ever have hoped: I hope they do not settle for the path of least resistance and always remember to believe in themselves.

Jeanette Tolbert and Yvette Taylor of the National Defense University headquarters staff are always helpful and smiling. Carolyn Turner, Alta Linthicum, and Bruce Thornlow, who make our library the most delightful and easiest to use in the world, were extremely helpful in chasing down those final resources. It's no wonder the NDU Library was named the Best Federal Library in 2001.

I want to note the privilege of working at the National War College. A largely unheralded institution, the War College is full of dedicated educators who do not allow self-promotion to outweigh overall learning objectives for the students in the classroom. With its blend of uniformed officers, senior agency specialists, and experts hired directly from the scholarly community, the National War College is a unique place, and the taxpayer ought to be proud of this shining example of public service on an issue that matters day and night, national security strategy.

Over the years, John "Cip" Cipparone, Jack "Jacko" Glasgow, and Mark Pizzo instilled in me an incredible respect for the Marine Corps, while naval aviators Tom Kilcline and Wild Bill Tyson made me appreciate why the car pool rules prohibit two pilots from sitting in the front seat of the car—too much talking with their hands. Dan Gaske was a tremendous economics colleague. George Murphy's steadiness is striking; nothing rattles him and I respect him tremendously. I am awed to work with Marvin Ott and Paul Godwin because of their incredible knowledge of Asia and security issues. Dick Melanson directed me to some very useful references, and Bruce Gregory helped me with Web resources. Janet Ballantyne, Lani Kass, Moshe Goodman, and Carole Palma reminded me to keep a balanced perspective in all things. Bud Cole's support was and remains, as always, invaluable and irreplaceable.

1

Introduction

After fighting the hard battles of World War II on the fields of France and Germany and in the southwest Pacific, the United States waged an enduring ideological battle against its former ally, the Soviet Union (1947–1989). After this prolonged period of actual and ideological conflict, the transition to a post–Cold War environment was expected to be simple and much cheaper. We know now that this is not the case; indeed, the period since the fall of the Soviet Union has been far *more* complicated in many ways, culminating with the tragic events in the United States on September 11, 2001.

The changes in U.S. national security concerns since 1989 have been truly breathtaking. Indeed, a distinct shift in focus was symbolized by several events that year: the fall of the Berlin Wall in Germany, China's slaughter of its own people in Tiananmen Square, and the Gorbachev government's decision to stop reinforcing the East German government and to acknowledge the failure of the Communist state. The end of the Cold War has had tremendous immediate, medium-range, and long-term effects on U.S. national security. This volume will consider those changes for readers who are seeking to understand how national security policy is made. One must grasp the security concerns that existed during the Cold War, generally considered to be 1947 through 1989, in order to recognize the changes that have occurred since 1989. Thus chapters 1 and 2 of this book will discuss both the Cold War and the post–Cold War decade, briefly identifying the changing threats to national security and introducing the agencies and individuals that shape national security policy. Chapters 3 through 7 provide more detail on the events, the people, and the policies in modern U.S. national security history, including key documents that have expressed U.S. policy, some of the organizations concerned with national security, and resources for further research.

What Is National Security?

Crucial to our understanding of national security today is its definition. For the purposes of this book, former Secretary of Defense Harold Brown's definition of national security seems most basic: "National security, then, is the ability to preserve the nation's physical integrity and territory; to maintain its economic relations with the rest of the world on reasonable terms; to protect its nature, institutions, and governance from disruption from outside; and to control its borders."[1] But a few words about the specifics of this definition are in order because they change over time.

Clearly, national defense is the most basic ingredient of national security. The Constitution requires the national government to defend the country through a militia, an army, and a navy. But throughout U.S. history, our national security concerns and strategies have changed, influenced by a myriad of circumstances, both at home and abroad. Each generation of leaders has had to ask: What is the government's responsibility for maintaining the national security? What does this entail? Who is involved? How is it achieved? How is its success measured?

For example, the definition is arguably broader today than it was at the beginning of the new millennium. For those who will always recall where they were on the morning of September 11, 2001, the outlandish, remote idea that the United States could be attacked by outsiders seeking to injure the national psyche was suddenly no longer distant, infeasible, or unthinkable. National security had come to include protection of our homes and offices as it never had before.

However, the height of our current concern for homeland security has not been a constant in the definition of U.S. security. The United States has had almost unparalleled geographic isolation from the threats of the world, back to the founding of the Republic. Two hundred twenty years ago foreign threats were the basic danger to the United States—the fear that Britain would attempt to retake its former territory. The threats have, of course, changed since then. During the nineteenth century, the United States was never seriously challenged (after the War of 1812) by any outside state having the ability to take over the country, and the nation focused not on securing what we had but on expanding our reach. During the period of Manifest Destiny, we spent our energies on expansion.

In the nineteenth and early twentieth centuries, arguments about the scope of national security frequently revolved around whether the United States was responsible for its citizens overseas. Moves to enforce U.S. law against foreigners infringing on the rights of our citizens in other countries generated some debate about respect for the legal systems of other countries, but public support generally favored extending U.S. law to protect U.S. citizens. For example, in the Caribbean in the initial years of the twentieth century, the United States frequently invoked its law, even over international law or the laws of other nations, to promote the defense and security of its citizens. The idea that "sending in the Marines" was more appropriate than going through legal channels exemplified the steadfast U.S. belief in the primacy of national security, regardless of law. Although perfectly understandable from the U.S. perspective, such actions evoked considerable distrust and anger abroad, where many felt the United States was arbitrary and pernicious in its definition of national security and its methods for protecting it.

It was in the twentieth century that the United States first believed another state had the potential to control our destiny. What we really feared was not that another state would physically conquer the national territory stretching from Canada to Mexico or from the Pacific to the Atlantic coasts; the country was too big for that. Instead the concern was that another state might control our ability to make our own choices and our own decisions about the economy, the political system, social standards, and religious and other freedoms.

The effect of this shift in national security focus is that for the better part of a century, particularly with the war against Hitler's Nazi state and even more so with the Cold War against Soviet Marxist-Leninist ideology, the United States defined national security not only as the defense of U.S. territorial integrity but also as the defense of our ability to choose our economic system, our political path, our religious orientations, and other personal freedoms, all described in the phrase "the American way of life." Even though the Soviet Union had the military might to annihilate many urban areas of the United States, our main concern during the Cold War was actually that we might be subjected to a political and ideological system that would suppress the exuberance and individual decision-making freedom of U.S. citizens. We took for granted, in fact, that the conflict would occur elsewhere (such as the plains of Central Europe or the lands of Asia) rather than in the U.S. homeland.

Gradually, the definition of national security became less coherent and more debatable. Beginning in the late-1960s, challenges to the economic and social consensus of the immediate post–World War II period gave rise to decidedly different views of what constitutes security, forged in the national debate about Vietnam. Toward the end of the Vietnam War, more people began to question the primacy of Cold War concerns, especially as details about a number of Cold War strategies became public knowledge. The public did not entirely support all U.S. actions during the Cold War, some of which were seen as short-term solutions that actually hurt U.S. interests in the long run. Examples of such actions include not only continuing U.S. involvement in Vietnam but CIA support for coups that overthrew governments in Iran (under Muhammad Mossadegh) and Guatemala (under Jacobo Arbenz Guzmán) and CIA and FBI involvement in domestic spying against U.S. citizens. The airing of these issues led many to question whether national security was being used to justify activities actually disruptive of domestic security. The debate thus sought to expand the definition of national security to include things like respect for human rights and healthy social and economic conditions.[2]

Today, the definition of national security in the United States has expanded again, as we recognize that conflict can occur on U.S. soil. The events of September 2001 illustrate that in a world of increasingly open commercial, transportation, and communication links, the centers of U.S. power and cultural life here at home can be hit and affected by outside forces bent upon our destruction. We do not yet know for certain the magnitude or endurance of the changes to national security resulting from September 11, but the potential does exist for considerable change in the national priorities and in the balance between civil rights and defense. At the same time, the United States is also asking whether threats to our way of life might not include other things as well, such as environmental destruction, which may have long-term effects on our ability to prosper as a society,

HIV/AIDS, and drug trafficking—none of which would have mattered to the national security strategist three decades ago.

The Old Days: Cold War, 1947–1989

At the end of World War II, victors and vanquished were easily identifiable. The United States was allied with Great Britain, France, China, the Soviet Union, and many other nations. Their main adversaries, Germany, Italy, and Japan, had been defeated. The Soviet Union had yet to recover from the terrible destruction of the war, including the death of as many as 20 million people, many of them innocent civilians who starved. Colonial transitions to independence were still in progress; Latin America was independent, but most of the Middle East, Asia, and Africa was still under colonial domination. The end of the terrible conflict, which had cost up to 40 million lives, was expected to bring world peace.

But significant changes in the global environment soon became clear—changes that drove the international community into a different, more dangerous war. From 1947 until 1989, U.S. national security was largely defined and measured in terms of a single conflict: the Cold War.

The fundamental differences between the United States and the Soviet Union had been temporarily overlooked during World War II for the sake of defeating Hitler. But in fact, their approaches to economics, social structure, politics, human rights, law, and virtually every other aspect of domestic governance, along with national security and international relations, were diametrically opposed. Because their goals appeared conflictual and their systems seemed intolerant of each other, the fact that these two victors retained large standing armies in the aftermath of global conflict and possessed the world's most powerful economic structures probably made the fear of conflict unavoidable.

Historians will long argue, however, about the causes and responsibilities for the Cold War, a period of identifiable threat to U.S. national security that lasted, in varying degrees of intensity, from 1947 to 1989. It was almost never a direct fighting war between the two major protagonists, as had been true in World War II. In 1945 the United States developed a new type of weapon, the atomic bomb, which the Soviet Union obtained four years later. Nuclear weapons elevated war to a deadlier level and deterred leaders in either state from launching the direct assault on the adversary that would have been expected in earlier conflicts. Instead, these two different social/economic/political/legal systems fought a long series of ideological battles, accompanied by periodic shooting wars between surrogate states.

For the United States, the Cold War began with concerns about a large standing army in the hands of a dictator who supported global expansionism aimed at extinguishing competing ways of life. The most prominent clarion call was issued by a young Foreign Service officer, George Kennan, in two documents written in the years immediately following World War II. In his "Long Telegram" from Moscow in 1946, Kennan wrote an exceptional analysis of the differences between the Soviet and Western systems. He believed that the Soviet Union would eventually collapse under its own weight. A year later, as the international affairs advisor at the newly formed National War College in Washington, DC, Kennan penned another article on the topic. The so-called Mr. X article in *Foreign Affairs,* entitled "The Sources of Soviet Conduct," was seized upon as a call to "contain" Soviet expansionism. Although Kennan has argued for decades that his prescription was misunderstood, this article, along with the Truman administration's 1950 decision to build up the national security apparatus (advocated in a report known as NSC 68), became the primary justification for the development of the world's most sophisticated military machine between 1948 and 1989.

Throughout this period, national security threats were generally defined as external to the United States rather than of domestic political or economic origin. The enemy was isolated to the Soviet Union and its surrogates, and the method of ending the conflict seemed easy to identify, understand, and measure—the United States had simply to defeat the Soviet ideology and military machine.

New Threats since 1989

The Soviet hold on Eastern Europe ended in November 1989, and the USSR itself dissolved just over two years later on December 31, 1991, when the Soviet flag was lowered for the last time. The threat that had terrified generations was ended. Yet the free, less-militarized world anticipated by most did not appear after 1989.

The United States soon recognized a new set of threats to its national security, both external and internal.

Even before Russia and the Commonwealth of Independent States succeeded the Soviet Union, the United States led a war against Saddam Hussein's Iraq, which had seized Kuwait and threatened petroleum-rich Saudi Arabia. The "peace dividend" so eagerly anticipated with the end of the Cold War was spent in a major effort in the Middle East, including a long-term commitment to maintaining a no-fly zone over Iraq and an apparently perpetual U.S. presence in the region.

As an enemy, Iraq is different than the Soviet Union; its conflict with the United States is not based on ideology. Indeed, Saddam Hussein is a dictator without any firm ideology except maintaining power. He does not seem to care what the rest of the world thinks or does, as long as he remains in power. Still in control in early 2002, he has been able to outlast at least two U.S. presidents and remains a frustrating challenge for the United States.

Further into the 1990s, the threat of genocide re-emerged as new adversaries, many of whom had long been considered countries that could be ignored, threatened the world order in ways completely unanticipated during the Cold War. Genocidal violence—a phenomenon generally thought eliminated by the superpower competition and international restraint that followed World War II—required the presence of military forces from the United States and other nations to impose or restore peace in highly emotional, bloody situations such as Rwanda, where in 1994 hundreds of thousands were killed in sectarian violence.

Additionally, new technologies produced new threats. As the new millennium dawned, the most important national security debate in the United States focused on ballistic missile defense (BMD). Introduced by the Reagan administration in 1983, BMD strove to banish war to space, rather than threatening the earth's surface. However, new technologies also allow "cyberwar," biological and chemical weapons, "smart" bombs, and other "improvements" in the art of warfare. Indeed, one of the major debates within the national-security community both in the United States and abroad revolves around whether the world is undergoing a "revolution in military affairs" (known as RMA), resulting from fundamental, enduring transformations in the art of war.

Another security factor introduced by the new technologies is the sheer volume of information that inundates the average citizen, much less the national security intelligence specialist. E-mail is an increasingly common form of communication in offices pursuing "paperless" and theoretically cheaper bureaucracy, and the World Wide Web is a seemingly endless source of information, with no way to ensure its accuracy. Unfortunately, the proliferation of material relevant to national security must be evaluated, catalogued, and prioritized. The Web also presents a new target to those who may wish harm to the United States, as recent concerns about viruses and hackers have shown.

Among other new threats is one that has not been regarded as a significant issue in the traditional national security field: the spread of the virus that causes the acquired immunodeficiency syndrome (AIDS), now most critically in Africa but in other parts of the world as well. AIDS is a blood-borne disease and can threaten the armed forces of any country. Environmental destruction and drug trafficking have also been identified as threats to our national security.

Many of the new technologies can be used by rogue states or even by nonstate entities, and this makes the threat of terrorism more serious than in previous years. Terrorists can now target larger populations, as September 11 so brutally illustrated, and protecting U.S. citizens and property from foreign and domestic terror has become the federal government's primary national security focus.

The Changing National Security Apparatus

Even before September 11, the U.S. national security apparatus was the most complex in the world, and the aftermath of the terrorism and recognition of the nation's vulnerabilities have made meeting security requirements even more difficult. The primary actors in creating and implementing U.S. national security policy now include the State Department, the U.S. legislature, the Department of Defense, the Department of Justice, the FBI, the intelligence community, the Department of Energy, the Federal Emergency Management Agency, and the Office of Homeland Security. All of these are outlined in the following.

Because the United States has such well-established democratic traditions, nothing can move us; not even the fears of vulnerability to global and insidious terrorism can make us abandon the checks and balances that we both cherish and take for granted. At the same time, the various social forces that believe they deserve a voice in the formulation of national security policy are wide-ranging and often surprising. Within the field, the term "national security calculus" (or "national security calculation") is often used to describe the balance between the threats facing our country, the tools available to defend against them, the freedoms and openness required by our democracy, and the various political and social interests and other variables that may enter the decision-making process. National security decision making is not, however, a mathematical equation wherein one side equals the other in precise, even terms. It involves weighing the various elements and identifying the best-case options. Every single calculation includes victories and losses; nothing that a national security strategist does is without costs of some sort.

The Legislative Branch

The complexity of making decisions about U.S. national security involves not only many levels of analysis but many different decision makers. One important difference between the United States and many other countries is the power of the U.S. Congress. The president of the United States is the commander in chief, but Congress has the power of the purse strings and the Senate declares war and confirms or rejects presidential appointments. Thus the overall congressional task of oversight gives lawmakers a major role in computing the national security calculus.

Furthermore, any committee in either body may become involved in specific national security issues. In the House of Representatives, the committees most involved in national security are the Ways and Means Committee, which is responsible for initiating tax bills; the Armed Services Committee, which is responsible for military affairs; the International Relations Committee, which covers relations with states around the world; and the Veterans' Affairs Committee, which works to guarantee that veterans of all wars receive the national support they have earned. Senate committees include the Armed Services Committee, which is responsible for military issues, such as the procurement of hardware for military uses; the Foreign Relations Committee, which focuses on the ties between the United States and foreign states and other topics in foreign affairs; the Appropriations Committee, where spending bills are created; the Special Committee on Intelligence, which oversees the vast world of intelligence, including and especially its possible use against domestic citizens; and the Caucus on International Narcotics Control, a group of senators working to stop the spread of narcotics in the United States. Each of these committees considers substantial issues related to national security policy and proposes budgets for different national security efforts. The range of their combined oversight responsibilities illustrates the broad and varied topics that national security encompasses.

The Executive Branch

The overwhelming bulk of the U.S. national security apparatus resides in the executive branch, under the control of the U.S. president. Subject to the checks and balances of our political system, all executive branch offices must be coordinated—an often difficult task. Indeed, in national security as in almost any other area, it often appears to the outsider that the goals and actions of various branches of U.S. government are in conflict with one another.

In the executive branch, most offices concerned with national security are Cabinet-level departments, although some exist in the White House itself and others are semiautonomous organizations within the U.S. government. The National Security Council (NSC), for example, was created by the National Security Act of 1947 as a coordination mechanism by which the secretaries of state, defense, and treasury, as well as other individuals, could meet to advise the president on national security. Chaired by the president, the NSC is advised on military and intelligence matters by the chairman of the Joint Chiefs of Staff and the director of the CIA, respectively. Council staff now work out of the White House complex with the president's special advisor for national security, called the national security advisor. Being part of the president's office takes them out of the line of Senate confirmation previously required by the Constitution. Presidents believe that by putting NSC members on their personal staff, they are protecting their ability to make policy without being undermined, in any way, by congressional intervention.

The Department of State

The secretary of state is the first Cabinet officer in the order of presidential succession, thus appearing to be first among equals in the president's Cabinet. However, the Department of State is the smallest of the Cabinet-level national security offices, with a smaller budget and workforce than any other Cabinet department. As U.S. presence around the world increases, State Department resources are stretched ever further. The department faces another difficulty: it is the only Cabinet office that has no natural constituency because its work focuses on U.S. interests outside of the country.

The State Department has always contained the Foreign Service, the elite corps (these select individuals must pass rigorous tests) that handles the complex issues facing the United States outside its territory. As a result of organizational consolidations in the 1990s, now the department also includes the Arms Control and Disarmament Agency, an artifact of the Cold War responsible for monitoring and assisting the negotiations and implementation of arms treaties, and the United States Information Agency, the public diplomacy arm of the government. Also operating within the State Department is the Agency for International Development, a formerly independent agency that fosters international development through grants, education, improvements in health care, and generalized technical assistance to developing societies.

The Department of Defense

The largest single Cabinet department in the United States is the Department of Defense (DoD), created in 1949 by an amendment to the National Security Act of 1947 as a coordinating department that creates policies for the Army, the Navy, and the Air Force. Within the DoD reside the Office of the Secretary of Defense, the Joint Chiefs of Staff, the Departments of the Army, the Navy, and the Air Force, as well as various other functions. Notably missing from the long list of DoD offices is the U.S. Coast Guard, which is part of the Department of Transportation even though there is a logical connection between the activities of the Coast Guard and various defense offices.

The myriad of institutions within the DoD can be mystifying. In addition to the department's primary offices there are a variety of commands and agencies. The National Security Agency, for example, is largely responsible for signal intelligence—that involving communication signals such as radio or TV, the Internet, and so on; its employees are skilled in the sciences and languages. Among all of these various offices considerable redundancy can be found. For example, the Defense Intelligence Agency duplicates the work of the Central Intelligence Agency (an independent entity, discussed in the following) but is theoretically able to answer DoD's needs more effectively. In addition, each of the Service Departments has both uniformed officers and a civilian workforce. For example, the various branches of the Navy are commanded by the Chief of Naval Operations, who sits on the Joint Chiefs of Staff. The Secretary of the Navy, however, is a civilian, and the secretary's parallel workforce also operates within the DoD bureaucracy. These duplications and parallels benefit the system in case of an attack on the nation, but they often result in competition between the civilian and uniformed spheres.

The Department of Justice

The Department of Justice has a role in national security because of its increased role in tracking illegal immigrants and in overseeing the methods by which the federal government pursues potential terrorists. In the immediate aftermath of September 11, the Justice Department under Attorney General John Ashcroft has generated much debate in its decisions to hold noncivil tribunals for those accused of acts related to the terrorism plot and to eliminate lawyer-client privilege, both seemingly significant transformations of U.S. judicial process.

The Federal Bureau of Investigation

The Federal Bureau of Investigation (FBI) has responsibility for domestic law enforcement, including counterterrorism and counterintelligence. The Bureau has major offices in cities throughout the country and branch offices in smaller locations. Created in 1908, the FBI has long been responsible for investigating federal crimes, and has not been involved in investigating violations of state and local government statutes, which are addressed by local police and sheriff's departments. However, today's FBI has a wider jurisdiction, including investigating economic espionage, monitoring immigration illegalities, and countering terrorism on the soil of the United States, such as the events occurring in Oklahoma City in 1995 and in New York in 1993 and 2001. The range of responsibilities facing the Bureau is similar to that addressed by the Office of Homeland Security.

The Intelligence Community

The best-known organization in the U.S. intelligence field is the Central Intelligence Agency (CIA), created by the 1947 National Security Law and today an independent agency. The CIA has an analytical side and an operations side, both with a role to play in learning more about the world around us. The director of the CIA also acts as the Director of Central Intelligence (DCI), leading the thirteen organizations making up the U.S. intelligence community.

The intelligence community has grown dramatically in the past fifty-five years, and today the CIA is joined by twelve other groups concerned with intelligence: The Department of Defense has eight different intelligence organizations (the Defense Intelligence Agency, the National Security Agency, Army/Navy/Air Force/Marine Corps intelligence offices, the National Reconnaissance Office, and the National Imagery and Mapping Agency), and the FBI and the Departments of Energy, State, and Treasury each have their own intelligence activities.[3] These various intelligence organizations engage in collecting and interpreting information and overcoming any barriers erected by foreign powers and organizations to keep secret their activities, capabilities, and plans.

The Department of Energy

President Jimmy Carter created the Department of Energy in the late 1970s to deal with the conservation and consumption of energy resources. One aspect of that job is nuclear power, which is directly linked to nuclear weapons production. This role gives the Department of Energy a voice in the discussion of national security.

The Federal Emergency Management Agency

The Federal Emergency Management Agency (FEMA) is charged with helping clean up damage and provide relief from events of natural or man-made disaster, including threats to our national security. FEMA gives citizens immediate aid and longer-term help in rebuilding and taking steps to prevent further difficulties.

The Office of Homeland Security

The greatest change to the national security environment over the past decade resulted from the awareness of threats to our homeland security. Prior to the 1990s, defense in the United States was almost always related to the task of "power projection," meaning the manner by which the United States was able to affect by military force things and events far away from the United States. Power projection is a feat available to only a few countries in today's world, namely the United States, Great Britain, France, and Russia; China and India are able to project their power, but only in an area relatively close to their national territories. Power projection is often used as a measure of a state's status in the international system. By that measurement, the United States is the global leader.

Homeland security, however, was not a variable in the national security calculus until the February 1993 attack on the World Trade Center. That bombing, which killed six people and was clearly a precursor of the 2001 attack, was the first indication that terrorists were thinking about attacking U.S. national territory. Islamic militants were arrested, charged, convicted, and incarcerated for the attack, but the very fact that it occurred was enough to reorient some national security priorities in the United States. Two years later, the demolition of the Arthur P. Murrah Federal Building in Oklahoma City at the hands of a former Army enlisted man made homeland defense unavoidably important to the country.

Homeland security and the related concept, homeland defense, are hard to define. In fact, at least one group specializing in this topic, the Anser Corporation's Homeland Security Program, claims there is no definitive U.S. definition of homeland security.[4] Both concepts raise as many questions as they answer: How can democracy coexist with heightened security? Should national security concerns outweigh traditional democratic values and practices? Is homeland security a military function or a civilian one? Is homeland defense the same as national missile defense? Does it include drug interdiction and policy?

While the terms appear interchangeable, homeland defense is not quite as encompassing as homeland security. Homeland defense involves taking steps to keep aggressors out of the country but does not work to prevent their rise elsewhere. Homeland security is an aggressive, active movement to prevent any sort of terrorist activity from ever occurring in the homeland. Homeland security moves actively to build the strongest, most comprehensive network of antiterrorist policies and pursues them in a much more deliberate, calculated manner. Keep in mind that this is my own definition, one that I've developed after years of working in the field on a daily basis. Other analysts would alter the definition somewhat, to be sure, but the broad understanding is that homeland security requires defense of our territory and way of life from outside forces, through the coordination of all instruments and organizations of national power (both governmental and private).

The creation of a homeland security office was accelerated by the events of September 11, but it was already in the works before the attacks. Soon after the attacks, President George W. Bush selected former Pennsylvania Governor Thomas Ridge as the first director of homeland defense, or special assistant to the president for homeland security. The "Homeland Security Czar," as Director Ridge is often called, shares the bureaucratic difficulties that have faced the "Drug Czar" (the director of the Office of National Drug Control Policy) since that office was created in the late 1980s. Both offices received their charges by executive order of the president of the United States rather than through Congressional mandate. This difference has profound implications: although the coordinators face the presidentially directed task of bringing together a wide array of civilian and military offices in a methodical, integrated strategy to deal with their particular concerns, the offices they seek to coordinate are often not under their control. These offices are active at the local, state, and federal levels of government, and their responsibilities often overlap; as a result, the efforts of the presidentially appointed policy czars are met with resistance, as the various offices fight to protect their bureaucratic turf.

At this point former Governor Ridge's role is quite difficult to pin down, in part because the office is a presidential creation rather than a congressionally mandated department. The general mission that former Governor Ridge has in his new job is as follows: "The mission of the Office will be to develop and coordinate the implementation of a comprehensive national strategy to secure the United States from terrorist threats or attacks. The Office will coordinate the executive branch's efforts to detect, prepare for, prevent, protect against, respond to, and recover from terrorist attacks within the United States."[5] The specific tasks of this mission include detection of terrorists; preparation for the state, local, and federal response agencies to address any conditions resulting from attacks; protection against attacks; prevention of terrorist incidents wherever possible; and coordination of the complex array of agencies that would have to respond to any event that threatened homeland security.

The special assistant for homeland security also coordinates the activities of the Homeland Security Council and its presidentially appointed members: the president, the vice president, the secretaries of treasury, defense, transportation, and health and human services, the attorney general, and the directors of the FBI and CIA. Others likely to attend meetings include the special assistant for national security affairs, the director of the Office of Management and Budget, and chiefs of staff to the president and vice president. The secretaries of state, agriculture, labor, veterans' affairs, commerce, energy, and the interior may participate if invited by the president. This varied group gives some indication of the range of concerns that the Office of Homeland Security must address. Homeland security is considered so important yet is so vaguely defined that it allows virtually any Cabinet agency to participate in consultations, a level of participation that might threaten to slow the office's rate of response.

One example of this difficulty is a conflict that arose over the specific place of the office within government. Governor Ridge initially was locked in a constitutional dispute over whether he could be summoned to testify on Capitol Hill. Although the Bush administration has since changed its position, it originally argued that Ridge was a presidential appointee, not a Cabinet official, and therefore did not have to testify. The Democrats in Congress argued that he was required to appear for reasons of national confidence and for constitutional reasons. Likewise, the Republicans were somewhat lukewarm in their support of the president's position. Clearly, at this point, less than a year after its creation, it is impossible to know how successful the Office of Homeland Security will be or how difficult its challenges will be. Its mission and structure are likely to evolve.

In the aftermath of September 11, our expectations about the requirements for protecting national security have grown, but we have not yet come to a consensus about how to measure either the threat itself or our success in protecting ourselves against the threat. Many would argue that one can never overestimate the threats to the survival of a way of life. Others reject such a view as overkill, recalling that in retrospect the Soviet threat during the Cold War was perhaps exaggerated at times. Some citizens seem to view "success" in this conflict as the absence of terrorist attacks. While perhaps adequate for some, such a measure of success is certainly not adequate for others. Some citizens ask whether we want to become a militarized society and risk sacrificing our basic democratic values to win this war. Others rebut that argument with the idea that we have already gone too far in protecting the rights of some against the needs of the majority.

The final measure of success will likely be a long-term one, impossible to evaluate as the evolving system is being put into effect and as people come to grips with the nature of the threat. We cannot know quite yet how important the threat to the United States is in the current environment, but it has certainly eroded our sense of fundamental security.

In June 2002, President Bush announced his intention of elevating homeland security to Cabinet status as, among other things, a new intelligence clearinghouse. The efficacy of such will be proven over time.

Notes

1. Harold Brown, *Thinking about National Security* (Boulder: Westview, 1983), p. 4.

2. Indeed, one could define national security exclusively in economic terms. Throughout this book I will try to outline some of the linkages between our national security strategy and economics.

3. For a pie chart illustrating the relationship between these agencies, see "United States Intelligence Community," Web site of the CIA. Online. Available at: http://www.cia.gov/ic/icagen2.htm. Accessed April 2, 2002.

4. Anser specialists make this point in the syllabus for the course on national security that they teach at the National War College.

5. "President Establishes Office of Homeland Security," Mission and Management. Web site of the White House, President George W. Bush. Online. Available at: http://www.whitehouse.gov/news/releases/2001/10/20011008.html. Accessed April 2, 2002.

2

Enduring Questions in U.S. National Security

Countless questions relating to national security have arisen over the past fifty years. The end of the Cold War resolved many of them, but since then a whole new batch have appeared for consideration. These questions provide lessons for current and future policymakers, instructing them about the evolution of various U.S. national security concerns, the roots of current threats, and potential difficulties ahead.

Past Controversies

How Serious Was the Soviet Threat?

U.S. national security concerns during the Cold War focused on the Soviet Union—the direct threat it posed to the United States and the indirect threat posed by its expansionism. Perhaps the most enduring controversies about this period revolve around the true nature of the Soviet regime. From the time of the Russian Revolution, people in the United States had a variety of radically different views on the nature of the regime: some found it aggressively expansionist, bent on international domination, and others thought it was merely seeking to protect itself from outside interference. In the post–World War II period, the question shifted to Soviet involvement in Eastern Europe: Was its basic goal to subjugate the rest of the world to global Communist domination, directed by Moscow at every turn? Or, were the Russians merely acting defensively? All prior Russian regimes had been invaded by neighboring states; was the Soviet Union simply seeking to thwart similar actions during a time of marked Soviet vulnerability?

Most often ignored by U.S. analysts has been the sheer magnitude of devastation the Soviet Union withstood between 1941 and 1945. World War II was fought as total war by the United States, including economic rationing and half a million deaths in the Asian and European theaters. But the scale and universality of loss for the Soviet Union was almost incomprehensible to Americans. In the Soviet Union the conflict cost 20 million lives, civilian and military, the same number as were lost by the rest of the world's nations combined. Millions of Russians and more than a quarter of a million Germans died in the battle of Stalingrad alone. Worse still, the war exacerbated an already terrible economic condition. By 1941, Soviet industry had not yet recovered from the devastation of the Russian Revolution (1917–1922). Stalin's first Five-Year Plan for industrialization had included collectivization, which had disastrous effects on local economies. The Soviet Union that emerged from war in 1945 had a greatly weakened economy.

However, the Soviet economy was enormous, and it had enormous potential. As national security strategists are required to do, many U.S. Cold War analysts chose to operate from a "worst-case analysis" of Soviet capabilities rather than focusing on the devastation World War II and the Soviet economic model engendered. Part of the concern that led analysts to fear the massive Soviet system was Stalin's decision in the 1940s not to participate in the Marshall Plan, hence refusing to accept outside assistance for reconstruction. This decision was seen at the time as signaling Soviet determination to carry on without external support, and thus as supposed evidence of its economic strength.

Winston Churchill's March 1946 "Iron Curtain" speech at Westminster College in Fulton, Missouri (see chapter 5), voiced the West's increasing worries about Soviet aggression around the world, particularly in Eastern Europe. Both George Kennan's 1946 "Long Telegram" and his article in *Foreign Affairs*, "The Sources of Soviet Conduct," heightened alarm about Soviet expansionism. Kennan's suggestion that U.S. policy should focus on containing Soviet expansionism was based not on fear of Soviet strength but on the premise that the Soviet system was not sustainable in the long-term and would ultimately collapse under its own weight. Containment would speed this collapse, not cause it. Kennan said many times in subsequent years that he did not mean to begin an aggressive campaign but rather meant to alert the policy community to fundamental Soviet instability. However, his article did give voice to current concerns, and, directly or not, it did inspire a foreign policy intended to "contain" Soviet expansion. Later in 1947, President Harry S. Truman's declaration of U.S. intent to protect democracies under siege from Communism, augmented by the Marshall Plan to rebuild Europe, was a move to implement a form of Kennan's "containment" prescription for dealing with Stalin. By the late 1940s, the United States had defined the Soviet regime as consummately expansionist, a view buttressed by Soviet espionage and the successful Soviet atomic bomb test in 1949.

In the five decades since those events, it has been difficult for observers to recall the "open" questions that still existed about the seriousness of the Soviet threat in the late 1940s. One of these questions concerns the timing of U.S. actions vis-à-vis the 1948 creation of pro-Soviet governments in Eastern Europe (Czechoslovakia, Hungary, Poland, Bulgaria, Romania; East Germany had been under Soviet occupation since the armistice in May 1945). Were these pro-Soviet regimes evidence that Moscow was expanding its tentacles, as Churchill and others surmised, or were they reactions to the aggressive U.S. financial support to a weakened Europe, seen by the Soviets as an attempt to encircle them? The Cold War International History Project at the Woodrow Wilson Center indicates that Stalin was quite consciously expanding his territorial power. However, some still wonder whether the unswerving U.S. perception of the Soviets as a danger in effect heightened the Cold War, producing an even more serious threat.

For most in the United States at that time, the U.S. interpretation of Soviet intentions and capability was made irreversible with the promulgation of a National Security Council decision in April 1950 (NSC 68) that advocated the most negative view of the Soviet Union, including further Soviet expansionism. This decision required the United States, which had effectively demobilized its vast armed forces by that time, to reverse that trend and build up U.S. military power. The assumptions behind NSC 68 about the Soviet threat led ultimately to the creation of the U.S. hydrogen bomb in 1953, and in turn, the Soviets developed their own bomb a year later. Competition in nuclear weapons capabilities also led to the development of ICBMs (intercontinental ballistic missiles) and MIRVs (multiple independently targeted reentry vehicles) by the United States and the Soviet Union in the following decade.

Another question still remains: how did the conflict between the superpowers and the primacy of the Soviet threat in our national security calculation affect ties between the superpowers and the rest of the world, especially "second-tier" states such as Britain and France and Third World countries in Asia, Africa, and Latin America? For example, almost coincident with NSC 68 was the Korean War, lasting from 1950 through 1953. For the United States, this conflict seemed a mere diversion from Soviet activities in Europe. The United States actually moved more troops into Europe to prevent a tightening of Soviet control around Berlin or the movement of the Red Army across the Fulda Gap than it did into the Korean conflict. Korea was seen less as a conflict between the two states on the peninsula than as a conflict between two proxies for the superpowers. It was assumed that the ideological differences between the United States and Soviet Union were being played out on a global chessboard.

Similarly, other Soviet actions around the world raised the question of the ideological versus the pragmatic nature of Soviet intentions. Insurgencies in Malaya, Vietnam, the Philippines, Indonesia, Burma, and Thailand were all thought to be Kremlin-controlled conflicts rather than anticolonial protests or manifestations of the socioeconomic inequalities characterizing many former colonial states. Many in the United States automatically assumed that these small, armed groups could not have taken these steps on their own but must have been the puppets of Stalin.

Meanwhile, the United States viewed its own actions in the Cold War as pure and without ulterior motives, although they were not always seen as such elsewhere (with the Southeast Asia conflict from 1954 to 1975 and U.S. interventions in Guatemala in 1954 and in Chile in 1970–1973 offering notable cases for discussion). Indeed, much of the world believed that the United States was only marginally less dominating and self-interested in its actions than was the Soviet Union. Thus the true nature of Soviet behavior lay in the eye of the beholder. For its part, the United States did not believe Soviet actions were anything other than an assault on democracy, freedom, and the "American" way of life.

Were U.S. Actions after World War II Justified?

Less often asked in the United States than elsewhere are questions about the legitimacy of U.S. interests in the world immediately after World War II. The traditional motives given for U.S. foreign policy focused on its idealistic goals, including the promotion of prosperity and democracy for all and the belief that war is merely a temporary condition in the international community to be overcome at all costs, and this description made it unthinkable for the average U.S. citizen to assign any sinister motives to U.S. actions abroad. The rest of the world, however, along with some analysts at home (particularly during the 1970s), were far more willing to believe that the Marshall Plan, the Truman Doctrine, and other national security decisions were less altruistic and more calculated in their intent.

In the eyes of many around the world, the Marshall Plan was a vehicle by which the United States guaranteed its predominance in the post–World War II period: U.S. goods were purchased with funds the plan had sent for the reconstruction of Europe. If reconstruction led to a boom in U.S. exports needed to help in the effort, then the world was going to become more highly enmeshed in a U.S.-based economic system. In short, some wondered whether the United States invested such an astronomical amount in the redevelopment of Europe in order to perpetuate the economic benefits of U.S. dominance in the international marketplace. If Britain had been the economic driver for the nineteenth century through the expansion of its colonies, then Washington's actions in the twentieth century were equally influential and more enduring. For those who believed this interpretation, U.S. actions under the Marshall Plan were intended to prevent any independence on the part of Western Europe and Japan, leaving them instead squarely in the Bretton Woods orbit around the U.S. economy.

The Truman Doctrine, similarly, was seen by many abroad as Washington's justification for its efforts to establish regimes friendly to its interests around the world and, by extension, to oust regimes antithetical to its interests. Critics frequently cite the examples of U.S. intervention, largely under the auspices of the Central Intelligence Agency, which was supposedly dominated by big corporations run by the likes of John Foster Dulles and his brother Allen. These U.S. forces worked in Iran, for example, to prevent petroleum nationalization by ousting Prime Minister

Muhammad Mossadegh and restoring the shah, Muhammad Reza Pahlavi, in 1953, fearing that the loss of petroleum sources and "listening posts" in Iran could be fatal to the U.S. moves to curb Soviet expansionism. The issue of whether the United States ought to have reimposed the more pro-Western shah is rarely discussed in this country, but it has long been a topic for argument abroad.

The 1954 ouster of the elected president of Guatemala, Jacobo Arbenz Guzmán, to prevent his moves toward land reform remains one of the most bitter lessons of the Cold War for Latin Americans. Whatever his proclivities, Arbenz Guzmán was the democratically elected president of Guatemala. He became inconvenient for the United States when his land reform efforts came into conflict with U.S. desires to retain economically beneficial conditions for the United Fruit Company. His ouster, conducted by Guatemalan exiles trained in neighboring Nicaragua but supported by the Central Intelligence Agency, did little to convince Latin Americans of the purity of U.S. motives; on the contrary, it illustrated that democracy and self-determination were applicable policy goals only when they worked in concert with U.S. interests.

U.S. efforts did not ignore Africa, where the fear that newly independent Congo and its vast resources would fall prey to Soviet expansionism led the United States in 1960 to prevent the consolidation of a regime by Patrice Lumumba. The actions, again taken with massive CIA support, replaced Lumumba with one of the continent's most ill-famed dictators, Mobutu Sese Seko, and led many critics to seriously doubt whether Washington's commitment to "free peoples" was anything more than selective support for like-minded regimes.

The longest running U.S. intervention has been the attempt to oust Fidel Castro Ruz from Cuba. This island, merely one hundred miles off the coast of Florida, had been a de facto U.S. economic and cultural colony since the Platt Amendment was added to the Cuban Constitution in 1910, guaranteeing the United States the ability to intervene in Cuba. When Castro Ruz and his insurgents managed to drive Fulgencio Batista from power in 1959, the United States had to recognize that Batista's rule had been one of the most dictatorial and least concerned with the rights of citizens. For his part, Castro Ruz had to make the decision that had faced all of his predecessors since independence from the Spanish in 1898: should he side with the Yanqui government or take a more nationalist position that would ultimately free Cuba and make it a sovereign state?

Unlike his predecessors, Castro Ruz chose independence from Washington and sought aid from the Soviet Union. For several reasons, Washington would not see this as a form of Cuban nationalism but assumed it had to be an extension of Soviet control into the "backyard" of the United States. To purge the threat, the United States has tried repeatedly to get rid of Castro Ruz, but he has outlasted ten U.S. presidents, an embargo by the world's greatest economy, and at least one invasion by Cuban exiles with U.S. support. For many in the Cuban exile community, Castro Ruz remains a serious threat to the United States, but for the rest of the world he is an anachronism who makes the U.S. embargo look foolish.

Finally, the United States moved to prevent the election and then the inauguration of Salvador Allende Gossens in Chile and to oust the Sandinistas in Nicaragua. These regimes were considered threatening because of their moves to nationalize U.S. assets—in Chile, those of the International Telephone and Telegraph Corporation and in Nicaragua those of other U.S. firms. For many analysts outside of the United States, none of these "enemies" presented an explicit threat to U.S. national security; rather the U.S. actions were part of a comprehensive goal of retaining hegemony in the world.

For the United States, however, this dark view of its role is virtually impossible to accept. Instead, Washington continues to believe only that it did what had to be done, perpetuating the spirit of responsibility so apparent in World War II. A parallel can be seen now, more than fifty years after the beginning of the Cold War, as the United States describes its global responsibility as fighting terrorism anywhere around the world while even some of its closest allies grow increasingly uneasy at this unilateral view of the issue.

Why Is U.S. Support for Israel Crucial to National Security Policy?

Another issue that the United States views differently than do many other states around the world is the creation and support of the state of Israel. Democratic and Republican administrations alike have universally supported the independence of Israel since its creation in 1948. The reasons for this commitment are historic and cultural: Israel's role as a firm democracy in this region of monarchies is just as notable as the U.S. concern that the Jewish people have their own country from which to protect themselves from the threat of another Holocaust.

The roots of the current crisis have as much to do with troubles between the West and the Islamic part of the world as with the problems between Israel and its Palestinian and Arab neighbors. U.S. interests in the region date back to the middle of the twentieth century, when the British and French were withdrawing from their extensive colonial holdings in the region to the metropolitan areas. Since the United States had not been engaged in colonizing, it was seen as an "honest broker" in the various conflicts in that part of the world. At a meeting between President Franklin D. Roosevelt and Saudi monarch Ibn Saud in February 1945, Roosevelt gave the Saudis the impression that the United States would protect their petroleum supply in exchange for guarantees of U.S. access, forming the basis for a half century of U.S. commitment to that desert kingdom. During the Cold War, U.S. involvement in the region increased as the United States became more committed to a relationship with the shah of Iran, who could provide an intelligence base on the southern belly of the Soviet Union as well as petroleum supplies.

U.S. interests in Israel date back to Israel's founding as a safe haven for a people persecuted and subject to a systematic campaign of annihilation during World War II. But U.S.-Israeli ties were of only secondary importance until the 1967 Six Day War, when Israel occupied the West Bank, Golan Heights, and Gaza Strip. At that point, the Johnson administration began to provide more overt help to Israel because European supporters of Israel were withdrawing in fear of alienating the Arab states. This withdrawal was particularly true of the French, who had supplied many of the armaments for Israel through 1967. As the French shifted toward the Arab view and Israeli vulnerabilities became apparent in the 1973 Yom Kippur War, Washington increased its support of Israel, and the U.S. position is today seen by many in the Middle East as being pro-Israel rather than that of an honest broker.

Today the United States is increasingly caught in the middle of a global struggle between a variety of cultures and socioeconomic classes and amidst a variety of unmet expectations. As economic prosperity and technological advances have taken hold in the industrialized states of North America, Japan, and Western

Europe, the states of the Middle East, with the notable exception of Israel, have remained relatively stagnant or have actually gone backward in their development. Members of the middle class are becoming more frustrated every day, as educated citizens find that their job prospects are dwindling. Much of the region is gripped by a feeling of futility, a sense that the Arab world of the twenty-first century cannot keep up with the rest of the world, and many have turned to their religion and its glorious past for solace.

At the same time, the United States is held up as the exemplar of the West, and its non-Islamic, secular way of life seems to conflict with the tenets of Islam. Indeed, for many in the Islamic world, but particularly among people who question U.S. intentions in helping Israel even as it opposes a resurgent Iraq, the United States appears an ever more remote country, far from being a partner or an honest broker.

Making matters worse, fears that the United States is interested in the Arab portion of the Middle East exclusively to exploit its petroleum resources only add to the disillusion. Many people note that they are seeking a more overt role for Islam in their societies, only to see it thwarted by repressive regimes that want no public discourse and use heavy-handed tactics to prevent it. For far too many people in the region, Washington appears to be supportive of such repression even as it claims that the spread of democratic values is one of its national goals and that it supports Israel because of that state's historic commitment and practice of democracy.

Some are using this criticism to justify more militant and violent actions against the United States, often in the name of protecting Islam or Arabs or repressed peoples. The irony is that the United States is not in any way seeking to promote the views or values of any particular nation or religion or people, and it continues to view its position as truly that of an honest broker.

The recent dramatic increase in violence in the region, associated indirectly with terrorist attacks against the West, is thus a result of a confluence of events. Certainly, the Israeli-Palestinian conflict is a key ingredient; the United States had invested tremendous political capital in the Palestinian-Israeli peace process by the summer of 2000, when President Clinton spent so many hours in negotiations. But the problems are not merely those between Israel and the Palestinians, nor are they just about the conflict between Western democratic values and Islamic revivalism. The conflict has developed in a complicated crucible of different perceptions, goals, and issues that appears to be getting more complex and volatile by the day. How to solve these problems or even determine which path the United States should pursue may be the most intransigent challenge facing the national security community today.

Who Lost China?

Another question about the Cold War has to do with the U.S. role in China during China's civil war, which ended in the creation of the People's Republic on October 1, 1949. Beginning in the nineteenth century, the United States believed it had a "special relationship" with China, partially because of its perceived wealth, both as a mission field for U.S. churches and as a huge potential market for business. Indeed, the United States business community has long believed that China is the last great trade frontier, promising dazzling success to any who would cross it, and opening up China's huge market still remains a tantalizing goal for Western entrepreneurs.

The United States had not been part of the formal process of economic colonization in China during the period after 1840, as had been the British, the French, and other European powers. The 1842 Treaty of Nanking ended the First Opium War by opening certain cities as "treaty" ports to Western trade. From then on, European states demanded and received more lucrative arrangements that granted them greater freedom to trade in China. Although it was not a party to these arrangements, the United States did benefit from them.

The Chinese, for their part, did not particularly differentiate between U.S. actions and those of Europeans, subjecting all Westerners to the same sort of abuse in the Boxer Rebellion (1900) and other anti-Western movements. Now, as the Chinese look back upon and bemoan what they call the "Century of Humiliation," running from about 1842 to Mao's declaration of the People's Republic of China in 1949, they generally see the United States as one source of that humiliation, holding the United States accountable for a variety of vaguely defined crimes.

Mao Zedong expressed this view clearly in 1949—Western nations had subverted China's development; hence, their dominance had to be ended. He was determined to follow Moscow as part of a global attack on U.S.-led democracy and capitalism. Yet because of the "special relationship" with China identified by U.S. missionaries, businessmen, and average citizens, people in the United States were shocked when China adopted a Communist government, finding it hard to understand how China could have gone to the "other camp." At the time, the Cold War was intensifying, creating such a completely bifurcated world that there were only two sides, and nations were either for us or against us. In the United States, supporters of the defeated Republic of China reacted strongly and ignorantly, arguing in their frustration that the United States had "lost" China to the other side.

The very question "Who lost China?" implied that the Truman administration, entrusted with maintaining the momentum of success that started with World War II, had let the country down by losing something that had been "ours," as if it were a book that had been lost on the way home from school. The question implied that the adoption of Communism by China could not have been a choice inspired by long-standing and complex regional and international forces, but rather must be the result of a mistake made by someone in the U.S. State Department.

It was in this context that a large number of State Department officials were accused of being pro-Communist and failing to support the Chinese Nationalists, led by Chiang Kai-shek. In fact, the United States had supported Chiang throughout World War II, with General Joseph Stilwell as his principle military advisor, but Chiang had been unwilling to lead the Chinese against the Japanese. His regime and army were wracked with corruption, which exacerbated tensions and prevented the establishment of an effective national government.

Because both Chiang and Mao were more interested in pursuing the civil war than in defeating the Japanese, much of Stilwell's advice had gone unheeded. Chiang developed a strong dislike for his advisor and was insulted by the reports to Washington that questioned his capabilities and interests. Despite his obvious inadequacies and corruptness, Washington did not worry enough about the Chinese leader's inability to govern a unified China, nor was this inability remembered as a possible answer to the "Who lost China" question.

During the remainder of the Cold War, the United States often viewed its relationship with China only in terms of its relationship with the Soviet Union, using China to improve its position vis-à-vis Moscow. The fact that, like the Soviet Union, China was Communist remained in the background. Then at the end of the Cold War, new questions arose: first, questions about what type of government was likely to continue in Beijing and second, questions about whether the United States was in fact willing to see Taiwan reunited with the mainland under a central Chinese government of some sort. Today, U.S. relations with China remain exceptionally difficult as we are challenged to answer not the old question of who lost China but the new question: what is China?

Taiwan, separated geographically from the mainland and still maintaining its own government, seeks a status that is somewhat undefined. It sees itself as neither independent nor under the control of Beijing. But Beijing sees Taiwan differently, rejecting even the hint of a claim that Taiwan is a sovereign, independent nation that can operate as an equal state in the international community.

Washington remains pivotal to the equation. The United States, which recognized Taiwan as the legitimate government of China from 1949 through 1979, has subsequently moved diplomatic recognition to Beijing. At the same time, Taiwan retains the unparalleled relationship with Washington expressed in the 1979 Taiwan Relations Act, which states Washington's responsibility for helping Taiwan in case Beijing would attempt some sort of nonpeaceful reunification. Beijing wants the United States to declare unambiguously that it will not defend Taiwan in case of armed conflict over what Beijing considers an internal issue, whereas Taiwan wants a guarantee that Washington will not abandon it should Beijing engage in military action to reunify the island with the mainland. Washington, particularly under the administration of President George W. Bush, wants not only to maintain the ambiguity of the U.S. stance but increasingly to assuage both sides. This most exceptional national security challenge may lead to all sorts of unintended consequences.

Would John F. Kennedy Have Withdrawn from Vietnam Had He Not Been Assassinated?

November 22, 1963, was a defining date in the lives of all Americans. It is an especially critical date for critics of the Vietnam War, since many of them believe that President Kennedy, instigator of the growing role of U.S. "advisors" in Vietnam, would have withdrawn those advisors had he lived to serve a second term. There is no way to know what Kennedy would have done later in Vietnam, although President Ngo Dinh Diem's assassination, occurring just three weeks before Kennedy's own death, may well have changed his decision to intensify U.S. presence in the former Indochina.

One empirical piece of the puzzle of Kennedy and Vietnam is the number of high-level Kennedy advisors who remained during Lyndon Johnson's presidency. These included Johnson himself, of course, National Security Advisor McGeorge Bundy, Secretary of State Dean Rusk, Secretary of Defense Robert McNamara, and several military officers. These individuals largely held the same positions—both analytically and literally—in both administrations. Although Johnson ended up deepening the conflict with tragic results, the analytical bases for his decisions were clearly present prior to November 1963. As the years passed, Johnson added to his team many more hawkish individuals, such as Walt Whitman Rostow and General William Westmoreland, but the basic problem was already in place—the U.S. failure to assess accurately what it would take to defeat the Viet Cong and North Vietnamese regular forces.

Why did the Johnson administration continue President Kennedy's policy of involvement in Vietnam? This begs the broader question as to whether decision making in U.S. national security affairs, both during and since the Cold War, has a momentum of its own that makes it difficult to reverse a decision once it has been taken. The discussion of nuclear weapons and how to deploy them, related indirectly to the potential for their use in various places during the Cold War, would appear to have a similar momentum.

Did Civilian Protest Tie the Military's Hands in Vietnam?

One of the most passionate issues of the post–World War II period has to do with the role of civilian protest and policymaking in the Vietnam conflict. For many who served in the military during that conflict or who serve today, more than a generation after the war ended, this wound is still open and painful: Many believe that civilians did not allow the military to conduct a fair fight in Vietnam but tried to hamper its efforts with unrealistic expectations and restrictions. Many believe that most civilians were and remain antimilitary, and some believe that people who disagreed with the war were unpatriotic.[1] This sentiment was revisited in the 1990s, when bitterness at President Bill Clinton's known efforts to avoid serving in the war boiled over many times. (Not as frequently discussed, however, was the lack of service on the part of then House Speaker Newt Gingrich, Texas Senator Phil Gramm, or Dick Cheney, among a long list of prominent individuals.)

Those who believe that civilian leaders were to blame for the U.S. loss in Vietnam frequently cite the experiences of commanders in Vietnam who were not allowed to pursue "complete" courses of action, thereby restricting military operations geographically or substantively. A frequently noted example is the restrictions on engaging the military outside Vietnam proper, such as in Cambodia or Laos. Those restrictions were lifted in 1970, however, and the war was still lost.

Part of the problem is that those who claim civilian betrayal often confuse the civil-military disputes about courses of action in Vietnam with political intent and national objectives. In a stunning analysis, H. R. McMaster's *Dereliction of Duty* argues that both sides failed equally to request what was necessary, or even to analyze national goals adequately. The "civil-military gap" over Vietnam illustrates an important policy tenet: A good relationship between the military and civilians is a crucial element of national security. If the two sectors become too deeply estranged, the danger of massive civilian unrest, a military violation of civilian chain of command, or even a military coup increases. Thus national security policy must ensure good communication between the two sectors so that civilians understand and support U.S. military expenditures and efforts and so that the military keeps in mind its ultimate goal—the protection of civilian life and institutions.

The question of whether the United States has a civil-military gap remains important today. If such a gap exists, the potential for misunderstanding on national security issues is great because both sides might eventually lose trust that the other will be truthful in national debate. The issue of a potential gap attracted much public attention in the 1990s as U.S. society wrestled with a number of involvements in overseas crises, such as those in Somalia, the Balkans, and Haiti, as well as in certain enlarged missions for the military such as countering drug trafficking and engaging in civil affairs (often labeled "nation-building"). Although it would be wrong to portray citizens, either those in uniform or civilians, as having monolithic views on any topic, at that time it did seem that the military generally preferred to limit its actions to "traditional" security affairs while civilians were often espousing expanded involvement. The war against terrorism, with all its attending concerns about civil rights and foreign intervention, might accentuate this nascent division. Again, the key to preventing a critical civil-military gap is open and honest communication between the two sectors.

Did the United States Destroy the Soviet Union, or Did It Collapse under Its Own Weight?

Just over a decade after Ronald Reagan's victory over Jimmy Carter in the 1980 presidential election, one of the greatest empires of all times collapsed. After a period of supposed U.S. weakness during the Carter administration, President Reagan was elected in part on a platform of "closing the window of vulnerability" to the Soviet Union. From this point on, the fall of the Soviet Union—and the end of its supposedly massive threat— was amazingly rapid. The question that emerged from this brief time was whether the Soviet Union was defeated by the Western allies under U.S. leadership, or whether it was in fact an extremely vulnerable system that had precariously teetered on the brink of failure for much of the Cold War period.

Supporters of the Reagan and George H. W. Bush presidencies have maintained that the Soviet Union was destroyed because it was pressured to match the massive research and development efforts involved in President Reagan's Strategic Defense Initiative (enunciated in a March 23, 1983, speech; see chapter 5). Other supporters believe it was the massive increase in defense expenditures in general that forced the Soviets into ruin. In the end, George Kennan's view that the Soviet Union would collapse under its own weight was accurate. Whether U.S. actions increased that weight or whether collapse was inevitable on its own schedule remains unknown.

The former Soviet Union and its leadership have not answered the question. We do know that Gorbachev's economic and political reforms of the late 1980s put serious stress on the Soviet system, which had long been overproducing goods that were left unsold, thus keeping workers employed but not productive. This excess of labor was exacerbated when political reforms allowed Soviet citizens to criticize their country's poor standard of living.

Additionally, the Soviet Union suffered tremendous internal debate and recrimination over its failed attempt to conquer

Afghanistan. The fierce Afghani response produced a vicious guerrilla conflict that the Soviets were never able to win, forcing the Red Army to withdraw in 1989. The end of that decade-long incursion has long been compared with the ignominious U.S. withdrawal from Vietnam fifteen years earlier. The defeat raised serious questions within the Soviet Union about the nature of the conflict, the true intentions of Kremlin leadership, and the efficacy of the Soviet armed forces. Instead of proving the Soviet Union to be the overwhelming force that had been described during the 1980 U.S. presidential campaign, the Afghan experience raised serious questions about Soviet military morale, capabilities, and endurance. As happened to the United States in Southeast Asia, many in the Red Army returned home with drug problems, only exacerbating the self-doubt and the disciplinary difficulties inflicted by military defeat. Like the United States, the Soviet Union also found that open-ended conflicts without an identifiable objective in mind can erode public support, cause self-doubt among the forces involved, and seriously undermine the national will that is necessary if national security strategists and uniformed leaders are to carry out a mission.

Current Controversies

Is China a Threat to U.S. National Security at the Beginning of the New Millennium?

One of the most controversial national security issues facing the United States today has to do with the nature of its evolving relationship with the People's Republic of China. The question of whether China is seeking modernization and economic development only to project itself onto the world stage is far from settled. Some analysts believe that China is successfully modernizing, and others have concluded that China is merely establishing a sham prosperity that is so uneven across the country that it threatens the survival of the state. Additionally, it is not clear whether the changes China is undergoing will allow it to continue under Communist Party rule or whether some alternate form of government will replace the Communist leadership.

Many analysts charge that Chinese military modernization since the early 1980s is designed to allow China a global presence. This modernization includes development of a more high-tech, more educated military that is taking the first steps toward joint operations, in which the various services coordinate their activities. The People's Liberation Army (PLA), which includes the PLA Navy (PLAN) and the PLA Air Force (PLAAF), is largely a ground force, with a traditional orientation toward the defense of China against threats from the north and west. Although the Soviet Union was identified as a diminished threat after 1985, when Deng Xiaoping reoriented the PLA to threats from other areas, Russia's looming presence to the north remains an important issue to which the PLA is likely to return. The PLA and the Chinese leadership, in general, have taken a much more positive view of the former Soviet Union since 1990 than was traditionally the case. Whether this closer relationship will endure once Chinese military modernization is firmly established or whether the economic improvements of the PRC will endure past "first-generation" reforms remains an open question.

Military modernization does not necessarily prove that China seeks a global presence. Many analysts believe that the PRC seeks to be the dominant state only in East Asia, rather than globally. These scholars, including Bernard Cole, Bates Gill, and Michael O'Hanlon, argue that the PLA reform is a gradual, measured program of modernization, and that the PLA is not as big a threat as it is often portrayed. Others, including Edward Timperlake and William Triplett, James Lilley and Carl Ford, see a much more alarming Chinese buildup, at least in comparison with other states in the region.

The answer to this question is important for U.S. strategists, because the United States would find unacceptable any constraints on its freedom of action, which the dominance of a single power in Asia (China or anyone else) would imply. The need to prepare for an "aggressive" China versus a modernizing but status quo China would require different levels of forces in the region. In any case, debates about the PLA and China, in general, continue to be many and broad.

How Should the United States Combat Terrorism?

Both in the late Clinton and the early George W. Bush administrations, national security analysts were still trying to assess the significance of the terrorist threat. But everything changed dramatically on September 11, 2001, when four jets filled with travelers hit the 101-story twin towers of the World Trade Center in lower Manhattan, the Pentagon in Washington, DC, and a field in Pennsylvania, leading to the deaths of several thousand people on the ground. This event forced the United States to recognize that it is vulnerable to international terrorism despite its security blanket of two oceans and two peaceful neighbors.

Even prior to the attacks, the United States had suffered from smaller, more isolated terrorist incidents. In 1993, in an eerie precedent, a bomb in the parking structure of the World Trade Center revealed terrorist interest in bringing down this symbol of U.S. wealth, culture, and prestige. In a more chilling act two years later, a U.S. citizen, angry at his government for actions taken against a cult, detonated a homemade bomb in Oklahoma City, destroying a federal office building and killing more than 160 citizens. Overseas, U.S. citizens have been targets of random acts of terrorism for decades, particularly in the highly charged 1970s. In 1998, two U.S. embassies in eastern African capitals were attacked by bombs on the same day, drawing U.S. attempts at retaliation that proved futile. The accused ringleader of both the embassy bombings and the September 11 attacks, exiled Saudi millionaire Usama Bin Laden, remains at large as of early 2002. The audacity of the 2001 attacks indicates not only the intensity of the terrorists' anger against the United States but also their high level of commitment, coordination, funding, and long-term dedication.

The appropriate response to these attacks in the long term is now the main topic of public policy debate, and the threat of terrorism will drive national security questions for the foreseeable future. When President Bush declared that the war against terrorism will be long, enduring, and potentially deadly for U.S. citizens, he raised profound questions. These involve the nature of U.S. commitment and resolve to stay the course and to redefine national security while moderating some traditional, cherished domestic liberties and rights. Six months after the initial attacks, the U.S. response appears to be a global war on terrorism fought with the widest possible definition and in as many locations as practicable. The Bush administration has taken the conflict to the al Qaeda and the Taliban in Afghanistan, and the widely hated Taliban regime has been replaced with a somewhat fragile pro-Western government under the temporary leadership of Hamid Karzai. The linkages between al Qaeda elements in the Middle East, Central Asia, and other places around the world are being investigated with more clarity than ever before, and steps have been taken to protect the homeland of the United States, ranging from increased airport security to enhanced Immigration and Naturalization Service monitoring to the introduction of military tribunals to try the accused accomplices to terrorism. Both President Bush and Director of Central Intelligence George Tenet have warned U.S. citizens to anticipate and fear more terrorism, also stating emphatically that the United States will react forcefully and deliberately against such attacks. The unknown in 2002 is how effectively these words and actions will deter individuals determined to attack the United States, its values, and its aspirations.

Will the U.S. Responses to the Attacks of September 11 Erode the Basic Democratic Norms We Seek to Protect?

The response that the Bush administration has mounted to the terrorism of 2001 has been swift and mighty. Most of it has focused on al Qaeda and allied terrorists in Afghanistan and other locations around the world. So far, less emphasis has been placed on the responses to terrorism that affect life at home, but when the United States has taken several months to ponder the events, more questions about this domestic response will arise. In particular, the use of military tribunals to try accused terrorists appears to some as a violation of basic constitutional rights that are foundational to the democracy we are seeking to protect.

There is little, if any, consensus on this issue. Attorney General John Ashcroft and Secretary of Defense Donald Rumsfeld have both argued repeatedly that military tribunals are appropriate because they would not be used against U.S. citizens; "terrorists" do not have the same rights as citizens and should not expect equal treatment. Further, this argument goes, the tribunals are not all that different from those used against war criminals at the end of World War II.

Opponents fear that the tribunals set a bad precedent in a number of ways. First, there is the question of whether one should undercut democratic principles in trying to preserve them; to some this appears a fundamental contradiction. Additionally and equally worrisome to many is the fear that if the United States ignores its basic legal standards when dealing with terrorists— standards that the United States almost always proclaims to be the global model for fairness and equity—then other nation states might feel justified in ignoring internationally recognized standards of jurisprudence when dealing with U.S. citizens.

Considering how many times the United States has argued that it would not allow its citizens to be tried in international courts that might be prejudicial, the current policy on military tribunals appears to many to be hypocritical.

The post–September 11 judicial process is only beginning to be formulated, so the final outcome is unclear. It does present a number of controversies that are likely only to grow in the future.

What Role Should the United States Play: Hegemon or Benevolent Participant?

Finally, the question of what pose the United States should strike in the world remains as relevant today as it was fifty-five years ago. There has long been an isolationist strain in U.S. national security policy, one that is as firmly proposed today as it was during World War I. Few people seriously argue that the United States should withdraw from the international community, but such a policy was discussed in the 1996 presidential campaign by fringe candidate Patrick Buchanan. The Republican Congress that assumed the majority in 1994 appeared less than eager to answer foreign concerns at the perceived sacrifice of domestic needs. Many of these legislators were uncomfortable with former Secretary of State Madeleine Albright's term "the indispensable nation." They thought that the United States needed to "come home," to curtail many of its international financial and military commitments. These individuals did not subscribe to the idea that the United States has global responsibilities, either as police officer or financial savior. Instead, in their view, the United States should limit its role and protect its citizens by staying home.

Perhaps the events of September 11 will cause U.S. citizens to petition their government to pull back from global commitments, to build a wall that will seal out others while keeping ourselves safe, and to close the door to a role in the global arena. This appears unlikely, however, as the United States seems far more likely to pursue a role in the world that involves both leadership and participation. The dramatic increase in budget allocations that President Bush received after September 11 probably foreshadows a much fuller U.S. participation in international affairs, in the tradition of the Republican "internationalist" school. It is now clear to most that the United States is the only honest broker that can mediate conflict, provide assistance, lead coalitions, and work to maintain international dignity. Engagement is required to keep the world peaceful and to ensure general global economic growth and prosperity. As the war on terrorism continues, however, this view may wane as people ask whether that commitment to a presence around the world is what led to infiltration by terrorists.

Since September 2001 the people of the United States have been at least as concerned with the question of why the rest of the world misunderstands our good intentions as we operate throughout the world. Few people among the citizenry of the United States would ever accept the verdict that we aim to dominate the world or to cause others to behave contrary to their national interests. Indeed, one characteristic of this nation, back to its founding days as a haven for those excluded from various societies in Western Europe, has been the assumption that the United States is a "City upon a Hill," with "the eyes of all people upon us," as John Winthrop said in 1630. But many around the world do not believe that the United States, as a whole, has acted as a genuine partner in the world arena.

Now more than ever, it is important to look at the global effect of U.S. efforts to protect national security in the last two generations. Which elements of U.S. policy have succeeded in protecting the nation's citizens and interests? Which elements have inflamed anger toward the United States, thus threatening the nation's security in the long run? How has the definition of national security changed over the years? The chapters that follow provide some of the details needed for such a policy examination, outlining the events, the people, the documents, and the organizations that have shaped our nation's attempts to protect itself. From this kind of analysis will come new definitions of security, new strategies and approaches, and new resolve.

Notes

1. The National War College operates on a strict "not for attribution" policy to protect the views of its students and faculty as well as any and all outside speakers; to protect free discussion, no individual's views are associated with his or her name. As a result, I can only say that in my experience it is a commonly held, albeit not monolithic, view that civilians and military personnel differ on the use of force in general and on the U.S. experience in Vietnam in particular. This anecdotal evidence seems to be buttressed by the public opinion data taken by Ole Holsti, professor emeritus at Duke University (*Public Opinion and American*

Foreign Policy, University of Michigan Press, 1996), as well as the work of Richard Kohn and Peter Feaver (*Soldiers and Civilians: The Civil-Military Gap and American National Security,* Cambridge: MIT Press, 2001). Kohn and Feaver have named this phenomenon the "civil-military gap."

3

Chronology

This chapter lists events from the end of World War II to the present that have been relevant to the course of U.S. national security strategy. At first glance, the overwhelming majority of these seem to involve the Soviet Union and are recognized today as important moments in the Cold War. But many are also relevant to an understanding of the context in which we now operate. The most obvious examples are in the Middle East, where decisions taken between 1948 and 1991 now appear as relevant to the problem of global terrorism as they were to the Cold War. Of course, such a list cannot be exhaustive, and other scholars might have chosen different incidents. In any case, I hope that this broad review of key events in the recent history of U.S. national security will help explain both the development of U.S. Cold War policy vis-à-vis the Soviet Union and other countries and the background of our current national security concerns.

1945   President Franklin D. Roosevelt dies in April and is succeeded by Vice President Harry S. Truman.

The United States, the first nation to develop atomic weapons, drops two atomic bombs in August on the Japanese cities of Hiroshima and Nagasaki.

World War II ends with the U.S.-led coalition victorious over the Axis powers of Germany, Italy, and Japan. Upon movement across Germany by the victorious French, British, Soviet, and U.S. forces, the territory of Germany is divided into four zones, including

1945 *(cont.)*	Berlin as an occupied city. Those zones remain in place throughout the Cold War. With the British, French, and Soviet states in ruins, the United States is unquestionably the greatest power in the world. The Soviets, however, have the largest standing army and do not demobilize it when hostilities cease, as do the Western allies.

The Arab League is born to fight the establishment of a Jewish state in the British-controlled area called Palestine.

China resumes the civil war that consumed the country in the decade before Japanese invasion.

In October, the United Nations replaces the League of Nations, established after World War I, as an international body intended to prevent global conflict. The United States, modifying its previous policy of nonengagement, actively participates in the United Nations.

Various former European colonies in areas such as Southeast Asia are reoccupied by colonial powers, but nationalist, pro-independence movements begin to challenge their rule more forcefully.

The Bretton Woods Agreements, signed in July 1944 and intended to regulate the post–World War II economic environment, begin to regulate the international political economy. The agreements stipulate the establishment of two major organizations, the International Monetary Fund—intended to create a reserve to help nations over immediate, short-term cash crises—and the International Bank for Reconstruction and Development (better known as the World Bank)—created to assist in long-term economic development needs in the aftermath of the conflict. These institutions will remain active through the Cold War period and beyond. The Bretton Woods Agreements also stipulate the creation of the International Trade Organization, but the latter is defeated in the U.S. Senate.

General George C. Marshall, former U.S. Army chief of staff, goes to China as President Truman's envoy to mediate between Communist insurgent Mao Zedong and the Nationalist president of the Republic of China, Generalissimo Chiang Kai-shek. Marshall's mission lasts a year but does not resolve the conflict.

1946   In February, State Department Foreign Service Officer George F. Kennan pens an assessment of Soviet prospects and possible future ambitions, called the "Long Telegram" (see chapter 5). Like Churchill's "Iron Curtain" speech, the Long Telegram causes U.S. decision makers concern about Soviet expansionism.

In a speech on March 5 at Missouri's Westminster College, former British Prime Minister Winston Churchill warns that an "iron curtain" has descended over Eastern Europe (see chapter 5). This is the first public expression of misgiving about the Soviet Union, the World War II ally that is acting aggressively and still has an extremely large standing army two years after the war ended.

The Atomic Energy Act of 1946 establishes the Atomic Energy Commission to monitor, regulate, and direct the creation of atomic energy, replacing the Manhattan Project. The commission will be subsumed into the Department of Energy in 1977.

1947   In response to Britain's admission that it cannot prevent a Communist takeover in Greece, in March President Truman declares U.S. support for any state threatened by Communism. This policy is called the Truman Doctrine (see chapter 5).

The British suggestion for dividing its mandate in Palestine is rejected by both Arabs and Jews. The issue is turned over to the UN.

The Western Hemisphere nations agree to collect security efforts under the rubric of the Inter-American Treaty for Reciprocal Assistance, often called the Rio Treaty.

1947
(cont.)

In apparent recognition that economic reconstruction is stalled and that Communists threaten to win elections in Italy and France, Secretary of State (and former wartime chief of staff) George C. Marshall unveils in a commencement speech at Harvard University a massive foreign assistance program, which becomes known as the Marshall Plan (see chapter 5).

George F. Kennan authors an anonymous article that discusses the Soviet Union and its ability to survive current global pressures. The so-called Mr. X article, appearing as "The Sources of Soviet Conduct" in the July issue of *Foreign Affairs*, coins the term "containment"—a policy designed to curb Soviet expansionism.

The British Raj in India ends in August, resulting in the partition of the country into the newly independent states of India and Pakistan, and the independence of Burma.

1948

In February a Communist coup in Czechoslovakia solidifies the wall of Communist governments west of Josef Stalin's Soviet Union.

In May Sir Winston Churchill leads the Hague Congress for European unity.

The British Mandate of Palestine ends in May with the founding of the Jewish state of Israel. Immediately upon Israel's recognition as a sovereign state by the United States and the Soviet Union, Palestinians flee into neighboring Arab states, and Egypt, Lebanon, Syria, Transjordan, and Iraq declare war on Israel. This is the first of many Arab-Israeli wars.

Tito (Josip Broz), the head of Communist Yugoslavia, begins to distance himself from Stalin, but it takes two generations for the United States to recognize the break.

Harry S. Truman defeats New York Governor Thomas Dewey in the U.S. presidential elections.

1949   The states of Western Europe, along with the United States and Canada, are concerned about the large Soviet standing army, and in April they create the North Atlantic Treaty Organization (NATO) as a self-defense organization (see chapter 5).

On May 11 Israel is admitted to the United Nations.

The Federal Republic of Germany (West Germany) and the German Democratic Republic (East Germany) are established on May 23 and October 9, respectively.

The Soviet Union tries in June to completely seal off the British, French, and U.S. sectors of Berlin, contrary to the 1945 agreements ending World War II. The Allies, under U.S. leadership, initiate and conduct an eleven-month resupply of the city known as the Berlin Airlift.

On August 29, the Soviet Union detonates its first atomic bomb, which U.S. sensors pick up as radiation floating across the West Coast of the United States.

Mao Zedong declares the establishment of the People's Republic of China on October 1, and Chiang Kai-shek and the Nationalists move the Republic of China to the island of Taiwan, off the mainland coast of Fujian Province. At this time, anti-Communist fears are growing markedly stronger in the United States, and critics of the Truman administration, particularly in the Republican Party, ask who allowed the "fall of China?"

Apartheid laws promoting extreme racial segregation are promulgated in South Africa, eventually making South Africa both a trusted ally in the fight against Communism and an international pariah.

1950   In January, Secretary of State Dean Acheson gives a speech at the National Press Club where he identifies a "defense perimeter" for the United States in East Asia, including Japan, Okinawa, and the Philippines but not Korea or Taiwan (see chapter 5). The speech

1950
(cont.)

will be blamed for the invasion of South Korea by North Korea six months later.

An agreement in February between Mao Zedong, the newly successful leader of Communist China, and Josef Stalin of the Soviet Union leads to a settlement of territorial disputes, creates a foreign aid program between the two states, and begins a mutual defense pact that will fuel U.S. concerns about the spread of Marxist-Leninism around the world.

In a February speech in West Virginia, Senator Joseph R. McCarthy charges that the State Department is harboring Communists. McCarthy's fervor sets off a Communist scare that will destroy the careers of many civil servants and a generation of China scholars and will bring the senator into conflict with Presidents Truman and Eisenhower, particularly when he challenges the loyalty of former Secretary of State and General George C. Marshall.

In April the National Security Council (NSC) offers several options for dealing with the Soviet threat and the global political environment in NSC memorandum 68 (see chapter 5). Additionally, President Truman chooses to pursue the development of a thermonuclear (hydrogen) weapon, possibly in response to Soviet atomic bomb development.

The 38th Parallel, dividing North and South Korea into Communist and capitalist states, is overrun by North Korean troops on June 25, beginning the Korean War.

1952

Riots protesting British influence erupt in Egypt, and King Faruk I is ousted in a military coup.

Thousands of people escape from East Germany to West Germany in August.

On October 3, Great Britain tests its first atomic weapon, making it the third atomic power.

On November 1 the United States tests its first thermonuclear (hydrogen) weapon, much more powerful than prior weapons.

World War II Supreme Allied Commander Dwight D. Eisenhower defeats Illinois Governor Adlai E. Stevenson for the presidency.

1953   Soviet premier and dictator Josef Stalin dies on March 5 and is succeeded by Georgy M. Malenkov.

In June, worker riots break out in East Germany—one of the first signs of popular unrest in the Soviet Union, which calls itself "the workers' paradise."

Despite questions about the fairness of their trial, Julius and Ethel Rosenberg are executed in the United States on June 19 for sending atomic secrets to the Soviet Union.

In July the UN forces under U.S. command sign an armistice with North Korean forces at the demilitarized zone (DMZ) dividing the two Koreas. Five decades later, the war has still not formally ended, and the two sides maintain a heavily armed DMZ.

The Soviet Union tests its first hydrogen weapon on August 12, less than a year after the United States.

Iranian Prime Minister Muhammad Mossadegh, who has been showing nationalist tendencies against the West, is overthrown on August 19 by royalist forces assisted by the U.S. Central Intelligence Agency (CIA).

1954   In a speech on January 12, U.S. Secretary of State John Foster Dulles enunciates a new military doctrine of response to Soviet aggression that becomes known as massive retaliation (see chapter 5).

In January, the first televised hearings on Senator Joseph McCarthy's charges of Communism in the U.S.

1954   government are televised, and by December he will be
(cont.)   censured by his Senate colleagues.

During an April 7 news conference, President Eisenhower elucidates his fear of the spread of Communism around the world in a concept later dubbed the "domino theory."

At Dien Bien Phu in May, Vietnamese forces hold French forces hostage and force their withdrawal from Indochina, ending the era of French colonization in Vietnam. As a result of subsequent discussions at an international peace conference, the Geneva Accords divide Vietnam into North and South (see chapter 5). During the Geneva conference, U.S. Secretary of State John Foster Dulles refuses to shake People's Republic of China Premier Zhou Enlai's hand.

The leftist president of Guatemala, Jacobo Arbenz Guzmán, is overthrown in June by an army of political exiles supported by the CIA. This is followed by decades of political upheaval in Guatemala and much of Central America.

Gamal Abdel Nasser, an Army officer, seizes power in Egypt, and on July 27 he signs the agreement by which British forces will evacuate from their base along the Suez Canal.

The U.S.-Taiwan Mutual Defense Treaty ties the United States to the defense of Formosa until the treaty is abrogated in 1979, when the United States will shift its recognition from Taiwan to Beijing.

1955   Soviet Premier Georgy Malenkov resigns in February and is succeeded by Nikolay Bulganin.

The Bandung Conference in Indonesia, the initial meeting of African and Asian states that consider themselves neither capitalist nor Communist but "nonaligned" in orientation, is held in April. The goal of the meeting is to promote economic and cultural cooperation and to oppose colonialism. Leaders include President Gamal Abdel Nasser of Egypt and Prime Minister Jawaharlal Nehru of India, along with the host, Indonesian President Sukarno. China also plays a prominent role, trying to advance its leadership role in the evolving Third World.

Sir Winston Churchill resigns in April, and Sir Anthony Eden assumes the prime ministership.

The Warsaw Pact, a Soviet-controlled military alliance against NATO, is signed by six states in Eastern Europe under Soviet suzerainty (Albania, Bulgaria, Czechoslovakia, East Germany, Hungary, and Poland) and the USSR on May 14.

In July, U.S. President Eisenhower meets with Soviet leaders at a summit in Geneva, Switzerland. Eisenhower proposes an "Open Skies" policy, under which both sides would give each other full descriptions of their military capabilities and allow for aerial inspections. The Soviets do not accept the proposal.

1956   On March 2, Pakistan adopts a new constitution that declares the nation an Islamic republic.

The Suez Crisis in Egypt causes a split between the United States and its NATO partners Britain and France.

War in the Middle East again pits Arab states against Israel. The United States sends aid to Israel.

President Eisenhower defeats Illinois Governor Adlai E. Stevenson for a second term.

A popular uprising in Hungary leads the Soviet Union to send the army to crush resistance to Communist rule in November. The West stands idly by as hundreds of Hungarians are executed and thousands are arrested or flee the country.

1957   In January, President Eisenhower asks Congress to "assist countries besieged by international Communism" in the Middle East, a policy later called the Eisenhower Doctrine.

The Treaty of Rome is signed in March by West Germany, France, Luxembourg, the Netherlands, Italy, and Belgium, beginning the European integration process and paving the way for the creation in 1958 of the European Economic Community (known as the Common Market). This process will eventually lead to economic union.

Under the leadership of Kwame Nkrumah, the British colony of the Gold Coast in west Africa becomes Ghana and achieves independence. The nationalism of this and other newly independent states is thought to be a magnet for Communism, and Washington begins to see Communist expansion in many peripheral places around the globe.

Sputnik I, the first satellite to circle the globe, is launched on October 4 by the Soviet Union, sparking fears of invasion in the United States.

1958   In July, President Eisenhower stations U.S. ships off the coast of Lebanon, landing twenty thousand Marines in response to a severe political crisis provoked by pro-Nasser elements, one of the first of many in that nation.

Beginning in August, Communist China bombards the islands of Quemoy and Matsu, controlled by Taiwan's Nationalist Guomindang (GMD) government, and threatens to invade. The United States sends forces to the region in support of Taiwan. The crisis continues until October.

1959   With small insurgent forces, Fidel Castro Ruz overthrows the long-standing dictator of Cuba, Fulgencio Batista y Zaldívar, who had been supported by the United States.

1960   France tests its first nuclear weapon on February 13, making it the fourth nuclear power.

On April 12, Soviet Cosmonaut Yuri Gagarin becomes the first person to circle the globe in space.

A U.S. nuclear submarine, the USS *Triton*, completes the first underwater circumnavigation of the globe on April 25.

The United States develops the first lasers, which will be crucial for the potential of ballistic missile defenses and other important technological uses.

Soviets shoot down U.S. spy planes in May and July, and U.S. pilot Francis Gary Powers is put through a show trial to embarrass the United States. Powers will be released in 1962.

The Organization of Petroleum Exporting Countries (OPEC) is created in September, largely at the behest of Venezuela. The original signatory states, Kuwait, Iran, Iraq, Saudi Arabia, and Venezuela, hope to raise petroleum prices by controlling the oil supply.

In September, Prime Minister Patrice Lumumba is overthrown in mineral-rich Congo. The United States had feared the expansion of the Cold War in the region, as Lumumba had advocated anticolonial measures that appeared to lean toward Communism. Never formally a Communist, Lumumba will be assassinated the following year.

Massachusetts Senator John F. Kennedy defeats Vice President Richard Nixon in a close election for president of the United States.

1961   In his farewell address to the nation on January 17, President Eisenhower warns that overly close ties between the military and business interests could be deleterious to the nation.

1961
(cont.)

President Kennedy proves unwilling to provide complete support to an ill-organized invasion of Cuba by anti-Communist refugees, supplied and trained by the United States. This effort, called the Bay of Pigs invasion, takes place in April and fails entirely.

In an attempt to stem the flight of people from Communist East Berlin to the West, the Berlin Wall is built in August across the politically divided city.

1962

In what will become known as the Cuban Missile Crisis, Fidel Castro Ruz agrees to Soviet Premier Nikita Khrushchev's deployment of medium-range ballistic missiles on Cuban soil, provoking President Kennedy to threaten a nuclear response or invasion of the island.

In a policy called "mutually assured destruction" (MAD), the United States and the Soviet Union begin creating a vast arsenal of nuclear warheads on missiles, bombers, and ships that can target civilian populations to hold them "hostage." Although the U.S. military never officially states that civilians are appropriate targets for nuclear forces, the size of the arsenals leads to no other logical conclusions.

The Catholic Church ends its decades-long defensive posture against modernism in the Second Vatican Council, known as Vatican II. Among other things, the council proposes significant changes in liturgy, increases the role of lay leadership, advocates dialogue among church leaders throughout the world, and encourages criticism of poverty and inequitable social conditions. For the United States, this more activist stance among church leaders will become somewhat of a fracture point in domestic politics, particularly in the 1970s and 1980s with regard to nuclear proliferation and U.S. intervention in support of nongovernmental regimes in Central America.

1963

In early November, the inept pro-Western president of South Vietnam, Ngo Dinh Diem, is assassinated in

Vietnam and replaced by a military government in a coup sanctioned by President Kennedy.

President Kennedy is assassinated on November 22 in Dallas, Texas, and Vice President Lyndon Johnson is sworn in as president.

1964   The Palestine Liberation Organization (PLO) is founded in May with support from the Arab League and with Yasser Arafat as its head. Its goal is to represent Palestinians in their efforts to regain territory from Israel, if not to entirely eliminate the Jewish state.

The Group of 77, consisting of seventy-seven former colonies, is established on June 15 to create a bargaining bloc at the United Nations in an attempt to better their economic and political positions.

In June anti-apartheid activist Nelson Rolihlahla Mandela is sentenced to life in prison in South Africa. Mandela becomes an international symbol of social justice efforts, and his plight is linked to U.S. support for the Afrikaner government in South Africa. This support raises questions about whether the United States is genuinely motivated by its belief in democracy or supports only those countries that further its interests.

In August, President Johnson seeks increased presidential powers from Congress in response to the Gulf of Tonkin incident.

The People's Republic of China tests its first nuclear weapon on October 16, becoming the world's fifth nuclear power.

Soviet Premier Nikita Khrushchev is replaced by Leonid Brezhnev in the aftermath of the Cuban Missile Crisis and other policy fiascoes.

President Lyndon Johnson defeats Arizona Senator Barry Goldwater for a full term as president.

1965   Sir Winston Churchill dies on January 24.

On January 25, Mao Zedong announces that his chosen successor, Liu Shaoqi, must be removed and the Communist Party reconstructed. This is the first step of the Great Proletarian Cultural Revolution, aimed at upending the traditional social, economic, and political structures of China and leading to millions of deaths through purges and starvation.

In February, the United States begins bombing operations in North Vietnam. In March, President Johnson sends U.S. ground troops to combat the Communist threat to South Vietnam.

On April 17, the first major antiwar demonstration takes place in Washington, DC.

In April, the United States sends 28,000 Marines to assist fewer than 1,000 U.S. citizens against a possible Communist threat in the Dominican Republic.

President Sukarno of Indonesia is politically weakened in an attempted coup on September 30, and the subsequent purges of Communist Party members lead to the death of perhaps 1 million citizens.

1967   Fifteen Latin American states meet in Mexico City and on February 14 sign the Treaty of Tlatelolco, which creates the Latin American Nuclear Free Zone, banning nuclear weapons in their part of the hemisphere.

On June 5, Israel launches a preemptive attack against Egypt, Syria, and Jordan and in a brief conflict known as the Six Day War, seizes the West Bank territory from Jordan, the Golan Heights from Syria, and the Sinai Peninsula from Egypt, and reunifies Jerusalem under Israeli control. The United Nations responds with UN Security Council Resolution 242, which requires Israel to return all territory gained in the war. The United States begins to increase its involvement in the conflict.

1968   On January 31, the Viet Cong launches a new military campaign, the Tet offensive, which will last for weeks. Contrary to the expectations of top U.S. officials, American success against the offensive does not help turn public opinion toward support for the war. On the contrary, the audacity of the Viet Cong in this effort and television pictures of battles on the grounds of the U.S. Embassy in Saigon convinces the U.S. public that a quick end to the conflict is not likely. The event occurs simultaneously with the siege of U.S. Marines at Khe Sanh and the devastation of Hue in northern South Vietnam.

In March, U.S. troops massacre civilians in the village of My Lai, increasing public anguish about U.S. behavior in the war.

A moderate regime under Alexander Dubček takes power in Czechoslovakia in March. Five months later, Soviet-led Warsaw Pact forces invade the country to curb its growing independence.

On April 4, civil rights leader and Nobel Peace Prize winner Martin Luther King Jr. is assassinated in Memphis, and riots break out across major metropolitan areas.

The number of airline hijackings, a relatively new form of political dissent, begins to climb.

The escalation of U.S. ground force deployments in Vietnam creates global protests against U.S. actions. In August, rioting in the streets of Chicago by students opposed to U.S. military involvement in Southeast Asia mars the Democratic Party's presidential convention. This street violence, which was broadly televised, illustrates the split within the nation about national security goals.

The United States and the Soviet Union begin tentative steps toward arms control talks, but they do not progress far.

1968 (cont.)	Claiming to have "a secret plan to end the war," former Vice President Richard Nixon defeats Vice President Hubert Humphrey for the presidency.
1969	Former President Dwight Eisenhower dies on March 28.
	On July 25 President Nixon, in a stopover in Guam, announces that the United States will support its allies' efforts to defend against Communist threats. This becomes known as the "Vietnamization" of conflict under the Nixon doctrine.
	Vietnamese nationalist Ho Chi Minh dies on September 3 in Hanoi.
1970	The Nuclear Nonproliferation Treaty (see chapter 5), with more than one hundred signatory states, goes into effect on March 5.
	In April, President Nixon sends U.S. forces to pursue Vietnamese opponents into Cambodia, an invasion that creates massive protests at home.
	The first Earth Day is proclaimed in April, bringing attention to the idea that the physical state of the planet is potentially as important as more traditional definitions of security.
	On May 4, four students protesting the expansion of the war from Vietnam into Cambodia are shot by Ohio National Guardsmen at Kent State University.
	On September 4, Socialist candidate Salvador Allende Gossens is elected as a minority president in Chile.
	A crisis called Black September begins on September 6, when the Popular Front for the Liberation of Palestine, supported by Syria, seizes four European airliners and brings them to Jordan, demanding the release of its members imprisoned in Europe and Israel. One of the hijackings fails, and the airliner is brought to London, where the surviving terrorist,

Leila Khaled, is imprisoned. The PFLP demands her release, hijacking another plane and holding over three hundred people hostage. The event threatens the overthrow of King Hussein of Jordan, who appeals for help to England and Israel. England releases Khaled in exchange for the hostages, and Hussein retains power in Jordan, perhaps aided by Israel.

President Gamal Abdel Nasser of Egypt dies on September 28 and is succeeded by Vice President Anwar el-Sadat.

Air Force officer Hafez al-Assad seizes power in Syria in December. Al-Assad will prove an enduring leader in the region as well as being extremely repressive, as shown by his harsh crackdown on the Muslim Brotherhood in the western city of Hama in 1982.

1971 Bangladesh declares its independence from Pakistan on March 26. Pakistan subsequently carries out a brutal attack on independence forces and civilians. The conflict ends in December, when India intervenes on behalf of Bangladesh, which will establish an independent government in January 1972.

Beginning on June 13, portions of *The Pentagon Papers* are published in the *New York Times*. The Nixon administration will take out a restraining order against the paper to stop publication, but by the end of June, the Supreme Court will rule that publication can continue.

In August, President Nixon unilaterally takes the United States off the gold exchange, effectively destroying the 1944 Bretton Woods Agreements. The action is required because the United States is no longer able to back up its currency with gold.

In October, the Republic of China on Taiwan, ruled by the Nationalists under Chiang Kai-shek, is ousted from permanent membership on the UN Security Council and replaced by the People's Republic of

1971
(cont.)
China, acknowledging Beijing's status as the legitimate government of China by the international community.

1972
President Nixon's visit to Beijing in February is the first by a U.S. senior official since the Communist victory in 1949, thus "opening" China to the West and improving U.S. relations with the Chinese Communists. This historic meeting is described in the Shanghai Communiqué (see chapter 5).

In May, President Nixon visits Moscow, where he signs the Strategic Arms Limitation (SALT I) and Antiballistic Missile (ABM) Treaties (see chapter 5) with Soviet Premier Leonid Brezhnev, culminating four years of arms control negotiations between the nuclear superpowers.

The Democratic Party headquarters is burglarized on June 17 by operatives tied to President Nixon's re-election campaign. The cover-up of this and other acts of espionage by the administration will lead to an enduring political firestorm that deeply affects the nation and undermines public trust in government.

The summer Olympics in Munich are interrupted by terrorism against Israeli athletes, illustrating the depth of feeling and the violence engendered by the Palestinian-Israeli conflict.

President Nixon defeats South Dakota Senator George McGovern for a second term.

Former President Truman dies on December 26 at the age of eighty-eight.

1973
Former President Lyndon Johnson dies on January 22, only a few days before the formal end of the Vietnam War.

On January 27, the Paris Peace Accords are signed by the United States, South Vietnam, and North Vietnam, putting an end to hostilities and requiring the withdrawal of all U.S. troops from South Vietnam within sixty days.

Chilean President Salvador Allende Gossens is overthrown on September 11 in a coup orchestrated by the CIA and Augusto Pinochet Ugarte, chief of staff of the Chilean Army.

On the highest and most solemn holy day in Judaism, Israel is attacked by Egypt and Syria, beginning the Yom Kippur War on October 6. As a result of U.S. assistance to Israel during the conflict, OPEC members agree to cut back petroleum production and to embargo sales to some states. Petroleum prices increase dramatically worldwide, proving that the Third World has commodities and power that can be leveraged against the developed world, especially the United States. Petroleum prices will remain elevated for almost a decade.

Congress, alarmed by virtually open-ended executive branch powers over the past decade, passes the War Powers Resolution on November 7 (see chapter 5). The resolution has never been signed into law, so its constitutionality remains in question, although U.S. presidents have acted in the spirit of the resolution.

1974   In May, India tests a "peaceful" nuclear explosive ("peaceful nuclear activities" being allowed under the Nonproliferation Treaty) and becomes the first Third World state to have nuclear capability.

As a result of the Watergate break-in and subsequent cover-up and investigation, President Nixon resigns on August 9. Vice President Gerald Ford is sworn in as president.

1975   Communist Parties win in elections in Vietnam, Cambodia, and Laos.

Chiang Kai-shek, president of the Republic of China, dies on April 5.

1975
(cont.)

The Communist Khmer Rouge, led by Pol Pot, seizes power in Cambodia on April 17, instituting a violent national upheaval that will result in over 1 million deaths in the next few years. Many are executed en masse in "killing fields," the title of a movie that will later reveal the extent of the violence to the Western public.

Lebanon has witnessed growing tensions between the Christian majority and the growing Muslim minority, allied with the Palestine Liberation Organization, and now civil war begins over power sharing in government. This destroys Lebanon's position as the "Switzerland of the Middle East" and leads the Palestinians to take a more prominent role in the country.

In November, the United Nations debates the issue of Zionism as a form of racism, casting a negative light on U.S. support for Israel.

1976

Chinese Premier Zhou Enlai dies on January 8.

Argentina, which has descended into a de facto civil war, deposes the sitting president, Isabel de Perón, on March 24 and imposes a "national security state." Thereafter, the military junta will violate the human rights of anyone thought to be an insurgent, regardless of juridical principles. Over the next eight years, thousands of Argentine citizens will "disappear" because of their political views or merely because they are "in the wrong place at the wrong time." Argentina's "national security" government will help the United States with several Cold War actions, including the training of right-wing counterinsurgencies in Central America, but it ultimately will feel betrayed by Washington.

Communist Party Chairman Mao Zedong dies on September 9. Together with the death of Premier Zhou Enlai, Mao's death formally ends the Great People's Cultural Revolution. Communist China begins the first post-Maoist purges, which include Mao's most recent wife, Jiang Qing, and the other three members of the Gang of Four.

Georgia Governor James "Jimmy" Carter defeats President Gerald Ford, who finished the second Nixon term.

1977   In March President Carter sends Secretary of State Cyrus Vance to Moscow with proposals for furthering the SALT II agreement. This takes place during a period of relative calm in the U.S.-Soviet relationship, known as détente.

In Israel, which had been founded as a socialist state by Ashkenazi (European) Jews, the leftist Labour Party suffers its first electoral defeat in May. The victorious Likud coalition, largely aimed at Sephardic (Spanish and Mediterranean) Jews, has a stance decidedly more opposed to ceding territory in the occupied West Bank. The tensions between Israeli settlers and West Bank Arabs grow.

In a commencement speech at Notre Dame University in June, President Carter declares that major national security concerns must include human rights and energy as well as traditional military forces and threats.

In August, the Palestinian Central Council declares the right of the Palestinians to "self-determination, to establish a national state" on their "national soil."

On September 7, President Carter completes negotiations with Panama and signs the Panama Canal Treaty, by which control of the canal will be returned to Panama on December 31, 1999.

In November, Egyptian President Sadat flies to Jerusalem to meet with Prime Minister Menachem Begin. He is the first Arab leader ever to do so.

1978   New Chinese leader Deng Xiaoping gradually begins an economic opening and dramatic reorientation of his society.

The Camp David Accords, brokered by President Carter between Israeli Prime Minister Menachem Begin and Egyptian President Anwar el-Sadat, are signed in September to bring peace to the Middle East. Although the accords will not be successful in bringing peace to the entire region, these two countries today remain formally at peace.

The CIA begins a new, decidedly unfavorable appraisal of Soviet intentions, known as Team B. This appraisal is consistent with views of many neoconservative skeptics of détente.

1979   In January, President Carter shifts U.S. recognition from Taiwan to Beijing. This ends a thirty-year policy of supporting Taiwan as the legitimate government of China. Conservatives in the United States, led by Arizona Senator Barry Goldwater, file suit to challenge the president's constitutional right to make this change, but the Supreme Court does not take the case. As a result, Congress passes the only law on U.S. relations with Taiwan, the Taiwan Relations Act (see chapter 5).

On January 16, Iran's leader, Muhammad Reza Shah Pahlavi, is forced from Iran by a revolution fomented by the Ayatollah Ruholla Khomeini, who is hostile to the United States and to Westernization and declares an Islamic Republic in Iran. In November, Khomeini encourages radicals to seize fifty-two U.S. hostages, who will be held for 444 days in Teheran.

On May 3, the Tory "Iron Lady," Margaret Thatcher, defeats the Labour Party's James Callahan to become the first woman elected prime minister in Great Britain.

SALT II is formally signed by the United States and the Soviet Union on June 18, but it is seen as a dangerous sell-out by U.S. conservatives, led by Ronald Reagan.

Pro-U.S. Nicaraguan dictator Anastasio Somoza Debayle flees to Paraguay on July 17, as the Frente Sandinista de Liberación Nacional (called the Sandinistas) increasingly dominates Nicaragua. Sandinista rule will last a decade, galvanizing the United States to support counterrevolutionaries (contras) and creating a scandal in the Reagan administration in the 1980s.

A U.S. satellite detects a mysterious "flash" over the southeast Atlantic in September, leading some to charge that Israel and South Africa are covertly working to develop nuclear weapons.

The Soviet Union invades Afghanistan on December 25, drawing global condemnation.

1980   Fidel Castro Ruz temporarily lifts Cuban exit restrictions, offering thousands of people the chance to leave Cuba. The United States offers asylum to a limited number of people, with political dissidents having first priority. All told, over 100,000 people flee to U.S. shores in the Mariel boatlift, from April through September. As this exodus proceeds, it becomes apparent that Castro has dumped many criminals and mentally disabled people instead of political dissidents.

The most unconventional leader in the Communist bloc, Josip Broz Tito, dies on May 4 in Yugoslavia. Tito had encouraged détente with the West, pluralism within the Communist world, and nonalignment for Third World countries. His death will lead to the breakdown of the Yugoslav entity into the composite national entities, resulting twelve years later in a brutal series of wars.

Iraq attacks Iran in September to gain access to the Shatt al Arab waterway. The eight-year-long conflict will cost more than 2 million lives.

1980 (cont.)	The Cable News Network, CNN, begins operation from Atlanta. This round-the-clock news access alters the Pentagon's control over the media in war and brings into people's homes from around the world an unending stream of news and images of events, many of which might otherwise have been historically minor occurrences.
	Former California Governor Ronald Reagan defeats President Carter for the presidency.
1981	On June 5, a mysterious new autoimmune deficiency is reported to have killed five young men in Los Angeles. It soon becomes apparent that the disease leads to high death rates and is prevalent among gay men in the Western world, centered in New York and San Francisco. It will eventually be called AIDS, or acquired immunodeficiency syndrome.
	On June 7, Israeli Prime Minister Menachem Begin sends jets to destroy the Osiraq nuclear reactor outside Baghdad to prevent Iraq from producing nuclear weapons. This move makes the United States more concerned about instability in the Middle East, but it does not dissuade the U.S. government from a tacit tolerance for Iraqi President Saddam Hussein.
	Egyptian President Anwar el-Sadat is assassinated on October 6 during a military parade in Cairo. The assassins are members of the Islamic Brotherhood who feel that Sadat has sold Egypt out to the Jewish state and is not abiding by the Sha'ria (Islamic law).
	The International Business Machines Company (IBM) introduces the personal computer (PC). The PC will make text communication even faster and more thorough than previous innovations. It will have a major effect on press coverage, the development of the Internet, and public access to all forms of international information.

1982   In April, Britain suffers an Argentine assault on its South Atlantic territories, the Falkland Islands, which Argentina also claims. Eventually a task force is dispatched to the area and the Argentine forces are hurled back, leading to the fall of the military regime in Buenos Aires in 1983.

Israel invades Lebanon in June to wipe out the PLO headquarters. Israeli Defense Minister and former General Ariel Sharon continues the invasion north of the Litani River, the psychological barrier above which Israel had not previously passed. Israel is condemned by the international community for daily airstrikes on the Muslim quarter of the city of Beirut.

In August, President Reagan deploys U.S. Marines to Beirut as a show of U.S. presence and as peacekeepers to Lebanon. The Marines serve as a peacekeeping force until September. They return again later that fall, after Phalangist allies of the Israelis carry out massacres at the Shatilla and Sabra refugee camps, killing hundreds of Palestinians.

NATO begins a "two-track" approach to missile modernization: continuing negotiations with the Russians for arms reductions while increasing the newer, more capable missiles deployed in Europe. Massive anti-U.S. protests cover Europe.

Low on cash reserves, Mexico acknowledges on September 6 that it must suspend payment on its foreign debt, setting off a Latin American debt crisis. By the mid-1980s, Mexico, Brazil, Venezuela, and Argentina all have serious debt, which threatens the international banking sector. Eventually, the debt will be renegotiated, but the net outflow of foreign exchange for debt-servicing will outweigh any foreign assistance that comes into the region. This is known as the "Lost Decade" in the region because standards of living fall so dramatically in the 1980s.

1982	Leonid Brezhnev, general secretary of the Communist
(cont.)	Party Central Committee in the USSR, dies in Moscow
	on November 10.

Fearful of Soviet expansionism in Central America, the United States begins arming and training counterinsurgents in the region. This involvement provokes charges of human rights violations because the militaries in the region, working with right-wing, anti-Communist death squads in the area, try to "purge the society" from elements seen as undesirable without recourse to any system of justice. Comparisons to Stalin's purges of political opponents are clear.

1983   In a televised speech on March 23, President Reagan endorses the Strategic Defense Initiative (see chapter 5), a defense strategy based on still-to-be-invented technologies for space-based systems. In the same speech, he calls attention to his concerns about a growing Soviet and Cuban base in the Caribbean island of Grenada.

On October 23, more than 230 U.S. Marines die at the hands of a suicide bomber in barracks outside Beirut, proving that peacekeeping is an exceptionally dangerous enterprise.

On October 25, the United States invades Grenada, ostensibly to protect U.S. students.

Argentina elects a democratic government in October, when the military government is forced out by protests against its regime and elections are held for the first time in a decade. The criticism focuses on the regime's military incompetence in the Falklands (Malvinas) war in the South Atlantic; on its ineffective economic policy, as it built a massive external debt; and on its human rights abuses, which have become increasingly apparent as the group of protesters called the Grandmothers in the Plaza gather every Wednesday afternoon across from the Presidential House to ask where their "disappeared" children are.

1984   New Zealand refuses to allow the United States to sail into its harbors any ships that are carrying nuclear weapons or that are powered by nuclear fuel. In response, the United States refuses to acknowledge whether its ships carry nuclear weapons. The following year New Zealand will be suspended from the ANZUS (Australia, New Zealand, and United States) Treaty, signed in 1951, over its refusal to adhere to stipulated procedures for nuclear weapons.

Prime Minister Indira Gandhi is assassinated on October 31 by her Sikh bodyguards in response to the suppression of insurgents at the Sikh temple in Amritsar earlier that year.

President Reagan defeats former Vice President Walter Mondale for a second term.

1985   Mikhail Gorbachev takes control in the Soviet Union after Konstantin Chernenko's death on March 11.

A spy ring headed by Arthur John Walker, an enlisted Navy man, is unearthed by the U.S. government, with evidence of many years of damage to U.S. national security. The men are indicted on May 28.

In a speech to the Central Military Committee in June, Chinese Communist Party Chairman Deng Xiaoping enunciates a major reorientation of China's defense strategy—from thwarting a possible Soviet invasion to responding to "wars around the periphery," the borders that China shares with fifteen other states.

Gorbachev and President Reagan meet at the Geneva Summit in November. Among other things, they discuss the need for improved dialogue between the two superpowers, for a ban on chemical weapons, for improved cooperation in research on nuclear fusion, and for increased cultural exchange between the two nations.

1986   The Ukrainian nuclear power plant at Chernobyl suffers a massive disaster on April 26, contaminating surrounding areas and shutting down the reactor.

In a September speech, President Reagan declares narcotics a national security issue for the United States.

The Goldwater-Nichols Military Reform Law is passed by Congress, intending to alter the military's ability to work together in a "joint" fashion while enhancing the leadership and management of the armed forces of the United States.

In October, President Reagan and First Secretary Gorbachev meet at the Reykjavík Summit in Iceland to discuss new arms reductions proposals.

1987   The March report of the Tower Commission, headed by former Senator John Tower of Texas, former National Security Advisor Brent Scowcroft, and former Senator and Secretary of State Edmund Muskie, condemns the Reagan administration for lax supervision of a complicated national security debacle, known as Iran-Contra.

1988   An agreement is reached in April regarding Soviet withdrawal from Afghanistan, ending a bitter chapter for the declining empire as its vaulted Red Army admits that it cannot defeat the more primitive Afghan forces. This was in part a victory for the United States, which gave significant support to the Afghans, but that victory will have its own cost since anti-Soviet Afghan forces will eventually turn on their U.S. patrons and plant the seeds of the al Qaeda network now involved in global terrorism.

In August, strongman Saddam Hussein of Iraq uses chemical weapons against the Iraqi Kurds, the first known use of such weapons since World War I.

U.S. Vice President George H. W. Bush defeats Massachusetts Governor Michael Dukakis for the presidency.

In December, a massive earthquake in the Soviet province of Armenia kills thousands of people. The government's inability to respond reveals the extent of Soviet military ineptitude.

1989   In January, the U.S.-Canada Free Trade Agreement, intended to lower the trade barriers between the North American neighbors, goes into effect, forming the basis for the subsequent North American Free Trade Agreement (NAFTA) with Mexico in 1994.

The Soviet Red Army withdraws from Afghanistan by February.

In June, the Chinese Communist Party crushes a protest movement in Tiananmen Square, killing some three thousand Chinese students. The incident chills the budding Chinese-Western relationship as it becomes clear that, unlike Gorbachev, who is seeking to modernize politically, the Chinese are interested only in economic modernization.

The East German government, with Soviet backing, admits it can no longer effectively control migration between the two Berlins. On November 9, protesters begin to tear down the wall. In the next two years, Communist regimes will fall throughout Eastern Europe.

The United States intervenes in Panama in December to seize strongman Manuel Noriega Morena, ostensibly because of his ties to drug traffickers.

1990   In Nicaragua, the Sandinistas lose a public election in February and surrender office more than a decade after seizing power and raising U.S. fears of Communist victories in Central America. The party will rapidly lose its influence in Nicaraguan society.

In August, Saddam Hussein seizes Kuwait. In the Persian Gulf War, called Operation Desert Storm, the United States and Britain build a coalition against

1990
(cont.)

Iraq, including France, Syria, Egypt, and Saudi Arabia. As Saddam Hussein attacks Israel with Scud missiles, the Bush administration convinces Israel not to launch missiles or atomic strikes in retaliation.

Soviet leaders agree to the eventual reunification of the two Germanies within NATO in the September "Two-Plus-Four" Treaty. Ratification will occur the following year.

President George H. W. Bush declares his intent to form a Free Trade Zone of the Americas, expanding on President Reagan and Canadian Prime Minister Brian Mulroney's U.S.-Canada free trade arrangement.

In November, the Iron Lady, Prime Minister Margaret Thatcher, is ousted from power in Britain amidst criticism of her economic policy and her unwillingness to support economic integration with the European Community. She is succeeded by John Major.

1991

In February, South African anti-apartheid leader Nelson Rolihlahla Mandela wins release from Robben Island prison, where he has spent almost thirty years. His release is one of a series of steps leading to the fall of apartheid rule in South Africa.

After careful preparation and buildup, a U.S.-led coalition defeats Saddam Hussein, forcing Iraqi forces from Kuwait but not ousting Saddam from power. A permanent cease-fire is reached on April 6. In the aftermath of the war, the United States begins talking about a much more prominent and enduring role in the Middle East, including the long-term stationing of troops in Saudi Arabia.

The provinces of Croatia and Slovenia declare their independence from Yugoslavia in May and June, respectively. Bosnia-Herzegovina and Macedonia will follow suit within the year.

Former Indian Prime Minister Rajiv Gandhi is assassinated by a Tamil suicide bomber on May 21 at a campaign rally, just as he is hoping to retake control of the Indian Parliament as leader of the Congress Party.

Serbian President Slobodan Milosevic and Croatian President Franjo Tudjman have been manipulating nationalist feeling in what was then Yugoslavia. The two republics skirmish, and war breaks out in July.

The Strategic Arms Reduction Treaty (START) I is signed by the Soviet Union and the United States in July, specifically attempting to reduce arms levels rather than merely stabilizing them.

The Soviet Union ceases to exist on December 26. A former Communist Party leader, Boris Yeltsin, becomes president of the newly independent Russian Federation.

The Maastricht Treaty is negotiated by most European Community members in December, creating a European central currency, the euro, and a central European bank. It will be signed the following February and ratified in November 1993. Belgium, Denmark, France, Germany, Greece, Ireland, Italy, Luxembourg, the Netherlands, Spain, and Portugal together create the European Monetary System, feared by some as a major competitor to the United States.

1992   In April, ethnic violence escalates in the former Yugoslavian province of Bosnia-Herzegovina.

Civil war in Somalia disintegrates into chaos and starvation, convincing President Bush to send troops there for food distribution. The U.S. troops begin to arrive in December, the first part of a larger UN force sent to restore order. The U.S. military will not be comfortable with the peace operations role, and much national debate ensues, much of it centered on whether the United States ought to participate in UN peacekeeping operations that might be under foreign control.

1992
(cont.)

Haitians, classified by the United States as economic rather than political refugees, flee to the Florida coast. The U.S. Coast Guard and President Bush attempt to convince them to stay home rather than taking flimsy boats across the sea.

A significant recession that has affected the U.S. economy since 1990 raises the specter of white-collar layoffs, and many fear that U.S. economic growth has stalled. Though nearly over by late 1992, the recession is a major contributor to Bill Clinton's presidential victory. Among other things, Clinton's campaign highlights the danger of defense spending that produces large deficits.

Arkansas Governor Bill Clinton defeats President George H. W. Bush for the presidency.

1993

On February 26, a bomb in the underground parking garage at the World Trade Center in New York City kills six people. U.S. officials charge Islamic radicals with the crime. Among those convicted is Egyptian cleric Omar Abdel-Rahman, who has been inciting violence against the United States. This attack also appears to be the initial action of the al Qaeda network funded by Saudi millionaire Usama Bin Laden.

The Oslo negotiations between Israel and the Palestinians, carried on in secret over several years, result in a peace accord signed by Prime Minister Rabin and Chairman Arafat at the White House on September 13. The right wing in each camp is unhappy with the agreement, and tensions continue.

An attempted coup against Russian President Boris Yeltsin in Moscow, led by his vice president, is met with severe force on September 28. The clash is seen on global television, resulting in a serious credibility problem for Yeltsin and for democracy in Russia.

The UN mission in Somalia shifts from providing humanitarian aid to "nation-building," forcing a deadly encounter with local warlords and causing the death of a number of international peacekeepers, including eighteen Americans in October.

In November, apartheid ends in South Africa, ending pressure on the United States to end its support for the racist regime, which was a major anti-Communist ally.

The European Union is formalized with ratification of the Maastricht Treaty in November, creating one large market and monetary system. This triggers concerns that its goal is to displace the United States as the world's economic leader.

1994   The North American Free Trade Agreement (NAFTA) takes effect on January 1, provoking violence in Mexico but expanding trade among the United States, Canada, and Mexico (see chapter 5).

Career CIA employee Aldrich Ames and his wife are arrested on February 24 for more than a decade's worth of spying for the Soviets and the Russians. The U.S. government believes Ames's actions have compromised U.S. national security to the core and have led to the death of several covert agents.

Beginning in April, ethnic conflict in Rwanda and Burundi leads to massacres of thousands, mostly Tutsi and moderate Hutu, while the international community does little in response.

Nelson Mandela is elected president of South Africa in April. Mandela's presidency creates a new ally for the United States in this region, which is plagued with nontraditional threats such as money laundering and AIDS.

The World Trade Organization is formally established on April 15 to lower trade barriers and arbitrate in trade disputes. The WTO will come into force the following year.

1994 (cont.)	The violence in Bosnia-Herzegovina, which began with its declaration of independence from the former Republic of Yugoslavia, escalates as the Serbs seek to enhance their position. Eventually, protecting Muslims in Bosnia becomes a NATO activity.
1995	The Arthur P. Murrah Federal Building in Oklahoma City is destroyed by a bomb on April 19, killing 168 people. A former enlisted soldier, Timothy J. McVeigh, is soon caught and will be convicted of the crime. The bombing reveals the vulnerability of the United States to terrorism.
	Despite strong protests by the People's Republic of China, Taiwan's president Lee Deng-hui receives a visa to visit his alma mater, Cornell University, hence setting foot on U.S. soil as president of Taiwan. He visits the university and delivers a speech in June.
	In September, NATO launches air strikes against Serbs engaged in ethnic cleansing in Bosnia, thus using force for the first time in its history.
	The Dayton Accord, which is intended to resolve the Bosnia-Herzegovina conflict, is initialed by Presidents Tudjman and Milosevic on November 21 near Dayton, Ohio, and signed in Paris a month later. U.S. troops, part of a large UN force, will begin an extended peace-keeping mission on the ground in 1996.
1996	Beijing launches missiles to intimidate Taiwan during the Taiwanese presidential elections in March. This will prompt U.S. President Clinton to send two carrier battle groups into the Taiwan Strait to reinforce the U.S. position that, regardless of explicit treaty obligations, it will protect Taiwan against Chinese aggression.
	The Comprehensive Test Ban Treaty is opened for signature on September 24 and brought before the U.S. Senate for ratification. Conservatives fear it will weaken the U.S. defense posture and treaty ratification efforts fail.

President Clinton wins a second term by defeating Senator Robert Dole.

1997   Former Communist Party Chairman Deng Xiaoping, the last of the Revolutionary Generation who fought the Nationalists with Mao Zedong during the 1920s, 1930s, and 1940s, dies on February 19 in Beijing.

Serbian President Slobodan Milosevic's continuing aggression begins to target Muslim Kosovars in the former Yugoslav Republic of Kosovo, leading the international community again to consider intervention.

Zaire's strongman Mobuto Sese Seko, an artifact from the Cold War, is overthrown by Laurent Kabila in May. The coup throws the vast area of central Africa into conflict and raises questions about the U.S. commitment to parts of the world with black populations.

On July 1, the British Crown Colony of Hong Kong reverts to the People's Republic of China for the first time in 150 years.

In July, the Asian economic crisis begins in Thailand and spreads through most of East Asia, with China the notable exception. This economic crisis shows the vulnerability of the global economy and requires the United States to support International Monetary Fund (IMF) economic reforms in the region. Unfortunately, these IMF-ordered reforms create further trouble and generate disappointment in the U.S. efforts, leading by May 1998 to the collapse of Indonesian President Suharto's thirty-one-year regime.

1998   India and Pakistan shock the world when they each test their rudimentary nuclear arsenals: India conducts five tests on May 11 and May 13, and Pakistan responds with tests on May 28 and May 30. Pakistan's are the first nuclear tests to be conducted directly in response to those of another state. The tests spark international concern that the nonproliferation regime has completely broken down.

1998
(cont.)

U.S. embassies in Dar es Salaam, Tanzania, and Nairobi, Kenya, are both bombed on August 7. The United States charges Saudi millionaire Usama Bin Laden with masterminding the assaults, but retaliatory actions fail to kill him.

Former General Augusto Pinochet Ugarte of Chile is arrested on October 16 in London, where he was receiving medical treatment. The surprise action comes under a Spanish warrant charging him with abusing the human rights of Spanish citizens in Chile. The arrest sparks an international debate about the immunity of former heads of state and the limits of human rights under international law.

1999

On May 4, the Oslo Accords expire without the establishment of a Palestinian state. The United States calls on both parties to rebuild a "relationship of trust."

Without UN sanction, NATO launches a massive air campaign to stop Serb actions against Kosovars. On May 7, a U.S. bomber involved in the campaign erroneously hits the Chinese Embassy in Belgrade. Beijing reacts with stunned fury, since not only was it unable to stop the action against Serbia but it also became a victim of the conflict.

The Panama Canal reverts to Panamanian control on December 31, in compliance with the Panama Canal Treaty signed by President Carter in 1977.

2000

On July 2, Vicente Fox becomes the first candidate outside the Institutional Revolutionary Party (PRI) to be elected president in Mexico since 1928.

In July, the U.S. Congress approves an aid package to Colombia in excess of $3 billion, known as Plan Colombia, to help fight the war on drugs. The plan is controversial because President Clinton, citing national security concerns, waives provisions requiring the Colombian military to be held accountable for human rights violations. Additionally, the plan has no clearly stated goal, reminding some critics of the Gulf of Tonkin Resolution and the open-ended U.S. involvement in Vietnam.

President Clinton spends much of the summer personally involved in negotiations between Israeli Prime Minister Ehud Barak and Palestine Authority President Yasser Arafat. Despite moderate optimism, the two sides are not able to reach an accord on settlement of the generations-long conflict over the West Bank, the Gaza Strip, and Jerusalem.

A bloody Palestinian uprising, or *intifada*, breaks out in September after Likud leader Ariel Sharon and several supporters visit the Temple Mount in Jerusalem, sacred to both Muslims and Jews. Sharon will defeat Prime Minister Ehud Barak in the 2001 elections for prime minister.

Texas Governor George W. Bush defeats Vice President Albert Gore in a highly contested election that will not be resolved until December.

2001   A Chinese Air Force jet collides with a U.S. EP3 reconnaissance plane over the South China Sea on April 1. The U.S. jet manages to land in southern China, where its crew is held for eleven days. The incident exacerbates growing tensions between the United States and China.

On June 11, three months to the day before the September 11 attacks, Oklahoma City bomber Timothy McVeigh is executed by the United States.

On June 28, Slobodan Milosevic, ousted from office through an open election in 2000, is surrendered by Serbian authorities to the International Court of Justice in The Hague, where he faces charges of genocide and crimes against humanity.

A career FBI counterespionage agent, Robert Hanssen, pleads guilty on July 6 to spying for the Soviet Union

2001
(cont.)

and then Russia in one of the most thorough infiltrations by a spy in the history of U.S. intelligence. Hanssen's betrayal, given his knowledge, shakes confidence in the efficacy of U.S. intelligence.

In the United States, four commercial jets are hijacked by Islamist extremists from the al Qaeda network on September 11. Two of the planes crash into the World Trade Center in New York, one crashes into the Pentagon in Washington, DC, and the fourth crashes into a field in Pennsylvania. In New York, just under three thousand people perish; the Pentagon deaths number just below two hundred. On the four planes, 256 people died. This audacious terrorist attack is the worst in history. The Bush administration, with support from Prime Minister Tony Blair's government in Britain, launches a "war against terrorism" that increasingly appears to many around the world to be a war against Islam.

In October, anthrax-laced letters arrive in the offices of Democratic Senators Thomas Daschle and Patrick Leahy. Several people die from the anthrax exposure and the government begins a massive campaign to sterilize the mail to prevent proliferation of the potentially deadly spores.

The United States works with Afghan forces to oust the Taliban government in Afghanistan, charging it with protecting Usama Bin Laden, a Saudi-born terrorist. Bin Laden is identified by Washington as the mastermind behind the network that brought about the September 11 attacks. Hamid Karzai, a U.S.-educated Afghan, assumes the job of interim head of state in Kabul, promising to bring democracy and peace to the broken and war-torn nation.

On November 10, the World Trade Organization admits the Communist-led People's Republic of China. China's accession to the WTO is a tribute to the influence of globalization and evidence of the desire of most countries to participate in normal international trade, whatever their ideology.

In December, President Bush announces that the United States will withdraw from the 1972 Antiballistic Missile Treaty, long identified as the bedrock of U.S.-Soviet arms control agreements.

2002   President Bush dramatically increases the budget for military spending.

The Palestinian *intifada* and the Israeli response in the West Bank and Israel accelerate, leading to much more violence in the Middle East.

India and Pakistan, both nuclear-armed states, stand on the brink of war for several months as New Delhi accuses Islamabad of allowing insurgents and terrorists to cross into India to cause conflict. This escalation of tension follows an attack on the Indian Parliament in December 2001 by unidentified armed men who India claims must be Pakistani. U.S. and other attempts to lower the tensions are only moderately successful, but the U.S. need for Pakistan's support in the war against al Qaeda in Afghanistan is a complicating factor.

Presidents Vladimir Putin and George W. Bush sign a markedly different arms reduction treaty aimed at reducing nuclear stockpiles to previously unheard of levels.

Russia is admitted to NATO, albeit in a reduced role compared to role of other NATO members.

4

Personalities

Perhaps the most difficult task in writing this volume was identifying the most important individuals for inclusion in an introductory book on national security. One is tempted to include people relating to only a single aspect of national security—say, the diplomatic realm or the political office-holders—but that would be incomplete. So I have tried to be as wide-ranging as possible in this chapter, acknowledging that other scholars would probably include (and exclude) other personalities than those I am highlighting here.

My decision to include these individuals relates to their pivotal role in some aspect of national security, including the effects on the United States of their significant involvement in an event. This chapter is written with a broader interpretation of national security than that used during the Cold War (for example, narcotics trafficker Carlos Lehder Rivas is included because the expansion of drugs into the national security calculation has been demonstrable), but it is still heavily biased toward those individuals who have played traditional security roles, such as presidents, military leaders, and foreign officials.

Dean Gooderham Acheson (1893–1971)

Dean Acheson served as secretary of state between 1949 and the end of the Truman administration in January 1953. Acheson was an ardent Europeanist, seeking to protect and enhance the European Recovery Program designed by his predecessor, George C. Marshall, and actively supporting the founding of the North Atlantic Treaty Organization (NATO), which endures today.

Acheson is often blamed for the beginning of the Korean War because he did not include South Korea within the U.S. "defense perimeter" in a January 1950 speech (see chapter 5), and the North Koreans invaded the South in June of that year. He also attracted controversy for defending accused Communist spy Alger Hiss, for which he was condemned and hounded by Senator Joseph McCarthy of Wisconsin during the Communist "witch hunt" of the early 1950s. McCarthy's suspicions were only exacerbated by the fact that Acheson was secretary of state when the Communist People's Republic of China was proclaimed in Beijing in October 1949.

Acheson's retirement years were almost as active as his earlier life, as he served as an envoy for President John F. Kennedy to European leaders during the Cuban Missile Crisis (October 1962) and advised President Lyndon Johnson to end the bombing of North Vietnam in 1968.

Konrad Adenauer (1876–1967)

First Chancellor of West Germany after its establishment in 1949, Konrad Adenauer was a Christian Democrat jailed for opposition activities during the Nazi era. Upon taking office as chancellor, Adenauer worked mightily to prove that West Germany was a bulwark against Soviet aggression in Europe. He began the improbable turnaround of Franco-German relations while solidifying ties with the United States. He brought West Germany into NATO and proved a major force in the establishment of the European Economic Community, today the European Union.

Yasser Arafat (1929–)

The most famous Palestinian in the world, Yasser Arafat was born in Cairo to Palestinian parents and spent only a portion of his childhood in Palestine. Educated as an engineer in his native Egypt, Arafat moved to Kuwait and, with friends, founded the Al-Fatah movement in 1959 to support the armed overthrow of the state of Israel. In 1964, the Palestine Liberation Organization (PLO) was created under the auspices of the Arab League to "liberate" Palestine for its exiled population. Arafat, relocated again to Jordan, increasingly took control of Fatah and waged guerrilla warfare against Israel, especially after the Israeli victory in the 1967 Six Day War. As Fatah became the dominant organized group within the Palestinian community, Arafat's role grew until he became the head of the PLO Executive Committee in 1969.

Over the next two decades, Arafat moved the PLO head-quarters to various locations to prevent Israeli attacks and to argue for a global recognition of the Palestinian cause. In September 1993, it was revealed that Arafat and King Hussein of Jordan had been negotiating with the Israelis for several months, leading to the Oslo Accords, which included a Palestinian Authority on the West Bank and the implication of a Palestinian state in the Middle East. Hussein had announced in the late 1980s that he had made peace with Israel, so a Palestinian state was not likely to be in Jordan; Arafat maneuvered for a state entity, under his presidency, in the West Bank. In 1993, he won the Nobel Peace Prize along with Israeli Prime Minister Yitzhak Rabin and Foreign Minister Shimon Peres.

After Rabin's assassination in late 1995, Israeli relations with the Palestine Authority deteriorated, particularly under Likud leaders such as Prime Ministers Benyamin Netanyahu and Ariel Sharon. After Sharon's September 2000 visit to the Western Wall in Jerusalem, an *intifada* (uprising) of Palestinians against Israel began that became the most violent in the history of the conflict. Arafat was blamed by the Israelis for not negotiating in good faith during the Camp David talks run by President Clinton in 2000, and the talks never reached any conclusion.

Beginning in December 2001, the Israeli government put Arafat under de facto house arrest because he proved unable to prevent suicide bombings against Israeli citizens. In March 2002, the Israeli Defense Force launched a coordinated assault against the Palestinian terror campaign, sending tanks into Palestinian cities and demanding that the terrorist infrastructure be shut down. Arafat became a symbol of the Palestinian people under siege when his headquarters in Ramallah was targeted by the Israeli Defense Force.

Jacobo Arbenz Guzmán (1913–1971)

A middle-class Guatemalan, Jacobo Arbenz Guzmán was minister of war after the overthrow of dictator Jorge Ubico. In 1950, he left the army and was elected president of Guatemala. Backed by the strong social concerns of his wife, María Cristina Vilanova, he began a social revolution to alter economic conditions in the country.

Although the resulting social upheaval was modest, Arbenz Guzmán's agrarian reforms led to expropriation of United Fruit Company holdings in 1953, sparking major concerns in the United States that Guatemala was "going Communist." The United Fruit Company began a public campaign against him, the U.S. State Department charged that the Arbenz Guzmán government was not paying "prompt, adequate, and fair compensation," as international law required, and an opposition led by Colonel Carlos Castillo Armas began arming for intervention from neighboring Nicaragua. The opposition received assistance from the Central Intelligence Agency, which was trying to prevent Communist subversion of the hemisphere.

In June 1954, Castillo Armas attacked the government and forced Arbenz Guzmán from office. In the remaining seventeen years of his life, he moved between Switzerland, Uruguay, Cuba, and Mexico, where he finally died in exile.

Menachem Begen (1913–1992)

Born in present-day Belarus, Menachem Begin was the first non–Labour Party prime minister of Israel (1977–1983). Upon his election in 1977, his Likud coalition began to assert its role as more confrontational and less patient with Israel's Arab neighbors about issues such as the occupied territories and the West Bank. Begin's election also marked the rise of the more conservative, Sephardic (non-European) Jews as a political power in traditionally liberal, Ashkenazi (European) Israel.

It was under Begin that the first Jewish settlements were started on the West Bank. Less than six months after Begin took power, Egyptian President Anwar el-Sadat flew to Jerusalem to open discussions with Israel. Sadat and Begin ultimately signed a peace treaty after negotiating the Camp David Accords, which ultimately cost Sadat his life and created a split within Israel. In June 1982, Israel invaded Lebanon, going further than the traditional intervention line at the Litani River to oust the Palestine Liberation Organization from its headquarters in Beirut and to stop it from shelling northern Israel. The invasion proved a public relations disaster, compounded by the Sabra and Shatilla refugee camp massacre in September. Upon his wife's death that same year, Begin's interest in governing faded, and he was living as a recluse when he died in 1992.

Ernest Bevin (1881–1951)

After serving as a labor activist early in the twentieth century, Ernest Bevin became a major figure in the British Labour Party and helped organize the General Strike of 1926. He joined the coalition government of Sir Winston Churchill in 1939, serving as minister of labor and national service. At the end of World War II, he took on a significant role in foreign affairs for Labour Prime Minister Clement Attlee, being an avowed supporter of stronger ties with the United States. He was an important organizer of the Berlin Airlift, which kept West Berlin fed and fueled as the Soviets cut off land links. Bevin was also an important figure in the founding of the North Atlantic Treaty Organization in 1949, in which Britain was a crucial member.

Usama Bin Laden (1957–)

One of the few, if not the only, non–head of state to provoke a war over his behavior, Usama Bin Laden, the son of a Saudi construction engineer, has been credited with creating the massive conspiracy that led to the World Trade Center and Pentagon terrorism in September 2001. In retaliation, the United States and a coalition of allies launched a military campaign against Bin Laden's terrorist organization, al Qaeda, and the Taliban government of Afghanistan that was harboring Bin Laden and his followers.

Bin Laden is one of many sons from the Saudi elite who helped the Afghan mujahideen in their fight against the Soviet intervention that began after 1979. Bin Laden spent much of his personal fortune, valued in the millions of dollars, to organize the al Qaeda network, which initially fought with the mujahideen against the Soviets. He also expended enormous sums to inject Wahhabi Islam (the sect of Sunni Islam centered in the Nedj area surrounding the Saudi capital, Riyadh) into Afghanistan. Afghanistan had been Islamic for well over a thousand years, but because Afghanistan was a highly decentralized state, a somewhat decentralized faith had taken root. In contrast, Wahhabi Islam is a more strict interpretation of Sunni Islam that relies on a rigid use of Sha'ria (Islamic law) for governing societies, and since the late 1970s, Wahhabi has been used as a method of bringing states firmly back into the Islamic fold. Eventually, the Taliban, a strict Islamic group with views coinciding with much of Wahhabism, ousted the post-Soviet government in Afghanistan, and Bin Laden's power in that country grew. By the late 1990s, he and his al Qaeda organization openly used Afghanistan as a base of operations.

In helping the Afghanis oust the Soviets in the 1980s, Bin Laden acted in concert with the United States. Within a few years, however, his irritation at U.S. ties to Israel, his abhorrence of U.S. military presence near the sacred Islamic sites of Mecca and Medina on the Saudi peninsula, and his objections to U.S. support for a Saudi regime that Bin Laden viewed as all too secular and pro-Western led Bin Laden to attack the United States. Although direct proof of Bin Laden's role in the 1993 World Trade Center bombing in New York City has never been made public, rumors of his involvement persist. More recently, he and his operatives stand accused of masterminding the 1998 bombings of U.S. embassies in Dar-es-Salaam, Tanzania, and Nairobi, Kenya, and of planning the bombing of the U.S.S. *Cole* while it was docked in Yemen.

In 2001, in the immediate aftermath of the September 11 terrorism, Bin Laden appeared on a number of videotapes taking credit for the attack. In October of that year, President George W. Bush launched an attack on Afghanistan and the al Qaeda organization, with the original intent of capturing Bin Laden and bringing down his network. As of May 2002, the Taliban government is out of power in Afghanistan. The Bush administration believes that al Qaeda has been broken up, but attacks on the U.S. forces that remain in Afghanistan lead to questions about this assessment. Finally, while Bin Laden has not been seen alive for certain since a December 2001 video, he does appear to have survived the savage attacks aimed at killing him and perhaps has managed to flee Afghanistan, possibly for the sanctuary of allied believers in neighboring Pakistan.

Willy Brandt (1913–1992)

Perhaps the fieriest chancellor of post–World War II Germany, Willy Brandt was a towering figure in international affairs in the middle decades of the twentieth century. Having fled from Germany during World War II, Brandt returned from exile in Norway to run for political office in the 1940s and 1950s. He was elected mayor of West Berlin in 1957 and ran for the Bundestag (the lower house of the legislature) as a socialist in the 1960s. In 1969, Brandt became chancellor and set about to lessen tensions between the Germanies in a policy that he labeled Ostpolitik, for which he won the Nobel Peace Prize in 1971.

Brandt was forced from office by a spy scandal in his office the following year, but he retained an international leadership role in promoting fuller ties between the Germanies. In the late 1970s he was known for the United Nations development report that carried his name. The Brandt Commission Report noted the growing gap between rich and poor and advocated steps to lessen these differences and promote better growth for the entire world. He was also a major figure in the Socialist International, an international federation of democratic socialist parties.

Leonid Ilyich Brezhnev (1906–1982)

Secretary general of the Communist Party and premier of the Soviet Union between Nikita Khrushchev's ouster in 1964 and his own death in 1982, Leonid Brezhnev was pivotal in the Soviet nuclear buildup and the rise and fall of Soviet foreign presence. His ascendancy to party leadership began after the Cuban Missile Crisis, in which the Soviet Union had been embarrassed and forced to back down, and in response he enunciated the Brezhnev Doctrine, which claimed that Soviet intervention in other Communist states was justified.

Under Brezhnev's leadership in the 1960s, the Soviet Union sent troops into Czechoslovakia in 1968 to prevent Alexander Dubček from taking a nonsocialist path, it supported so-called wars of national liberation in Africa and Southeast Asia, and it funded the modernization and proliferation of missile systems. Early the following decade, Brezhnev negotiated and signed the Antiballistic Missile Treaty and the Strategic Arms Limitations Treaty I with the United States (see chapter 5). In 1979, Brezhnev sent Soviet troops into Afghanistan, beginning a decade-long debacle that did not end until five years after his death, when the Soviets were forced to withdraw by mujahideen rebels. During Brezhnev's tenure, the détente with the United States turned to a frigid Cold War, and the poverty of the Soviet economic system became increasingly difficult to mask.

George H. W. Bush (1924–)

George H. W. Bush was the first sitting vice president in over one hundred years to win election to the U.S. presidency. He had been

Director of Central Intelligence, U.S. envoy to the People's Republic of China, head of the Republican Party, and a congressman from Texas. The Bush presidency (1989–1993) witnessed several major international events, including the end of the Soviet Union and the Eastern Bloc, which the administration was slow to recognize; the Gulf War with former ally Saddam Hussein over his seizure of Kuwait and his threat to confiscate petroleum fields in neighboring Saudi Arabia; the use of the U.S. Army and Marines in Panama to arrest dictator Manuel Noriega Morena on drug charges; the disintegration of the former Republic of Yugoslavia into warring ethnic enclaves trying to function as sovereign states; and the brutal repression in Tiananmen Square of a nascent Chinese prodemocracy movement that might have led to the end of the Communist Party in China. Bush's presidency was one of momentous global change, and the president prided himself on his personal connections and affiliations with world leaders. Sometimes these ties seem to have slowed the U.S. reaction to various events, such as the Tiananmen Square massacre in 1989. Bush was unable to win reelection despite his vast foreign policy experience because the public was more concerned with a severe recession and the apparent transformation of the U.S. economy than with the "management" of world affairs.

George Walker Bush (1946–)

George Walker Bush, son of U.S. President George H. W. Bush, assumed the office of the U.S. presidency in January 2001 under the greatest constitutional cloud in U.S. history, having defeated his opponent, Vice President Al Gore, by fewer than six hundred votes in Florida. The U.S. Supreme Court eventually decided the case in a controversial split decision, and Bush began his administration under a cloud of controversy. Before arriving in Washington, he had been a baseball team owner, energy entrepreneur, and governor of Texas. Bush led the country during the September 11, 2001, attack on the World Trade Center in New York and the Pentagon in Washington, the biggest international terrorist attack on the United States in history.

Soon after the attacks, Bush organized a coalition, primarily with the help of British Prime Minister Tony Blair, to pursue mastermind Usama Bin Laden, head of the terrorist al Qaeda network, in Afghanistan. Within three months, the United States led a military action that ousted the Taliban, an Islamic fundamentalist government with strong links to Saudi Islam, from its exceptionally repressive governance of Afghanistan, installing a pro-Western interim government in Kabul under Pashtun tribal leader Hamid Karzai. President Bush warned terrorists around the world that the United States would pursue them anywhere, and the war on terrorism that he declared soon led to a major expansion in defense spending and the establishment of an extensive "homeland security" program in the United States. All of this occurred during a period of economic recession in the United States, which President Bush addressed through a significant tax cut. Coming at the time of the war against terrorism and other domestic requirements, this policy returned the United States to deficit spending for the first time in several years.

James Earl "Jimmy" Carter Jr. (1924–)

President James "Jimmy" Carter may achieve more respect for his activities since his presidency ended than any other president. Son of a Georgia peanut farmer and a graduate of the U.S. Naval Academy, Carter returned to Georgia as a young man and eventually ran for governor. His announcement that he was running for president in 1976 was met with surprise around the country, but he defeated Gerald Ford in the aftermath of Watergate.

During Carter's presidency, the United States took a decidedly more vocal position on human rights questions in national security affairs, and the president himself emphasized energy conservation. Although today human rights and energy are no longer considered nontraditional concerns, both were controversial positions when Carter espoused them in the late 1970s. Carter's administration was also marked by problems in his relationship with Congress over domestic and foreign affairs, including his decision in late 1978 to normalize relations with the People's Republic of China while withdrawing recognition from Taiwan as the government of China. Carter also had problems with the Soviets, who invaded Afghanistan during the last year of his term, and with the Latin Americans over human rights questions. His greatest disappointment came in 1979, when he decided to admit the exiled shah of Iran into the United States for medical treatment and Iranian revolutionaries seized fifty-two U.S. Embassy employees, holding them hostage for 444 days.

In a particularly poignant speech in July 1979, President Carter described the national mood as being one of "a crisis of confidence," and this phrase might also describe the mood at the end of his administration. Ronald Reagan, former governor of California, defeated Carter for the presidency in 1980, largely on the charge that Carter had left the United States increasingly vulnerable to a Soviet nuclear arms buildup. Upon retirement, Carter established the Carter Center at Emory University, focusing on the peaceful resolution of international conflict and projects for improving the human condition.

Fidel Castro Ruz (1926–)

Cuban Premier Fidel Castro Ruz, or "Fidel," as he is known around the world, has survived countless assassination attempts and remains a thorn in the side of U.S. presidents, regardless of their party affiliation. Born into an upper-class farming family, Castro Ruz earned a law degree and proved far more interested in politics than farming. In the early 1950s, he and other radicals took up arms to overthrow the increasingly oppressive government of former reformist Fulgencio Batista y Zaldívar. They were exiled to Mexico in the mid-1950s, but by January 1, 1959, Castro Ruz and his men actually succeeded in ousting the dictator, largely because he lost the confidence of the United States, which was unwilling to protect him.

Castro Ruz recognized what prior reformers had never understood in Cuba: to maintain power, he had no option but to declare "war" on the United States government and other powers in the "colossus of the north," especially U.S. corporations, that had the island economy in a stranglehold. In the early 1960s, when it became apparent that the Eisenhower administration viewed him as unwilling to cooperate with U.S. business interests, Castro Ruz made the break by turning to the Soviet Union for assistance. Washington was increasingly frustrated at its inability to influence Castro Ruz, and under Kennedy administration encouragement, CIA-trained Cuban exiles mounted an unsuccessful effort to overthrow Castro, which came to be known as the Bay of Pigs. Castro responded by allowing Soviets to begin positioning missiles in Cuba, touching off the Cuban Missile Crisis in October 1962. The crisis brought the United States and the Soviet Union to the brink of war. The Soviets finally backed down, and in the aftermath Cuba was more dependent than ever on the Soviet Union for assistance.

There were some improvements to living conditions in Cuba

during the initial period of Castro Ruz's rule, when he introduced reforms in education, basic sanitation, and health care, and the standard of living increased slightly among Cubans who had been living in terrible conditions under the Batista regime. But Castro Ruz was unable to push the average income much above the poverty line, and the United States imposed an embargo against Cuba that dragged on for several decades. In 1980, Castro Ruz purged much of the political and social malcontents from his country through the Mariel boatlift, which sent to the United States many Cubans who had proven "difficult." In 2002, no viable political opposition to the aging Castro Ruz has been allowed to develop, and the U.S. embargo on Cuba remains in effect. The question of a post-Castro Cuba remains open.

Richard Bruce Cheney (1941–)

The most powerful vice president in recent memory, if not in U.S. history, Vice President Richard "Dick" Cheney served in a variety of positions in the U.S. government before joining President George W. Bush in the White House, including chief of staff to the Ford White House in the 1970s, conservative Republican congressman from Wyoming in the 1980s, secretary of defense under President George H. W. Bush, and architect of the Persian Gulf War in the late 1980s. He was also president of Halliburton, a major international corporation operating in energy issues. Cheney had considered his own presidential campaign in the 1990s, but health problems, including four heart attacks, prevented him from doing so.

President Bush chose Cheney as his vice president because he needed a solid individual who would bring strong credibility to the position, especially since the president was considered weak on national security affairs. President Bush turned to the vice president as a stabilizing and confidence-building presence during the immediate aftermath of the 2001 terrorist bombing. In the first months after the attacks, Cheney was kept from public view much of the time as part of an effort to protect individuals in the national chain of succession to the White House against possible terrorist action. Since taking office, Cheney has been a major figure in the White House's moves to strengthen missile defense and to curtail relations with China.

Chiang Kai-shek (1887–1975)

Generalissimo Chiang Kai-shek was a towering figure in the history of twentieth-century China. He took part in the overthrow of the imperial government and witnessed the beginnings of the Republic of China in 1912. He led the National Revolutionary Army and the Nationalist Party, or Guomindang (GMD). He was the leader of the Republic of China in 1949, when he and his followers were forced from mainland China to the nearby island of Formosa (Taiwan).

In the 1920s, the Nationalists were allied with the Chinese Communist Party. Chiang, a Nationalist, was the first commandant of the Whampoa Military Academy outside Guangzhou in southeast China, where his political commissar was Zhou Enlai, who would eventually be premier of Communist China. The two sides broke into warring factions in 1927.

During World War II, the alliance between the two groups was reestablished to fight against Japanese invaders under Chiang's leadership, with U.S. assistance from General Joseph Stilwell. But they resumed their war when Japan was defeated in 1945. The United States ultimately sided with the GMD and from 1949 through 1979 declared that Chiang's was the legitimate government of China, rather than that of Mao Zedong in Beijing.

After U.S. President Richard Nixon went to Beijing in February 1972, it became clear that the United States was no longer willing to protect Taiwan's representation in the United Nations as the recognized government of China, and Beijing had already assumed the permanent UN Security Council seat previously held by Taiwan. The GMD retained control of the presidency in Taiwan well past Chiang's death in 1975, surrendering it only upon Chen Shui-Bien's Democratic People's Party victory in March 2000.

Sir Winston Leonard Spencer Churchill (1874–1965)

The son of a Yankee socialite and a British peer, Sir Winston Churchill was a towering figure in world affairs in the mid–twentieth century. His work as a reporter during the Boer War was crucial to British war efforts, and he was a major politician in both Liberal and Conservative governments in the first decades of the twentieth century. He was especially interested in the Royal Navy and was a major proponent of sea power for the empire.

Churchill was elected prime minister in the dark days of 1940, after Nazi Germany had invaded Denmark and Norway and when it appeared likely that the Germans would invade Britain. Churchill understood the importance of bringing the United States into the European war to defeat the Germans and worked assiduously to encourage President Franklin Roosevelt to abandon neutrality in favor of weighing in on the Allied side. When the Pearl Harbor attack transpired in late 1941, Churchill got his wish. From then on, he worked with Roosevelt and his successor, Harry S. Truman, not only to win the war but also to shape the post–World War II world.

Churchill's role as a strategist was crucial to Britain's ability to retain a modicum of power in the aftermath of the war, when it became clear that the empire was in deep decline. Another of Churchill's important post-war contributions was the "Iron Curtain" speech, which he gave in March 1946 at Westminster College in Missouri (see chapter 5). Here he warned of the curtain of Soviet tyranny descending on Eastern Europe and stressed the important roles to be played by the United States and the United Nations.

Churchill lost the prime ministership in the late 1940s but returned to office in the 1950s. He finally retired the post in 1955. Active politically until well into his eighties, Churchill retained his seat in Parliament until 1964, and then he lost it only because he did not stand for reelection.

William Jefferson "Bill" Clinton (1945–)

Elected U.S. president during the recession of 1992, William "Bill" Clinton was in power when most of the "new" national security threats became overt challenges to U.S. leadership in the international community (1993–2001). Clinton faced several new threats: destabilizing drug violence surfaced as Colombia became a large exporter of illegal drugs, large-scale displacement and starvation among refugees in Somalia forced international action, equilibrium in Central Europe was imperiled by the disintegration of a former republic in Yugoslavia into several ethnic enclaves seeking nation-state status and survival, globalization exerted increasing pressure that took power from the president and gave it to central bankers and trade specialists, and finally, an increase in anti-U.S. terrorist activity led the administration to strengthen its antiterrorism forces and increase its vigilance. The Soviet threat diminished during the Clinton presidency, and many concluded that it had been replaced with a Chinese threat. Although elected on domestic economic issues, Clinton was personally committed to the peace processes in Northern Ireland and the Middle East.

Charles André-Marie-Joseph de Gaulle (1890–1970)

A veteran of the disastrous battle of Verdun in World War I, Charles de Gaulle became the best-known symbol of Free France during World War II. He spent the war in exile in London, from where he rallied French citizens with radio broadcasts and argued to British and U.S. leaders that France, upon recapturing its sovereignty, would return to its position as a dominant state in Europe. De Gaulle proved highly popular with the French people and was highly acclaimed when elected president of the Republic in 1945.

Governing as a civilian in the years after World War II proved more formidable than de Gaulle had anticipated, however. France faced many challenges that needed immediate attention if the French Communists and their assumed allies in Moscow were to be prevented from seizing power. De Gaulle, who served as president from 1958 to 1969, favored a strong hand in governing that was not quite as popular in a democratic setting as during a war. In particular, the turmoil over Algeria and similar independence movements during the 1950s led to tremendous dissent and upheaval within France itself, and Algeria ultimately achieved its independence in the 1960s.

French nationalism, which was to be expected with regard to Britain, produced conflict with the other European states and, indirectly, with the United States. More difficult issues between Washington and Paris included the question of sovereignty and leadership in NATO, leading de Gaulle to withdraw France from the alliance in 1967. At the same time, France chose to pursue its *force de frappe,* an independent nuclear guarantee aimed at preventing France from being dragged into a conflict because of U.S. "ineptitude." Ultimately, de Gaulle's strong hand proved too much during the tumultuous year of 1968, culminating in antigovernment and antiwar student protests and violence in the streets. He retired from the presidency after losing a referendum and lived out his last months frustrated by the course of events.

Deng Xiaoping (1904–1997)

Deng Xiaoping was one of the most remarkable survivors of the twentieth century—not only did he survive the Long March (1935–1936) across much of China under terrible conditions, but he was also purged by the Communist Party leadership and sentenced to "re-education" three times: in the 1950s, the 1960s, and again in the 1970s. Born in Sichuan Province, Deng was educated in the early 1920s in France, where he joined a branch of the recently formed Chinese Communist Party (CCP) headed by Zhou Enlai. He returned to Shanghai in 1927 and was assigned the job of establishing CCP military bases.

After the revolution succeeded in October 1949, Deng rose through party ranks to assume important roles in the economic revolution that was shaking China. Because he was a pragmatist rather than a pure ideologue, Deng was purged after the appalling effects of the Great Leap Forward in the 1950s. Again because of his willingness to adjust to changing conditions, he was arrested and his family profoundly affected during the Great Proletarian Cultural Revolution (1965–1976). Deng returned to the center of party activities upon Mao's death in 1976, only to be accused again by the Gang of Four and politically exiled for the third time.

By 1978 Deng had become the embodiment of the Second Generation of CCP leadership. With his fundamental commitment to working solutions rather than strict ideological answers, Deng began the "economic opening" now associated with the post-1978 period in China. His reforms have made state ownership of all aspects of the economy outdated, and the transformation of Chinese social and economic structures can be credited directly to Deng's willingness to allow private ownership and outside capital to spark economic development. In 1985 he redirected China's military doctrine, no longer identifying the major threat as a Soviet invasion but now concerned with wars along the periphery, the border areas that China shares with fifteen other states—a fundamental shift in global view that predated the fall of the Soviet Union by four years.

Deng's innate conservatism and insistence that the Communist Party retain power was evidenced, however, by the Tiananmen Square incident in June 1989, in which the party responded with massive force to demonstrations that had endured in Beijing for well over a month. Soon after Tiananmen,

Deng was forced to withdraw from active life because of his age, although he made periodic appearances until his death in early 1997.

John Foster Dulles (1888–1959)

Son of a Presbyterian minister and brother of the first director of the Central Intelligence Agency, John Foster Dulles was President Dwight D. Eisenhower's first secretary of state (1953–1959). Before entering the Cabinet, he had been a major corporate and international law specialist and a Republican activist for many years. He is remembered for his hard-core anti-Communism and for being the prime mover behind the international alliance structure that the United States orchestrated—including the Southeast Asia Treaty Organization (SEATO), the Central Treaty Organization (CENTO), and the Australia-New Zealand-United States Security Treaty (ANZUS)—to complement the NATO alliance and the Inter-American Treaty of Reciprocal Assistance (see chapter 5) formed by the Truman administration.

Dulles is also known for supporting CIA activities in 1953 against Iranian Prime Minister Muhammad Mossadegh, who was considered a potential threat to U.S. petroleum interests, and in 1954 against Jacobo Arbenz Guzmán in Guatemala, where Dulles's former client the United Fruit Company appeared likely to lose significant landholdings. Dulles is probably best remembered for two events in 1954: he refused to shake the hand of Chinese envoy Zhou Enlai at the Paris Accords meetings after the French defeat at Dien Bien Phu, and in a speech in early 1954 he coined the phrase "massive retaliation," which became the catchword for Eisenhower's nuclear and defense doctrine. Dulles died of cancer in 1959.

Sir Robert Anthony Eden (1897–1977)

A member of the Tory (Conservative) Party in Britain who supported the League of Nations and other international organizations aimed at preventing the horrors of world war, Robert Anthony Eden served in Foreign Office positions until 1938, when he resigned in protest after Neville Chamberlain's appeasement of Adolf Hitler. He returned to serve Winston Churchill and eventually became prime minister in 1955. He was the chairman of the Paris conference that brought a temporary cessation of hostilities to the former French Indochina and that divided Vietnam into north and south. Eden engaged in a major foreign policy debacle by using force in the Suez Canal Crisis of 1956, angering President Dwight Eisenhower. Eden resigned two years later.

Dwight David Eisenhower (1890–1969)

The Supreme Allied Commander in Europe during World War II, Dwight David Eisenhower became president at a time of virtually unparalleled U.S. power (1953–1961). A career U.S. Army officer, Eisenhower was a staff officer under Generals John J. Pershing, Douglas MacArthur, and Walter Kreuger before taking command in Europe and orchestrating the Normandy invasion in June 1944. After the war, he retained his political independence as Columbia University president until he ran for president on the Republican ticket in 1952 and 1956.

Eisenhower's tenure in office was marked by pressure to increase military expenditures, in contrast with his philosophical orientation toward reduced government. His secretary of state, John Foster Dulles, answered the challenge by arguing that the United States would engage in "massive retaliation" with nuclear weapons in response to any threats against its interests. Eisenhower had to respond to challenges to U.S. interests many times: in 1954 when Guatemala appeared to be leaning toward Communism; two years later when the Suez Canal Crisis coincided with the Hungarian uprising; in 1957, when the Soviets launched the first man-made satellite; and finally in 1958, when U.S. ships were stationed off Lebanon's coast in response to conflict in the Middle East. As Eisenhower left office, he warned of the potential for the development of a "military-industrial complex" that could take the country down roads it did not anticipate or desire.

Gerald Rudolph Ford (1913–)

The thirty-eighth president of the United States was unique in several ways among the men who have occupied the White House. He was the first president to assume office upon the resignation of his predecessor, which he did in August 1974 when President Richard Nixon left in disgrace. A month later he granted Nixon a pardon, becoming the first president to do so. President Ford was also probably the first president who was born with a completely different name; his parents divorced immediately after his birth, and his stepfather changed his name from Leslie Lynch King Jr. to Gerald Rudolph Ford.

Ford was actually more famous for events prior to his presidency than for most of his experience in the White House. He was a star football player at the University of Michigan during a championship season. He made a major impact on U.S. politics as the Republican leader of the House of Representatives during their long period of minority status in the 1960s and 1970s. He remained minority leader until Richard Nixon nominated him to replace Spiro T. Agnew upon the latter's resignation in 1973. Ford assumed the vice presidency during the burgeoning Watergate scandal, which cost Nixon his own presidency less than a year later.

During Ford's presidency, the United States saw the ultimate fall of the Republic of Vietnam, as the former capital of Saigon came under Communist control and was renamed Ho Chi Minh City. During this time the United States became increasingly concerned about Cuban actions in Angola and southern Africa. The relationship with the Soviet Union, which had appeared to warm earlier in the 1970s, began to freeze again. Unfortunately, Ford's most memorable national security moment as president came in a televised debate with his opponent, former Georgia Governor Jimmy Carter, when he declared, "Eastern Europe is not behind the Iron Curtain." Ford was defeated in the 1976 campaign and returned to private life.

Indira Priyadarshini Nehru Gandhi (1917–1984)

The only daughter of Jawaharlal Nehru, one of the grand political leaders of newly independent India, Indira Gandhi went from receiving an Oxford education and marrying to be a traditional, stay-at-home wife to being the prime minister of the first state in the Third World to detonate a nuclear weapon (in 1974). Gandhi was prime minister between 1966 and 1977 and between 1980 and 1984, during which time India fought a war and managed to separate Bangladesh from Pakistan, continued to beleaguer the United States by siding with the Soviet Union and other nonaligned states in the Cold War, and slowly helped many of the poor in India's burgeoning population to improve their living standards.

Although India has still not caught up with China in development terms, Indira Gandhi's terms in office sent an important message to many technologically oriented Indians, who saw their nation reach higher levels of development than in the past. She was assassinated in 1984 after having moved against Sikhs in Amritsar earlier that year. The Gandhi political dynasty appears to have ended when her younger son, Sanjay, died in an air accident in 1980 and her elder son was assassinated in 1991.

Mikhail Gorbachev (1931–)

Assuming office at what was thought in the West to be the height of Soviet power, Mikhail Gorbachev was the last general secretary of the Communist Party (1985–1991) and the last president of the Soviet Union (1990–1991). A party apparatchik from the Crimea, he took office in March 1985 upon Konstantin Chernenko's death. Almost immediately, Gorbachev had to respond to the growing pressures of the collapsing Soviet system: thirteen months into his regime, the Chernobyl nuclear plant in Ukraine suffered the worst nuclear accident in history; a year and a half after that, Soviet officials and troops proved unable to reach an earthquake-devastated Armenia, throwing into question the state's ability to mobilize against opponents; and finally, the Soviet Red Army began to withdraw from Afghanistan in much the same atmosphere that had surrounded U.S. forces leaving Southeast Asia in the mid-1970s.

In 1985 Gorbachev held a summit in Reykjavík, Iceland, with U.S. President Ronald Reagan, followed by another summit a year later in Geneva; both of these meetings focused on further nuclear arms cuts following on those of the early 1980s. By the late 1980s, Gorbachev was talking not only about arms cuts but also about considerably downsizing the Soviet Army as well. In 1989 he presided over the de facto end of the Iron Curtain, as the Berlin Wall was torn down and as pro-Soviet, Communist regimes fell like dominoes in Eastern Europe. In 1990 Gorbachev agreed that the two Germanies could be reunited in NATO. The following year, hard-line Communists, led by the vice president, attempted a coup against Gorbachev. Although the coup was unsuccessful, it revealed how controversial his program was. Gorbachev left office when the presidency of the Soviet Union, and the Soviet Union itself, ended in December 1991. Many of his reforms were ultimately saved by Russian President Boris Yeltsin.

Ho Chi Minh (1890–1969)

The leader of North Vietnam during most of its struggle against France, the United States, and South Vietnam, Ho Chi Minh was an intellectual who studied in Paris in the first decade of the twentieth century. There he joined the Communist movement that was trying to liberate his native country from French control. In the years immediately after World War II, when France sought to reimpose its control over Indochina after the Japanese were ousted, Ho argued that Vietnam should receive independence instead of returning to colonial status. He launched an insurgency against the French, finally ousting them after the decisive siege of Dien Bien Phu in 1954, a victory that led to the Geneva Accords. As a result of those negotiations, Vietnam was divided into North and South, with Catholic pro-Westerners in charge in the South and Ho in power in the North. He retained the goal of liberating all of Vietnam from Western imperialism, even if that required foreign assistance from Vietnam's historic foe, China, or the Soviet Union. Ho died in 1969, less than a decade before Hanoi achieved its final objective with the removal of U.S. forces from Saigon in 1975.

Saddam Hussein (1937–)

In many ways, Saddam Hussein is the new Fidel Castro Ruz for U.S. national security strategists: he continues to survive regardless of countless attempts to oust him, and his continued rule results in growing frustration for the White House. Originally a member of the Ba'ath Revolutionary Party in Iraq, Hussein seized power in 1979 from another dictator, soon launching a war against Ayatollah Khomeini's Islamic Republic of Iran. He never achieved a decisive victory over the Iranians, and the conflict cost probably 2 million lives over its eight-year duration. Additionally, Hussein was documented as the first world leader since World War I to use chemical gas, which he used against his own citizens in Kurdistan, attracting international condemnation.

With petroleum prices falling and Iraq's debts mounting, Hussein invaded and seized Kuwait in August 1990, prompting the United States and allied forces to launch a six-month buildup of troops in neighboring Saudi Arabia. Despite a massive UN-sanctioned air campaign beginning in mid-January 1991, Hussein refused to withdraw from Kuwait. In a ninety-six-hour land campaign by allied forces, Iraq's elite Revolutionary Guards were emasculated and driven from the emirate. Hussein, however, was never forced from power. In the years since the Gulf War, allied forces have tried in vain to force him from power through sanctions and embargoes, but his brutal rule guarantees that these actions hurt the Iraqi people, focusing international attention on their plight rather than on Hussein himself. Various covert and not-so-covert plots have proven unable to oust him.

Hussein's long-suspected intent to develop nuclear weapons was finally confirmed with UN inspections in the 1990s. The second Bush administration has sought to oust him, to a great extent because of concerns about these weapons of mass destruction, and has labeled Iraq as part of an "axis of evil," along with Iran and North Korea. U.S. allies are far more skeptical about the viability of direct action against Hussein.

Jiang Zemin (1926–)

This engineer from Yangzhou (Jiangsu Province) is the first civilian leader of China since 1911, when the Communist Revolution ended the Qing dynasty and began the turbulent era of modern China. A technocrat who spent most of his career in the Shanghai Communist Party apparatus, Jiang was mayor between 1985 and 1989, when he went to Beijing in the aftermath of the Tiananmen Massacre. Deng Xiaoping elevated him within the party hierarchy after 1989, but Jiang was considered by many a weak figure without staying power. He succeeded the elderly but virtually peerless Deng Xiaoping in the early 1990s, and upon the latter's death in 1997 he became supreme leader of the People's Republic.

Jiang has proven surprisingly adept at managing the huge country and calling for assistance from people he knows in Shanghai. In the late 1990s, Jiang chose another technocrat, Zhu Rongji, to be the economic architect of the reforms aimed at forcing China's political opening to continue past the initial stages. Jiang has overseen the admission of China to the World Trade Organization and the awarding of the 2008 Olympics to Beijing, both announced in 2001. He is scheduled to step down from the party leadership at the Sixteenth Party Congress in September 2002. However, his announced heir, Hu Jintao, will likely find Jiang unwilling to abandon all of his offices; for example, one might expect him to remain as chairman of the Central Military Committee.

Jiang has been president through the periods of turbulence in Sino-U.S. relations, including the accidental U.S. bombing of the Chinese Embassy in Belgrade in May 1999 and the U.S. EP3 reconnaissance plane incident just short of two years later. Although he has proven able in running the system, he has never reached the point of absolute power that characterized the generation of the Long March, the revolutionaries who led China out of the civil war into its current prowess.

Lyndon Baines Johnson (1908–1973)

One of the most frustrated presidents in U.S. history (1963–1969), Lyndon Johnson persistently tried to win the war in Vietnam while waging a domestic war against poverty and racism. He ultimately left office as a despised, defeated figure who had learned over a forty-year career that Washington can be a city of tremendous highs and lows in power.

After serving as a congressional staffer for six years, Johnson was elected as a Democratic congressman from Texas during Franklin Roosevelt's second term. After six terms in the House, Johnson served in the Senate between 1949 and 1961, and he was majority leader when presidential candidate John Kennedy asked him to join his ticket in order to win the anti-Catholic southern tier of the United States.

As Kennedy's vice president, Johnson was in charge of the space program. He was largely frustrated by the job until he was thrust into the presidency after the president's assassination in November 1963. Kennedy had been gradually increasing U.S. intervention in Vietnam, and in 1964 Johnson used the Gulf of Tonkin incident, long since a controversial event, to justify a major escalation in U.S. involvement. A year later, he began deploying U.S. ground troops to Vietnam, steadily escalating the war at the same time that he, his advisors, and the military commander in Vietnam, General William Westmoreland, proclaimed that peace was not far away. In 1965 Johnson sent Marines into the Dominican Republic to save U.S. citizens, and some critics believed that the president saw this action as an archetype for the hoped-for victory in Vietnam.

Beginning in 1964 and throughout his presidency, Johnson also worked toward a Great Society, where civil rights, economic conditions, voting rights, and protections for aging citizens were guaranteed by federal law. This set of programs, along with the war in Vietnam, were expensive in both political and social capital. When the Viet Cong proved able to attack the U.S. Embassy compound in the 1968 Tet offensive, much of the U.S. public, not only draft-age men, turned decisively against the war. Six weeks later the Tet offensive was defeated, but the course of events had psychologically broken Johnson's support at home. On March 31, 1968, Johnson announced he would not seek reelection.

George Frost Kennan (1904–)

The man most often cited for the development of the doctrine of containment toward the Soviet Union, George F. Kennan joined the Foreign Service after graduating from Princeton in 1927. Kennan served his first tour in Moscow in the 1930s, when the United States first opened an embassy in the Soviet Union. During a later tour there in the first months after the end of World War II, Kennan wrote an assessment of conditions in Josef Stalin's Soviet Union that became known as the "Long Telegram" (see chapter 5).

Upon returning to the United States, Kennan became the first international affairs advisor at the newly established National War College, where he wrote an article that he sent to the influential journal *Foreign Affairs* under the pseudonym "Mr. X." This article, "The Sources of Soviet Conduct," argued that the Soviet Union would ultimately implode from its own internal weakness, but Kennan's argument became used to justify a doctrine of "containing" the Soviet Union. Kennan bitterly resented this interpretation and left the Foreign Service in 1953 after briefly serving as ambassador to Moscow. He taught at the Advanced Studies Institute at Princeton University for the next twenty years, and the Russian Studies Center there ultimately became the Kennan Institute. Kennan espoused a minimalist approach to U.S. national security alliances with a focus on only a few core areas, which would not include many of the places the United States has engaged over the past forty years.

John Fitzgerald Kennedy (1917–1963)

Probably the most famous U.S. president around the world in the twentieth century, John Kennedy was an enigma in both political and more specifically national security terms. Elected as the first Roman Catholic and the youngest president ever, Kennedy had served roughly a term each in the U.S. House of Representatives and the U.S. Senate before aspiring to the highest office in the land. He had seen combat as a Naval officer during World War II and had written a best-selling book about his experience. Kennedy had spent time in Asia in the early 1950s, yet he agreed with the U.S. decisions to escalate U.S. assistance to former French colonial areas seeking to prevent the seizure of power by Communist nationalists, especially in Laos and South Vietnam.

Kennedy was president during a period of Soviet expansionism around the world, most chillingly illustrated by the discovery in October 1962 of Soviet medium-range ballistic missiles in the newly Communist island of Cuba, just off the coast of Florida. The missiles were ultimately removed, but the world underwent a tense thirteen days as Kennedy addressed the intolerable conditions of a nuclear threat in the Western Hemisphere. During his presidency he also had several disastrous meetings with Soviet Communist Party Chairman Nikita Khrushchev, after one of which Khrushchev erected the Berlin Wall to separate East and West Berlin and to prevent free movement within the city.

In addition to facing these Cold War challenges, the Kennedy administration initiated several lasting programs that engaged the United States in long-term humanitarian development in the Third World (the Alliance for Progress in Latin America, the Agency for International Development, and the Peace Corps being three notable examples). Kennedy also led the country during one of the largest expansions of the U.S. military in history. Especially important was the growth of the nuclear arsenal with the authorization of one thousand intercontinental ballistic missiles and a new submarine-launched ballistic missile fleet. Many supporters argue that had he not been assassinated in November 1963, Kennedy would have withdrawn support for the South Vietnamese government and the tragic increase in U.S. involvement would have ceased, but there is virtually no evidence to support these claims.

Sayyid Ruholla al Musan al-Khomeini Hindi (1900–1989)

A Muslim cleric who developed a pathological hatred for the Shah of Iran, Muhammad Reza Shah Pahlavi, and his perceived acquiescence to modernization, the Ayatollah Khomeini led a revolution that took down the shah and introduced a form of religious fundamentalism that would reverse centuries of modern-ization in Iran. Khomeini had been a minor cleric in Qom until 1963, when the shah exiled him to Turkey for opposing women's rights and land reform. He eventually moved to a religious cen-ter in Iraq, where he stayed for thirteen years before Iraqi officials forced him out. He then moved to Paris, where he had greater access to Shiite religious supporters in Iran.

Meanwhile, the shah's approach to dissent in Iranian society was becoming increasingly authoritarian, and his secret police had become notorious for torture and illegal detention of citizens. This by no means hurt Khomeini's cause. Through recordings of his speeches, religious texts, and other broad public appeals, Khomeini fomented a revolution that would drive the shah from Teheran. In 1978, demonstrators filled the streets of Teheran and Iranian soldiers threatened mutiny. The shah was then critically ill with cancer, and in January 1979, Washington allowed him to enter the United States for medical treatment. Khomeini arrived in Iran in February, declaring the revolution a success.

In November the U.S. Embassy in Teheran was seized by alleged students, who held fifty-two employees hostage for 444 days to show their fury, even though the shah had died in exile early in the hostage drama. Khomeini's vision of an "orthodox" Shiite religious society in Iran was virtually unchallenged until his death in 1989, even throughout the war with Iraq and relative isolation by the international community. Immediately before his death, Khomeini issued a *fatwa*, or legal decree, condemning to death the Indian writer Salman Rushdie and forcing the author to go underground for several years. No subsequent cleric in Iran has had quite the unchallenged power of Khomeini, and Iranian society appears to be evolving gradually to something less repres-sive by Western standards.

Nikita Sergeyevich Khrushchev (1894–1971)

The successor to Josef Stalin, Nikita Khrushchev was general sec-retary of the Communist Party for a decade after 1953 and Soviet premier from 1958 through 1964, when he was ousted in a de facto coup. Khrushchev stunned the world with his 1956 "secret speech" to the Twentieth Party Congress, in which he condemned Stalin for his purges and other actions over his quarter-century rule in the Soviet Union. However, Khrushchev proved equally as interested in promoting global Communism when he began supporting Fidel Castro Ruz, Ho Chi Minh, and insurgencies in other Third World areas where the Soviet Union could promote what it called "wars of national liberation" against Western colonialism. Khrushchev tried to seal off East Berlin from West Berlin by authorizing the erection of the Berlin Wall in 1961, soon after he had attended an unsuccessful summit in Vienna with the young new U.S. President, John Kennedy. In 1962, Khrushchev authorized the deployment of medium-range ballistic missiles to Cuba, but the missiles were discovered by the United States before their installation was completed. Kennedy and Khrushchev held each other at bay for thirteen days, with Washington imposing a blockade of Cuba to prevent Soviet ships from bringing in more parts to the weapons systems. In the end, the missiles were withdrawn, and this defeat led to Khrushchev's ouster the following year.

Henry Alfred Kissinger (1923–)

A Jewish refugee from Germany, Henry Kissinger would be secretary of state for four of the most turbulent years in U.S. national security history (1973–1977), and he was special assistant to the president for national security affairs, arguably the more important role, for eight years under Presidents Nixon and Ford. Kissinger was a Harvard professor in 1969, when his connection with Nelson A. Rockefeller gave him an entrée to the newly elected president, Richard Nixon. Kissinger had authored a famous monograph on the use of nuclear weapons, entitled *Nuclear Weapons and Foreign Policy,* but he had not been a figure in U.S. national security policymaking before Nixon asked him to be his special assistant for national security affairs. Kissinger immediately began to plan for the consolidation of national security decision making in his office while overseeing major shifts in the policy positions left over from the Johnson administration, first reaching out to Vietnam and later, to China.

Kissinger proved to be an extremely activist security advisor, involving himself and the United States in issues around the world because of his belief in Realpolitik and in creating linkages between issues as the basis of strategy. His role, with Nixon's agreement, in promoting U.S. expansion of the war from Vietnam into Laos and Cambodia sparked violence at Kent State University in Ohio and Jackson State University in Mississippi in May 1970. In 1971, Kissinger preceded Nixon to China to prepare for the historic reorientation of U.S. policy toward that nation. From 1970 through 1973, Kissinger worked with the Central Intelligence Agency and U.S. businesses to oust Socialist President Salvador Allende Gossens from office in Chile.

Kissinger won the 1973 Nobel Peace Prize for his negotiations with North Vietnam's Le Duc Tho after the Paris Peace Accords nominally ended the war in Vietnam. He was influential in negotiations with the Soviet Union that resulted in the Antiballistic Missile Treaty and Strategic Arms Limitation Treaty, both signed in 1972. His name was inextricably linked with "shuttle diplomacy" in the Middle East, as he tried to parlay Anwar el-Sadat's opening to the West into an enduring peace with Israel.

In 1973 Kissinger became secretary of state as well as special assistant to the president for national security affairs, and he held both positions until the Ford administration (1974–1977), when he was only the secretary of state. During his final years in office, Kissinger's policies drew more and more criticism because of the "fall" of South Vietnam, Laos, and Cambodia to the Communists in 1975, the problems of U.S. intervention in the Angolan civil war in the middle of the decade, and other challenges to the United States that remained unanswered.

Lee Kuan Yew (1923–)

Lee Kuan Yew was the first prime minister in independent Singapore (1959–1990) and a dominant figure in the rise of this island nation as an economic powerhouse in Asia. When Singapore was vulnerable to its larger neighbor Malaysia, Lee parlayed the economic prowess of the highly educated Singaporean population into a major international safe haven for stable government and investment and shrewd power politics in the international realm. Today, years after he left office, Lee is still seen as a major international statesman. He ran Singapore as a strict semiauthoritarian state, arguing that its success showed that the "Asian Way" was more productive and stable than the values of individual rights so earnestly championed in the United States and Western Europe.

Carlos Lehder Rivas (1949–)

One of the original members of the Medellín drug cartel in the north-central Colombian city of the same name, Carlos Lehder

Rivas realized the potential of a new type of criminal syndicate involving the importation of cocaine into the United States. Born to a German father and a Colombian mother, Lehder Rivas grew up near Detroit and was in jail on auto theft charges when he came into contact with a pilot who told him about the vast supply of coca in South America. Lehder Rivas immediately saw the potential for a network to distribute the drug via air routes across the Caribbean islands into various metropolitan areas of the United States. Simultaneously, several groups in Colombia, coincidentally located around Medellín, began to take interest in the coca being grown in Peru and Bolivia. Lehder Rivas's suggestions for a network of transportation became the origin of the Medellín cartel.

In a matter of less than a decade, the cartel became as wealthy as many nation-states and increasingly managed the entire stream of coca production, culminating with its transport from central South America. By the late 1980s, the major growth area for the commodity shifted to Colombia itself, and illegal drug profits took on a tremendous role in Colombian society. Lehder Rivas, who had begun abusing cocaine himself, was captured at his *finca* (estate) outside Medellín in a daring raid by Colombian police and U.S. Special Forces in 1987. He was tried before a U.S. court and sentenced to life in prison at a federal maximum security penitentiary. Colombia's problems with drugs continue, however, as the profits exacerbate a war between the political right and left and the state appears unable to stem the conflict.

Douglas MacArthur (1880–1964)

General Douglas MacArthur lived his entire life as a soldier; son of a Civil War officer, there was not a single day when he was not tied to the U.S. Army in some manner. Much of that time was spent in Asia, where MacArthur was first posted to the Philippines upon graduating at the top of the West Point Class of 1903. MacArthur thus arrived during the heady time when U.S. colonization was first taking hold in the islands. Promoted to brigadier general, MacArthur became the most decorated soldier in World War I on the battlefields of France. After serving as superintendent of the Military Academy, he also managed to irritate Army Chief of Staff General John J. Pershing, who "exiled" him back to the Philippines. There he felt quite comfortable, acting as the focus of U.S. presence in the colony. After a brief period stateside, MacArthur returned to the islands in the late 1920s as commander of the army's Philippine interests, a post he kept until President Herbert Hoover named him as chief of staff of the army in 1930. During the worst days of the Depression, MacArthur used troops to roust the broken-down World War I veterans who had formed the "Bonus Army" from their camps in southeast Washington, DC. This public humiliation made MacArthur willing to return to Manila yet again, this time to help prepare the colony for independence a dozen years later.

MacArthur was forced from Manila by the Japanese invasion in December 1941, and he took temporary refuge in Australia. With U.S. forces, he later moved from Australia back to the war against Japan. At the end of the war, President Harry Truman named MacArthur supreme Allied commander in Japan, where he ruled for five years. In 1950, despite a brilliant stroke at Inchon, he proved a disastrous choice to lead UN forces in Korea. MacArthur was so confident of his ability to judge Asian minds that he completely underestimated Chinese resolve when he crossed the 38th Parallel, provoking Mao's response. While MacArthur was acting under the assumption that China was moving aggressively in Asia, the Chinese assumed that the United States intended to invade China, and so they were ready for MacArthur when he arrived. MacArthur's hubris was a major problem for all. In one of the most heated civil-military conflicts of U.S. history, President Truman recalled MacArthur and stripped him of his command in 1951.

Nelson Rolihlahla Mandela (1918–)

Nelson Rolihlahla Mandela represents the tremendous changes that South Africa has undergone in the past fifty years. Born into an African royal family, he was trained as an attorney, but the apartheid laws of the 1940s made his work impossible to carry out. Mandela became a major figure in the African National Congress (ANC), the major political movement that blacks joined to try overthrowing the apartheid system. In the 1950s, the ANC adopted violence as the only approach that would draw Afrikaner (white) attention to their demands. In 1964 Mandela was put into the maximum security penitentiary at Robben Island, where he spent three decades, becoming the world's most famous political prisoner. The gradual opening of South African society in the late 1980s forced his release in 1990. In 1994

Mandela became the first post-apartheid president of South Africa. Mandela left office in 1998 to become a world statesman and one of the most respected world leaders. His struggle succeeded, as none other has, in bringing Africa to the attention of the United States.

Mao Zedong (1893–1976)

The father of the People's Republic of China (PRC), Mao Zedong was initially a teacher from Hunan Province in central China. In 1921, frustrated with the continuing deterioration and exploitation of Republican China (1911–1949), he joined the nascent Chinese Communist Party (CCP). Mao was an important but not dominant figure in the CCP through the 1920s and early 1930s, as it battled the Nationalist, Guomindang (GMD) Party under Chiang Kai-shek, later president of China.

As Chiang tried ever more diligently to wipe out the CCP, Mao and sixty thousand other supporters fled on what became known as "the Long March," a three-thousand-mile tramp across central China between 1935 and 1936. At the end of that experience, Mao emerged as the intellectual and ideological leader of the CCP, just when China was hit by a new threat—the Japanese invasion. Between 1937 and 1945, the CCP and the GMD formed a nominal alliance to oust the foreigners, but each side was preparing to return to civil war for control over China's future. Through superior organization, doctrine, and strategy, Mao ultimately drove Chiang Kai-shek and the GMD to the island of Taiwan, one hundred miles off the coast. Chiang claimed to have the legitimate government of China, known as the Republic of China, while Mao focused on creating his version of an ideal Communist society.

The United States had played an active role in the support of nationalist China's attempts to oust the Japanese during World War II. After the war, President Truman sent General George Marshall to try to arbitrate between Mao and Chiang. When Chiang fled to Taiwan, declaring it the Republic of China, the United States still supported the GMD.

Mao proved much less capable at governing than at leading a revolution. Beginning with the proclamation of the People's Republic of China on October 1, 1949, Mao launched a series of disastrous socioeconomic programs that swerved between centralized control over production, food, and governance and more decentralized control. The Great Leap Forward (1958–1960) and the Great Proletarian Cultural Revolution (1965–1976) were only the most obvious failures—the first causing millions of Chinese to starve to death and the second resulting in the purge of millions by radical Red Guards.

Mao remained interested in spreading revolution abroad but was primarily interested in domestic developments. He had sought assistance from the Soviet Union in the early 1950s because he had no other option, particularly after the Korean War left China even weaker than it was at the end of its own civil war. Josef Stalin proved a fickle benefactor, so Mao's travels to Moscow (his only trips abroad) were humbling and only marginally satisfactory. With limited Soviet support, China developed and tested its first nuclear weapon in 1964. Mao broke away from the Soviets in the early 1960s, and rather than depending on foreign assistance, China began creating an indigenous military capability in its large People's Liberation Army. The PRC provided significant aid to North Vietnam in fighting U.S. forces from 1960 to 1973.

U.S. President Richard Nixon turned away from the traditional U.S. ally Chiang Kai-shek in 1972 when he opened relations with Mao by visiting Beijing. Four years after Nixon's stunning visit, Mao died and China began even more draconian changes.

George Catlett Marshall (1880–1959)

The embodiment of the citizen-soldier-diplomat in the United States, General George C. Marshall was the chief of staff of the U.S. Army during World War II and then served as secretary of state (1947–1949) and secretary of defense (1950–1951) under President Harry S. Truman. A graduate of the Virginia Military Institute, Marshall served in World War I, where he witnessed the horrors of war and learned the importance of leadership under General John J. Pershing. In the interwar period, Marshall spent a period of time in Tianjin, China, where he observed the economic and social conditions of a country undergoing civil war. He was also an infantry instructor at Fort Benning, Georgia, a post that allowed him to view upcoming officers who would be called upon to lead the United States during World War II.

President Franklin Roosevelt named Marshall chief of staff of the army in 1939, a post he held even though he would have preferred to serve with the troops in-theater. Marshall was the strategic conductor for the entire U.S. campaign around the globe between 1941 and 1945. He selected General Dwight D. Eisenhower as supreme Allied commander in Europe for the Normandy invasion of 1944. Marshall also oversaw the retention of General Douglas MacArthur as commander in the Pacific, even when MacArthur wrangled directly with several navy admirals who believed their views to be equally important as, if not superior to, those of the temperamental general.

After the Allied victory, President Truman sent Marshall to China as special envoy to negotiate between Chiang Kai-shek and Communist leader Mao Zedong. Returning to the United States, Marshall accepted Truman's nomination as secretary of state in late 1946, serving in the post until 1949, when ill health forced his retirement. Marshall also served as secretary of defense after the death of James Forrestal and during NATO's formative years.

During his tenure as secretary of state, Marshall gave a famous commencement speech at Harvard University, in which he laid out the basis for a massive economic reconstruction plan for Europe. The plan, officially titled the Economic Cooperation Act, became better known as the Marshall Plan, and Marshall received the 1953 Nobel Peace Prize for his efforts. Marshall was also present at the Bogotá convention that created the Organization of American States in April 1948.

Marshall was secretary of state when the evidence of Soviet consolidation of influence in Eastern Europe was strongest and when the beginning of the Cold War was a growing issue in U.S. national security circles. Although he left office prior to the "fall of China" with Mao's victory over the GMD in October 1949, Senator Joseph McCarthy still attacked Marshall as a Communist sympathizer in his 1950s witch-hunt. It was this attack on Marshall that finally galvanized pressure on McCarthy to cease his activities.

Joseph McCarthy (1908–1957)

A Republican senator from Wisconsin, Joseph McCarthy launched his first charges of Communist infiltration into the U.S. government (primarily in the State Department) less than a year after the "fall of China" to Mao's Communist Party in 1949. Through hearings before the Congress, McCarthy increasingly sensationalized charges of Communist subversion and argued that the Truman and Eisenhower administrations had ignored or even abetted such subversion. The entertainment industry was particularly hard hit, and many people with real or perceived links to the Communist Party were blacklisted and unable to work in Hollywood. When McCarthy went after former Chief of Staff of the Army and Secretary of State George C. Marshall, public and governmental tolerance broke. McCarthy was ultimately censured for his activities, and he died a broken man in 1957.

Robert Strange McNamara (1916–)

The president of Ford Motor Company when President John Kennedy named him secretary of defense after the 1960 election, Robert Strange McNamara served in that office during one of the most controversial periods in U.S. history. McNamara had served in the Army Air Corps during World War II after graduating from the University of California at Berkeley. An ardent believer in the "systems analysis" approach to decision making, in which quantifiable materials are studied to give absolute answers, McNamara took office when the United States was worrying about Soviet expansionism and nuclear modernization as well as Soviet-supported "wars of national liberation" in the Third World. McNamara sought to modernize U.S. nuclear forces through the strategy of flexible response, requiring a number of different levels and types of systems to offer redundancy in case of attack.

McNamara was better known, however, for his role in escalating the conflict in Southeast Asia. Always arguing that optimistic analyses were needed because the war was about to turn in favor of the United States and the South Vietnamese, McNamara supported heightening troop levels throughout the 1960s to get the job done. After the war, he claimed that he had not believed the United States could win, but he is generally considered to be the architect of the war. He resigned in 1968 when he became president of the Bank of Reconstruction and Development, better known as the World Bank. Many critics found this a cruel irony because the work of the World Bank could not be conducted during the conflict in Southeast Asia.

Golda Meir (1898–1978)

One of the cofounders of the State of Israel and its third prime minister, Golda Meir was born in present-day Ukraine and emigrated with her family to Wisconsin in 1906. As active Zionists, she and her husband made aliyah (moved to Palestine) in 1921. She became active in a number of Zionist organizations, taking leadership positions, and she was the first ambassador to the Soviet Union upon the founding of Israel in 1948.

After serving as both the minister of foreign affairs and secretary-general of the Labour Party, Meir was elected prime minister by the Labour coalition government in 1969. She was serving as prime minister at the outbreak of the Yom Kippur War on October 6, 1973, when Israel was attacked by Syria and Egypt. Meir and Moshe Dayan, the defense minister, drew serious condemnation within Israel for the country's lack of preparedness in this conflict. Following general elections the next year, Meir was unable to form a coalition government and was forced from office. She died in Jerusalem in late 1978.

Slobodan Milosevic (1941–)

A minor Communist Party official until the late 1980s, Slobodan Milosevic became president of Serbia in 1989. He kept himself in power by using Serbian nationalism to galvanize Serbs in several areas of the former Republic of Yugoslavia to engage in "ethnic cleansing," or brutal purges, of non-Serbian peoples from these areas. Milosevic first came into conflict with Croatian and Slovenian nationalists in 1991, when he tried to retain Serbian dominance in the Yugoslav Republic, leading to the independence of Slovenia from Yugoslavia that year and Croatia a year later. In 1992, the ethnic cleansing and removal of Bosnian Muslims from various parts of Bosnia-Herzegovina began; it would last throughout the NATO campaign and the eventual Dayton Accord three years later. Soon, problems in the heavily Albanian province of Kosovo led to conflict there, and NATO members launched a full-scale air campaign and were anticipating a land war to stop the Serbian behavior when Milosevic caved in to NATO demands in mid-1999. In 2000, Milosevic tried to win the presidential election illegally, but he was defeated. In 2001 he was turned over to the United Nations War Crimes Tribunal, where he faced trial for the worst war crimes in Europe since the Nazi era of the 1930s and 1940s. The trial began early in 2002 and is expected to last more than a year.

Jawaharlal "Pandit" Nehru (1889–1964)

Jawaharlal Nehru, also known as Pandit, or Teacher, was the first prime minister of India upon its independence from the British Raj in 1947. Born in Allahabad in northern India, he studied at Cambridge and became a successful lawyer in the preindependence period. Elected president of the Indian National Congress in 1929, he fought for the nation's independence for another twenty years. Upon independence, Nehru set India onto a path of nonalignment, taking a major role at the 1955 Bandung Conference in Indonesia, along with Gamal Abdel Nasser of Egypt and Sukarno of Indonesia. He also introduced a form of industrialization that sought to protect Indian industries through import substitution.

Nehru was president during the war with China in 1962, when the Indians suffered a stinging defeat. Upon his death in 1964, Nehru's daughter Indira Gandhi became prime minister for most of the following twenty years until her assassination in 1984. His family appeared somewhat "cursed," since of his grandsons (and Indira's political heirs apparent), Sanjay was killed in an airplane crash in 1980 and Rajiv was assassinated eleven years later.

Paul Henry Nitze (1907–)

A successful businessman who became a bipartisan government fixture in many presidential administrations, Paul Nitze served in the Roosevelt administration on the Board of Economic Warfare and the Foreign Economic Administration and then went on to direct the U.S. Strategic Bombing Survey for President Truman. In the years immediately following World War II, Nitze worked in the State Department's Office of International Trade Policy. He eventually moved to the Policy Planning Staff at the State Department, where he was the main proponent of NSC 68 (see chapter 5), the rationale for increased U.S. military buildup to counter the perceived growing threat of Soviet power.

A decade later, President John Kennedy named Nitze the assistant secretary of defense for international security affairs and then secretary of the navy. In the 1970s, Nitze was a driving force behind the conservative Committee on the Present Danger, whose members (many of whom were former liberals who labeled themselves neoconservatives or "neocons") charged the Carter and Ford administrations with weakening U.S. defenses in the face of mounting Soviet superiority. With Ronald Reagan's election in 1980, Nitze returned to government service, primarily as arms control negotiator, reprising his Strategic Arms Limitation Talks negotiations with the Soviets from the early 1970s. Nitze was the primary voice behind the Intermediate Range Ballistic Missile Treaty with Moscow in 1984. He is often compared with his contemporary George F. Kennan because the two had such a profound influence on national security policy while differing greatly on how to deal with the Soviet threat.

Richard Milhous Nixon (1913–1994)

The only president to resign in disgrace, Richard Nixon was probably the most controversial president of the twentieth century. A Californian, he went east to Duke University for law school before serving in the navy during World War II. Returning to southern California in the mid-1940s, Nixon was elected to the House of Representatives, where he almost immediately became enmeshed in the anti-Communist campaign accusing Alger Hiss of spying in the Department of State. After two terms in the House, Nixon won a California senatorial seat in the midst of what was considered "Red-baiting" over the politics of his opponent, Helen Gahagan Douglas, whom Nixon accused of being "pink"—both a woman and a Communist; she in turn gave him the label "Tricky Dick," which stuck with him for decades.

Nixon won the election, but his willingness to tar his opponents prompted questions that stayed with him throughout his public career. Because of his prominence as an anti-Communist and after only two years in the Senate, Nixon managed to earn the second place on General Dwight D. Eisenhower's ticket in the 1952 presidential victory over Illinois Senator Adlai Stevenson. Nixon's role in the Eisenhower administration was always somewhat tenuous since his antics clearly made the president somewhat uncomfortable, but Nixon managed to survive through the 1956 campaign. In the later years of his term as vice president, Nixon attracted attention in several of his foreign policy appearances, including a controversial and dangerous visit to Venezuela when his car was attacked and he engaged in a debate with Soviet Premier Nikita Khrushchev.

In 1960, Nixon won the Republican nomination for president and was tantalizingly close to defeating Massachusetts Senator

John Fitzgerald Kennedy in the closest presidential election in history, which he probably lost in part because he had no visible support from President Eisenhower. Upon that defeat, Nixon tried for the California governorship, which he lost in 1962. Then, after a steady, calculated return to the public eye, Nixon again captured the Republican nomination in 1968, winning in another extremely close election.

Nixon won the 1968 presidential election at least partially because his opponent, Vice President Hubert H. Humphrey, served under an extremely unpopular President Lyndon B. Johnson and because Nixon claimed to have a "secret plan" to win the war in Southeast Asia. In the early months of his administration, Nixon and Special Assistant for National Security Affairs Henry A. Kissinger launched a massive reorganization and consolidation of the national security apparatus, but they did not manage to end the war. In 1970, the war expanded into Cambodia, leading to massive protests on college campuses across the United States and what became known as the Kent State massacre, where four students were killed by Ohio National Guard bullets. Arguing that he had the support of the "silent majority" in the country, Nixon proceeded with the war. It finally ended in January 1973, after Kissinger had spent several years in secret negotiations with the North Vietnamese in Paris.

Nixon's penchant for secrecy also led to a coup of balance-of-power politics. In 1972, Nixon, the arch anti-Communist, made the first trip by a U.S. president to Beijing, where he met Chinese Chairman Mao Zedong in February, shocking the international community and ending twenty years of Chinese isolation from the West and much of the international community. Later that year, Nixon visited Moscow, where he signed the Antiballistic Missile Treaty and the Strategic Arms Limitation Treaty I with Soviet Premier Leonid Brezhnev.

Unfortunately, Nixon's secrecy extended to his actions at home, where in 1972 his election campaign broke into the Democratic Party National Headquarters in the Watergate Hotel to bug the office. Compounding the crime of his subordinates, Nixon tried to cover up the crime, leading to a tortured national airing of dirty laundry on presidential lying, the taping of his office, and other issues. In the midst of this scandal, dubbed Watergate, Vice President Spiro T. Agnew was forced to resign over corruption charges in the autumn of 1973, and House Minority Leader Gerald R. Ford became vice president. The investigation into Watergate led to Nixon's impeachment by the House of Representatives in the summer of 1974.

Nixon tried to forge ahead on foreign affairs, continuing to work for peace in the Middle East, withdrawing U.S. forces from Southeast Asia, and enhancing relations with the People's Republic of China. Facing impending conviction by the Senate, Nixon announced his resignation on August 8, 1974, without admitting to any crimes. One month later, for the sake of national healing, his successor, Gerald Ford, gave Nixon a pardon for any crimes he might have committed.

After several years of political and personal exile in southern California, Nixon saw himself emerge as a father figure for many people in national security affairs as he advocated what appeared to many to be realistic, balanced views on Europe, China, and the U.S. power in the world. Never entirely able to return to the political stage, Nixon died somewhat more quietly than he lived in 1994.

Muhammad Reza Shah Pahlavi (1919–1980)

The title of shah of Iran dates back two thousand years into Persian history, and the Pahlavi dynasty adopted it early in the twentieth century. Muhammad Reza Shah was a young, inexperienced ruler when he assumed the Peacock throne in the early 1950s. His prime minister, Muhammad Mossadegh, appeared to be heading down a socialist path with his nationalist petroleum policies until the U.S. Central Intelligence Agency ousted him to solidify the pro-Western shah's rule. During the 1960s, the shah was considered a bulwark against Communist expansionism in the Middle East, but he actually proved to be quite antagonistic toward the West when petroleum prices rose with the 1973 Yom Kippur War.

An autocratic and highly repressive ruler who believed that economic modernization could be substituted for social and political freedoms, the shah suffered a serious loss of confidence as increasing numbers of Iranians became disillusioned and turned to Ayatollah Khomeini to restore meaning to their lives. Khomeini orchestrated a campaign, led by students and those seeking renewal in their lives, that ultimately forced the shah from Teheran in 1979. Seriously ill, he fled to Panama before entering the United States for medical treatment. He died in Egypt in 1980, but given the memory of his repressive rule, his death did not engender much sadness in Iran.

Colin Luther Powell (1937–)

The son of Jamaican immigrants, Colin Powell became the first African American to serve as special assistant to the president for national security affairs (1987–1989 under President Reagan), as chairman of the Joint Chiefs of Staff (1989–1993 under President George H. W. Bush), and as secretary of state (2001 to the present under President George W. Bush). Powell had an extraordinary career in the army, rising to the rank of four star general when he had graduated not from West Point but from the City College of New York, his home town. Powell served two tours in Vietnam and held other traditional army jobs before becoming a political fixture in the capital as a White House Fellow, a graduate of the National War College, and military assistant to several prominent Reagan administration officials. He became special assistant to the president for national security affairs in 1987.

Powell's time as chairman of the Joint Chiefs of Staff coincided with the first Bush administration, when he enjoyed the adoration of the troops and widespread public admiration as the chief architect of Desert Shield/Desert Storm, which ousted Saddam Hussein from Kuwait in early 1991. He was adamantly opposed to the efforts of the next president, Bill Clinton, to engage in humanitarian operations around the world, invoking concerns about the willingness of the United States to first commit troops and then see public opinion turn against those troops, as Powell had witnessed in Southeast Asia. Retiring in 1993 after two tours as chairman of the Joint Chiefs, Powell flirted with the idea of running for president in 1996 but decided against it in favor of running a private initiative aimed at raising the standards for inner city youth.

When he accepted the post of secretary of state under President George W. Bush, Powell was the single most popular figure in the new administration. He was later somewhat eclipsed by Secretary of Defense Donald Rumsfeld as a result of Rumsfeld's daily briefings in the aftermath of September 11 and the campaign against Afghanistan. However, Powell has been influential in raising morale at the State Department and has been challenged mightily by the deterioration of conditions in the Middle East since 2000.

Vladimir Putin (1952–)

The quiet, unassuming, but powerful successor to controversial, volatile Russian Federation President Boris Yeltsin, Vladimir Putin was a minor figure in Russian politics until his meteoric rise in the late 1990s. Born to a practicing Russian Orthodox family in Leningrad and a lawyer by training, Putin spent much of his career as a spy in Germany, where he became fluent in German. Returning to the Soviet Union as it was collapsing, in the early 1990s Putin became deputy mayor of St. Petersburg, the new name for Leningrad. In the mid-1990s he moved to Moscow, where he attracted President Yeltsin's attention as an important figure in the security apparatus, becoming a close confidant almost immediately. Many were surprised when Yeltsin named Putin prime minister in 1998. When Yeltsin suddenly announced his resignation on December 31, 1999, Putin assumed the job of president as an interim position and was elected president of the Russian Federation in March 2000.

President Putin has taken a decidedly pro-Western trajectory against the odds and against the desires of many people in the Russian Federation. When confronted by the decision of the Bush administration to abrogate the Antiballistic Missile Treaty of 1972, Putin raised objections but agreed to end the treaty. Similarly, he has sided with the United States in the campaign against terrorism in Afghanistan, even though this implies that U.S. troops will acquire long-term bases in the Central Asian republics along Russia's southern border. Many Westerners fear that Putin is consolidating much power internally, becoming something like a czarist ruler, but there appears to be no organized opposition in Russia that can force him to do otherwise. Putin has pledged to leave office by the middle of the first decade of the twenty-first century.

Yitzhak Rabin (1923–1995)

The first Sabra (native born Israeli) to serve as the prime minister of Israel, Yitzhak Rabin had first been an independence hero and then, early in the 1960s, served as army chief of staff. He was an active member of the Labour Party and served as prime minister in the mid-1970s (1974–1977). He was elected prime minister again in the early 1990s (1992–1995), and in 1993, after secret negotiations in Oslo with Yasser Arafat, he stunned the world by signing accords intended to lead to peace with the Palestinians. As the possibility of making peace with the Palestinians and the Jordanians (a much easier feat) dawned on Israel, radicals on the right rebelled, and an Israeli extremist assassinated Rabin at a Jerusalem peace rally in November 1995.

Ronald Wilson Reagan (1911–)

An actor and labor organizer in the 1940s and 1950s, Ronald Reagan abandoned his early commitment to the Democrats in the early 1960s and became involved in Republican politics. He rose in prominence to become governor of California in 1967, a post he held during some of the most controversial years of the 1970s. Finding himself the heir to Barry Goldwater's conservative movement within the Republican Party, Reagan became a heroic spokesperson for those fearing the United States was becoming vulnerable to Soviet superiority. Bolstered by warnings from the Committee on the Present Danger and other anti-Communist groups in the late 1970s, Reagan won the 1980 election over a weakened President Jimmy Carter just as Carter was trying to get fifty-two hostages back from Iran.

Charged by liberals with destabilizing the international community in the early months of his administration, the Reagan administration moved dramatically against the Soviet Union in a number of places around the world. In Central America, the administration armed counterrevolutionaries (contras) to oust the Sandinistas in Nicaragua while heavily funding the conservative government in El Salvador. Simultaneously, the Reagan administration funded the mujahideen in Afghanistan to resist the Soviet moves there. Most notably, the administration moved to modernize nuclear missiles in Europe even as it negotiated with its adversaries in the Soviet Union.

Although many were asking whether the United States was creating a worse situation, the United States managed to maintain the leadership that ultimately let it outlast the Soviet Union. Ultimately, however, the administration was tarnished when it became obvious that President Reagan had authorized a covert arms-for-hostages deal with Iran. Additionally, the 1983 attack on U.S. Marines in Lebanon was a tragedy of major proportions for U.S. forces abroad.

Condoleezza Rice (1954–)

This African-American Republican is the first woman in U.S. history to hold the position of special assistant to the president for national security affairs, the office she holds in the administration of President George W. Bush. She also served on the National Security Council staff in the administration of President George H. W. Bush (1989–1993).

Dr. Rice came to Washington from a career as a Russian Studies specialist at Stanford University, where she continued as provost after her first period of government service. Since the World Trade Center and Pentagon were attacked in September 2001, she has been a major figure in President Bush's global antiterrorism coalition team. Rice's position as special assistant to the president for national security affairs (a position colloquially but incorrectly known as the national security advisor) arguably makes her the most prominent woman ever to hold a national security position in the United States. She is credited with being one of the driving figures behind the White House campaign to hunt down Usama Bin Laden after September 11, 2001.

Thomas Ridge (1945–)

Former governor of Pennsylvania and Vietnam veteran Thomas Ridge is the first ever assistant to the president for homeland security, a position created after the terrorist attacks on September 11, 2001. Governor Ridge had been highly regarded as a potential vice presidential running mate for fellow Texan Governor George W. Bush in 2000, but many Republican Party activists considered him too liberal, even though generally considered a moderate Republican. As chief of homeland security, Ridge is responsible for coordinating the various agencies and offices of the federal government in the attempt to prevent another terrorist attack on U.S. soil. This highly complex job was designed to take pressure off the White House while providing the United States with ample protection of the national soil.

Anna Eleanor Roosevelt (1884–1962)

Eleanor Roosevelt was the most influential First Lady in U.S. history. In that capacity, she traveled extensively on behalf of the president and pushed the United States to consider human rights and civil rights and many of the other issues now considered to be part of the post–Cold War security agenda. While her husband, President Franklin Roosevelt, was in office, her work was largely domestic in focus. However, after his death she took prominent public positions on many issues ignored by prior administrations, and for a number of years she served as a delegate to the United Nations General Assembly. She was particularly instrumental in raising consciousness and ultimately support for the Universal Declaration of Human Rights and for commissions of the United Nations Education and Social Council (UNESCO).

Franklin Delano Roosevelt (1882–1945)

Arguably the most influential president of the twentieth century, Franklin Roosevelt served the longest term (1933–1945) of any U.S. chief executive. During World War I, Roosevelt was assistant secretary of the navy under President Woodrow Wilson, and then in the 1920s he served as governor of New York. Assuming the presidency at the depth of the Great Depression, Roosevelt pushed domestic legislation through Congress that left an indelible mark on the U.S. political and social scene.

Roosevelt's shaping of national security policy was equally impressive. Taking office at a time when defense spending was low because the country was internally focused, Roosevelt gradually strengthened new alliances (making marginal attempts to improve relations with Latin America) and old alliances (engaging in Lend Lease with Britain as war broke out in 1939). He raised concerns at home about the need for a stronger defense establishment, and his moves to ready the United States for war proved important when U.S. Pacific forces were attacked at Pearl Harbor on December 7, 1941.

The United States entered the war in Europe and in the Pacific simultaneously, waging the most impressive campaign in history during the next three and a half years, ending just after Roosevelt's death in April 1945. He also initiated one of the most intensive weapons programs in history, the Manhattan Project, which created the first atomic bomb in 1945. Roosevelt's contributions to U.S. national security were not merely military, however; his cooperative diplomacy with British Prime Minister Winston Churchill led to the post-war global economic architecture manifest in the Bretton Woods economic system, negotiated at a New Hampshire resort in 1944. Roosevelt's imprimatur was also stamped on the San Francisco negotiations leading to the United Nations Charter the following year.

Donald H. Rumsfeld (1932–)

The secretary of defense in the administrations of both Gerald Ford and George W. Bush, Donald Rumsfeld boasts a career as chief spokesperson on U.S. defense matters spanning more than twenty-five years. Serving as a naval aviator in the Korean War and a congressman from the north suburbs of Chicago, Rumsfeld then held prominent positions in Republican administrations back to the Nixon administration. Rumsfeld's foreign policy experience includes an appointment as U.S. Ambassador to NATO, and under President Ford he was the youngest secretary of defense in U.S. history, after which he returned to private industry for twenty years.

Rumsfeld returned to national prominence in the late 1990s as chairman of a committee to evaluate missile defense systems, which he strongly advocated. In 2000, he was a surprise choice by President Bush for defense secretary, but his political star appeared to be fading in the summer of 2001 because he seemed to be losing battles within the administration. Since the September 11 attacks, however, Rumsfeld has brought a strength to the job that has greatly supported the president. He achieved great international respect and some concern with the strong convictions he held during the Afghanistan campaign to find Usama Bin Laden. The war in Afghanistan made Rumsfeld a major media figure, and attention only increased with the Bush administration plans to increase U.S. defense spending back to early 1980s levels. When asked whether his policies would leave the United States open to charges of hegemony, Rumsfeld unabashedly said that the United States was defending itself at all costs.

Anwar el-Sadat (1918–1981)

Upon assuming office as president of Egypt in 1970 after the volatile Gamal Abdel Nasser died of a heart attack, Anwar el-Sadat was generally thought to be a placeholder, someone that would serve only until Egypt found another charismatic leader. Instead, Sadat, a former military man who had served under

Nasser when Egypt threw off monarchy and adopted a pro-Soviet stand in the 1950s, proved a skilled strategist and made much more sweeping changes to Egypt's global status than anyone anticipated.

To the surprise of both the United States and the Soviet Union, Sadat opened Egypt to the West in 1972, giving Soviet military advisors, a fixture in Egypt since the mid-1950s, twenty-four hours to leave the country. In conjunction with Syrian President Hafez al-Assad, Sadat launched the 1973 Yom Kippur War on the most solemn day of the Jewish calendar, catching Israel unaware. He later admitted that he had been defeated in this war, but he claimed to have accomplished his strategic goal of getting the United States to pay greater attention to Egypt, and indeed, Sadat gradually become a valued U.S. ally during the Nixon and Ford administrations.

In November 1977, Sadat stunned the world by flying to Jerusalem to open face-to-face negotiations with Israeli Prime Minister Menachem Begin. Long negotiations between the two resulted in the first peace treaty between an Arab state and Israel in 1979, and Sadat and Begin were jointly awarded the Nobel Peace Prize. The decision to make peace with Israel came at a time of rising Islamic fundamentalism in the Middle East, including Egypt, and Sadat paid the price. At a military parade in October 1981, he was assassinated by the Islamic Brotherhood.

Ariel Sharon (1928–)

Former general and hero of the 1956 Arab-Israeli War, Ariel Sharon became prime minister of Israel in 2000 after a controversial career as a soldier and politician. Born while the British Mandate governed Israel, Sharon served in the Israeli Defense Force after having been a fighter in the Haganah, the underground Jewish organization working for the creation of the state of Israel, during the 1940s. Sharon was an influential military leader before he achieved election to the Knesset under the Likud coalition in 1977. His role in the ill-fated Israeli invasion of Lebanon in 1982 to oust the Palestine Liberation Organization from Israel's northern neighbor led to his ouster from the political scene until the late 1990s, when he joined the coalition governments that ruled during that period. His visit to the Temple Mount in late September 2000 was blamed for starting a Palestinian *intifada* (uprising) that led to his election as prime

minister in early 2001 but also produced a much more generalized violence between Israelis and Palestinians in the West
Bank.

Josef Stalin (1879–1953)

The longest-serving head of the Soviet Union, Josef Stalin had
been one of the Bolshevik revolutionaries who, lead by Vladimir
Ilyich Lenin and Leon Trotsky, fought to found the Soviet Union
in 1917. Upon Lenin's death in 1924, Stalin gradually consolidated power as general secretary of the Central Committee of
the Communist Party, ousting Trotsky and other rivals to
become the most powerful man in the Soviet Union. Stalin "col-
lectivized" agriculture and worked to keep a highly centralized
governance over the far-flung Soviet empire. In the 1930s, he
purged millions of Russians, and his policies led to the death of
millions more from starvation as a result of the collectivization
campaigns.

Stalin recognized the growing power of Hitler's Reich and
signed a nonaggression pact with the Nazi leader in 1939, assuming it would free the Russians from that threat and allow continued
focus on domestic issues. In June 1941, however, Hitler turned his
war machine from the English Channel to the east, unleashing
one of the bloodiest campaigns in history in an attempt to defeat
the Soviets. Although the three-year Nazi onslaught failed, the
conflict on the Eastern Front cost tens of millions of Russian dead,
both uniformed and civilian, while decimating the already fragile
Soviet economy. A wartime alliance with the United States and
Great Britain led to a series of summits in Cairo, Teheran, Casa-
blanca, Yalta, and Potsdam, where representatives of the three
nations established the post–World War II global architecture.

Churchill and others feared the power of the Red Army,
which still occupied much of Eastern Europe in the aftermath of
the war, and a split in the alliance resulted, leading to an ideological battle called the Cold War. The advent of atomic weapons,
first in the United States, then in the Soviet Union, heightened
concerns that the next war would be much deadlier and all-
encompassing. Stalin's death in 1953 did not end the tensions but
passed it to new players, with the West certain that the source of
tension was not Stalin, but the nature of the two systems: capitalist versus Communist.

Edward Teller (1908–)

A Jewish refugee from Hitler's Europe, Edward Teller is a physicist who first convinced the Truman administration to pursue the "super" or hydrogen bomb, a much more powerful weapon than that detonated over Hiroshima and Nagasaki in August 1945. Two generations later, Teller also had the ear of President Ronald Reagan and lobbied for the research and development of space-based weapons and a ballistic missile defense system that became known, after President Reagan's 1983 speech, as Star Wars. Teller has retained his concerns about the potential for a resurgence of Soviet-type threats to the United States. He is one of the last survivors of the 1940s Manhattan Project.

Margaret Hilda Thatcher (1925–)

Margaret Hilda Thatcher rose through the ranks of the Tory Party to become the first woman to serve as Great Britain's prime minister—a post in which she earned the title "the Iron Lady" for her firm, unbending commitment to ideological purity. Coming into power on the heels of a decade of labor problems and economic stagnation, Thatcher quickly began undercutting labor's grip on major sectors of British industry, a condition dating back to the end of World War II, when Britain had "socialized" much of its industry and public sector. Like her friend and ideological soul mate Ronald Reagan, elected one year after her, Thatcher was convinced that private enterprise was a much more meaningful and fulfilling approach to governance, and she waged an unrelenting war against the large "socialized" sections of British society. The health care sector was an initial target because although socialized medicine was intended to provide health care for all, the real emphasis, in her mind, was its low quality. In a brutal coal strike lasting throughout 1980, she also effectively broke the back of the coal miners, long a powerful political force in Britain and in the rival Labour Party.

In foreign policy, Thatcher showed unending suspicion about the goals of the European Common Market and made it clear that Britain would remain British above anything else, regardless of complaints in the European Union. She was supportive of Reagan's nuclear modernization program, deploying shorter-range cruise missiles to British bases against widespread public protest. At the same time, when Mikhail Gorbachev assumed the presidency of the Soviet Union in 1985 and met Thatcher for the first time, she declared that he was "a man we can do business with," thus opening the door to greater discussion between the West and the Kremlin.

Thatcher served as prime minister from 1979 through 1990. In her later years in power she proved even less willing to negotiate with various sectors of British society, even though obvious gaps between the rich and poor had grown much wider and many felt that too much power and success was concentrated in London and the "home counties" (areas surrounding London). In the summer of 1990, in her last major national security crisis, she encouraged U.S. President George H. W. Bush to oppose Saddam Hussein's invasion of Kuwait. Thatcher was finally ousted from power by Tory moderates in late 1990. Taking a peerage as Lady Thatcher, she continues to present her strong views in speaking engagements around the globe.

Josip Broz Tito (1892–1980)

Josip Broz Tito was a skilled politician and Communist, able to maintain the unified state of Yugoslavia even while distancing himself from Stalin's Soviet Union. He had been a World War I hero and became general secretary of the Communist Party of Yugoslavia in the late 1930s by networking throughout the provinces of the republic. Although he was a Croat, he led the predominantly Serbian forces in World War II against the Nazis. Tito relied not only on Soviet assistance, but on British and U.S. forces eager to oust Germans from any conquered territories. This tie to Western governments gave Tito an opening when the military assistance he sought from Stalin at the end of the war was refused. Tito turned to the West and requested—and achieved— the removal of the Red Army from Yugoslav territory long before that goal was attained elsewhere in the Eastern Bloc.

Tito was always a committed Communist and governed as such. But Stalin never trusted him, and the West always harbored hopes that Yugoslavia would turn from Communism. Tito was able to keep the disparate parts of Yugoslavia together until he died in May 1980. Within a decade of his death, the evidence of his incredible skills was obvious as subsequent leaders fell prey to ethnic politics and Yugoslavia ultimately fell apart, particularly because of the nationalist manipulations of Slobodan Milosevic.

Harry S. Truman (1884–1972)

Known as the "haberdasher from Independence," Harry S. Truman experienced the horrors of warfare while serving as an artillery officer in Europe during World War I. After the war, he opened a clothing store in Kansas City, Missouri. In the early 1920s, he entered politics. In 1935 he became a U.S. senator from Missouri through the Kansas City Democratic "machine," and he was chosen as President Franklin D. Roosevelt's vice presidential nominee for the 1944 campaign. Upon Roosevelt's death in April of the following year, Truman assumed the presidency with no knowledge of the Manhattan Project or many other aspects of U.S. national security.

In July 1945, President Truman met with Winston Churchill and Josef Stalin at Potsdam, where he indicated that the United States had a major new weapon but was not yet sure it would work. He ultimately made the decision to drop atomic weapons on Hiroshima and Nagasaki, Japan, in August 1945, becoming the only person to have ever made the decision to use such weapons. With the end of the war, Truman had to orchestrate the demobilization of millions of U.S. forces while worrying about the increasingly apparent danger of the heavily armed and still massive army of the nation's former ally, the Soviet Union.

During Truman's presidency, the United States aggressively protected democracies under threat from nondemocratic (Communist) forces, a policy that became known as the Truman Doctrine. Truman sent General George C. Marshall to China as a special envoy to try to end the Chinese civil war, and Marshall later became the namesake for the massive U.S. rebuilding plan for European reconstruction. In 1948 Truman won perhaps the most famous presidential election of all time when he defeated New York Governor Thomas Dewey after newspapers had prematurely and erroneously proclaimed Dewey's victory. In 1950, after his secretary of state, Dean Acheson, proclaimed a defense perimeter excluding South Korea, Truman saw his nominal ally South Korea attacked by forces from the North. Truman sent U.S. troops to aid South Korea, and a three-year stalemate, costing more than fifty-five thousand U.S. deaths, began. Truman chose not to run for reelection in 1952 and retired to his childhood home of Independence, Missouri.

Arthur Hendrick Vandenberg (1884–1951)

A prominent Republican senator from Michigan between 1928 and 1951, Arthur Vandenberg was one of the most influential members of Congress in the reconstitution of post–World War II global affairs. Long a critic of U.S. involvement that would in any way hurt national interests, Vandenberg became a delegate to the San Francisco conference where the United Nations Charter was written in 1945. He also attended the Rio Conference that was held to establish collective defense arrangements in the Western Hemisphere two years later. His imprimatur as a leading senator on the Foreign Relations Committee guaranteed that Presidents Franklin Roosevelt and Harry Truman would not face the congressional backlash that President Woodrow Wilson had endured with his Fourteen Points Proposal in 1918 and the subsequent congressional defeat of U.S. entry into the League of Nations.

Lech Walesa (1943–)

Lech Walesa was an obscure electrician working odd jobs in the shipyard at Gdansk, Poland, when he became a labor activist arguing for more workers' rights. Eventually his work helped spark the Solidarity Trade Union movement that ultimately led to the downfall of the Polish Communist state. Walesa won the Nobel Peace Prize in 1983 for his continuing efforts to keep Solidarity going under tremendous pressure, as the Polish government and Soviet forces tried to stem the independent labor movement. In post-Communist Poland, Walesa became the first democratically elected president of the country in 1990, but he was defeated for reelection five years later. Walesa has credited the Catholic Church as his partner during the Solidarity struggle.

5

Documents

The documents discussed in this chapter have formed the basis of U.S. national security commitments and ideals since the end of World War II. They are listed in chronological order, and in studying them sequentially one can trace the development of security thought.

Many of the documents relate to the Cold War; these not only help explain that period of U.S. national security preoccupation, which ended more than a decade ago, but they also shed light on today's situation. Some of them remain guideposts for U.S. security today, having changed with the times. For example, the United Nations Charter, now more than fifty years old, has taken on a different, more important role than it had for much of its history. Likewise, the NATO alliance is much changed from its original Cold War character. A short annotation for each document explains its relevance to U.S. national security.

A good number of documents are reprinted in full here, but some are prohibitively long to include in a volume of this scope. In these cases, I have either included excerpts of the full text (e.g., the Taiwan Relations Act) or have provided source information, including a Web site address where possible, by which the reader can find the source document. Many of the materials discussed here are also available through either the Cold War International History Project, run out of the Woodrow Wilson Center of the Smithsonian Institution, or the National Security Archive. Both of these groups are in the process of making long-term hard copy and electronic compilations of Cold War documents.

United Nations Charter (1945)

The United Nations Charter is the founding document for the international community's supranational organization for world peace. The United Nations is fundamentally different in its organization from its most visible predecessor, the League of Nations, which was formed in the aftermath of World War I. The UN Charter identifies the purposes of the United Nations and describes the composition of the General Assembly, the Security Council and other councils, the UN Secretariat, and various other components of the body. It remains the basic document for much of the international regime under which the world operates.

The UN Charter is available on-line at: http://www.un.org/Overview/Charter/contents.html. Also available at the UN Web site (http://www.un.org/english) are Security Council and General Assembly resolutions, Economic and Social Council documentation, and other basic materials.

"The Long Telegram" (1946)

On February 22, 1946, George F. Kennan, the U.S. chargé d'affaires in Moscow, telegrammed to Washington an extended analysis of the immediate postwar situation in the Soviet Union. One of the most comprehensive views to come out of Moscow, it warned of the Soviet anticapitalist worldview and possible expansionism. When the concerns became public in July 1947 as "The Sources of Soviet Conduct" in the periodical *Foreign Affairs*, it caused more people to worry about Soviet intentions and capabilities, coming as it did not long after former British Prime Minister Winston Churchill raised questions about an "iron curtain" breaking Europe into two pieces. The telegram, eight thousand words in length, is excerpted at: http://www.mtholyoke.edu/acad/intrel/longtel.html, and the entire document appears in George Kennan, *Memoirs, 1925–1950* (Boston: Little, Brown, 1967), 547–559.

Winston Churchill's "Iron Curtain" Speech (1946)

Former British Prime Minister Winston Churchill presented this speech on March 5, 1946, at Westminster College, a small liberal arts college in east central Missouri where he received an honorary degree. The speech, which Churchill called "The Sinews of Peace," contained an allusion to an "iron curtain descending on Europe"— an image that was to remain powerful throughout the Cold War, especially in its early years. Churchill expressed the growing sentiment that the Soviet Union appeared to be establishing a system that was bound to come into ideological conflict with its former allies in the "free, capitalist" West. It appeared quite plausible that yet another global conflict could result, given that the "iron curtain" was prohibiting some states from exercising their freedom of government.

The speech is quite long, and so it has been excerpted here. The complete text of the speech can be found at: http://www.hpol.org/churchill/.

I am glad to come to Westminster College this afternoon, and am complimented that you should give me a degree. The name "Westminster" is somehow familiar to me. I seem to have heard of it before. Indeed, it was at Westminster that I received a very large part of my education in politics, dialectic, rhetoric, and one or two other things. In fact we have both been educated at the same, or similar, or, at any rate, kindred establishments. . . .

The United States stands at this time at the pinnacle of world power. It is a solemn moment for the American Democracy. For with primacy in power is also joined an awe-inspiring accountability to the future. If you look around you, you must feel not only the sense of duty done but also you must feel anxiety lest you fall below the level of achievement. Opportunity is here now, clear and shining for both our countries. To reject it or ignore it or fritter it away will bring upon us all the long reproaches of the after-time. It is necessary that constancy of mind, persistency of purpose, and the grand simplicity of decision shall guide and rule the conduct of the English-speaking peoples in peace as they did in war. We must, and I believe we shall, prove ourselves equal to this severe requirement. . . .

A shadow has fallen upon the scenes so lately lighted by the Allied victory. Nobody knows what Soviet Russia and its Communist international organization intends to do in the immediate future, or what are the limits, if any, to their expansive and proselytizing tendencies. I have a strong admiration and regard for the valiant Russian people and for my wartime comrade, Marshal Stalin. There is deep sympathy and goodwill in Britain—and I doubt not here also— toward the peoples of all the Russias and a resolve to persevere through many differences and rebuffs in establishing lasting friendships. We understand the Russian need to be secure on her western frontiers by the removal of all possibility of German aggression. We welcome Russia to her rightful place among the leading nations of the world. We welcome her flag upon the seas. Above all, we welcome constant, frequent and growing contacts between the Russian people and our own people on both sides of the Atlantic. It is my duty however, for I am sure you would wish me to state the facts as I see them to you, to place before you certain facts about the present position in Europe.

From Stettin in the Baltic to Trieste in the Adriatic, an iron curtain has descended across the Continent. Behind that line lie all the capitals of the ancient states of Central and Eastern Europe. Warsaw, Berlin, Prague, Vienna, Budapest, Belgrade, Bucharest and Sofia, all these famous cities and the populations around them lie in what I must call the Soviet sphere, and all are subject in one form or another, not only to Soviet influence but to a very high and, in many cases, increasing measure of control from Moscow. Athens alone—Greece with its immortal glories—is free to decide its future at an election under British, American and French observation. The Russian-dominated Polish Government has been encouraged to make enormous and wrongful inroads upon Germany, and mass expulsions of millions of Germans on a scale grievous and undreamed-of are now taking place. The Communist parties, which were very small in all these Eastern States of Europe, have been raised to preeminence and power far beyond their numbers and are seeking everywhere to obtain totalitarian control. Police governments are prevailing in nearly every case, and so far, except in Czechoslovakia, there is no true democracy. . . .

The safety of the world requires a new unity in Europe, from which no nation should be permanently outcast. It is from the quarrels of the strong parent races in Europe that the world wars we have witnessed, or which occurred in former times, have sprung. Twice in our own lifetime we have seen the United States, against their wishes and their traditions, against arguments, the force of which it is impossible not to comprehend, drawn by irresistible forces into these wars in time to secure the victory of the good cause, but only after frightful slaughter and devastation had occurred. Twice the United States has had to send several millions of its young men across the Atlantic to find the war; but now war can find any nation, wherever it may dwell between dusk and dawn. Surely we should work with conscious purpose for a grand pacification of Europe, within the structure of the United Nations and in accordance with its Charter. That I feel is an open cause of policy of very great importance.

In front of the iron curtain which lies across Europe are other causes for anxiety. In Italy the Communist Party is seriously hampered by having to support the Communist-trained Marshal Tito's claims to former Italian territory at the head of the Adriatic. Nevertheless the future of Italy hangs in the balance. Again one cannot imagine a regenerated Europe without a strong France. All my public life I have worked for a strong France and I never lost faith in her destiny, even in the darkest hours. I will not lose faith now. However, in a great number of countries, far from the Russian frontiers and throughout the world, Communist fifth columns are established and work in complete unity and absolute obedience to the directions they receive from the Communist center. Except in the British Commonwealth and in the United States where Communism is in its infancy, the Communist parties or fifth columns constitute a growing challenge and peril to Christian civilization. These are somber facts for anyone to have to recite on the morrow of a victory gained by so much splendid comradeship in arms and in the cause of freedom and democracy; but we should be most unwise not to face them squarely while time remains. . . .

On the other hand I repulse the idea that a new war is inevitable; still more that it is imminent. It is because I am sure that our fortunes are still in our own hands and that we hold the power to save the future, that I feel the duty to speak out now that I have the occasion and the opportunity to do so. I do not believe that Soviet Russia desires war. What they desire is the fruits of war and the indefinite expansion of their power and doctrines. But what we have to consider here today while time remains, is the permanent prevention of war and the establishment of conditions of freedom and democracy as rapidly as possible in all countries. Our difficulties and dangers will not be removed by closing our eyes to them. They will not be removed by mere waiting to see what happens; nor will they be removed by a policy of appeasement. What is needed is a settlement, and the longer this is delayed, the more difficult it will be and the greater our dangers will become.

From what I have seen of our Russian friends and Allies during the war, I am convinced that there is nothing they admire so much as strength, and there is nothing for which they have less respect than for weakness, especially military weakness. For that reason the old doctrine of a balance of power is unsound. We cannot afford, if we can help it, to work on narrow margins, offering temptations to a trial of strength. If the Western Democracies stand together in strict adherence to the principles of the United Nations Charter, their influence for furthering those principles will be immense and no one is likely to molest them. If however they become divided or falter in their duty and if these all-important years are allowed to slip away then indeed catastrophe may overwhelm us all.

Last time I saw it all coming and cried aloud to my own fellow-countrymen and to the world, but no one paid any attention. Up till the year 1933 or even 1935, Germany might have been saved from the awful fate which has overtaken her and we might all have been spared the miseries Hitler let loose upon mankind. There never was a war in all history easier to prevent by timely action than the one which has just desolated such great areas of the globe. It could have been prevented in my belief without the firing of a single shot, and Germany might be powerful, prosperous and honored today; but no one would listen and one by one we were all sucked into the awful whirlpool. We surely must not let that happen again. This can only be achieved by reaching now, in 1946, a good understanding on all points with Russia under the general authority of the United Nations Organization and by the maintenance of that good understanding through many peaceful years, by the world instrument, supported by the whole strength of the English-speaking world and all its connections. There is the solution which I respectfully offer to you in this Address to which I have given the title "The Sinews of Peace." . . .

Source: Churchill, Winston. "The Sinews of Peace." In: *Winston Churchill: His Complete Speeches 1897–1963,* Vol. 6, *1943–1949,* 7285–7293. Edited by Robert Rhodes James. New York and London: Chelsea House Publishers, 1974. Reproduced with permission of Curtis Brown Ltd., London, on behalf of Winston S. Churchill. Copyright Winston S. Churchill 1946.

The Truman Doctrine (1947)

President Harry S. Truman's address to a joint session of Congress on March 12, 1947, would be one of three major national security proclamations made within a sixteen-week period in 1947, the other two being George F. Kennan's "Mr. X" article and Secretary of State George C. Marshall's commencement speech at Harvard enunciating the Marshall Plan for reconstruction (see separate entries). Truman's speech articulated a policy, known thereafter as the Truman Doctrine, that identified U.S. interests in responding to free peoples threatened by "attempted subjugation by armed minorities or by outside pressures." This policy was ignored, however, when the United States did not intervene in the 1956 Hungarian uprising, to the chagrin of those who were committed to challenging the Communists.

Mr. President, Mr. Speaker, Members of the Congress of the United States:

The gravity of the situation which confronts the world today necessitates my appearance before a joint session of the Congress. The foreign policy and the national security of this country are involved.

One aspect of the present situation, which I wish to present to you at this time for your consideration and decision, concerns Greece and Turkey.

The United States has received from the Greek Government an urgent appeal for financial and economic assistance. Preliminary reports from the American Economic Mission now in Greece and reports from the American Ambassador in Greece corroborate the statement of the Greek Government that assistance is imperative if Greece is to survive as a free nation.

I do not believe that the American people and the Congress wish to turn a deaf ear to the appeal of the Greek Government.

Greece is not a rich country. Lack of sufficient natural resources has always forced the Greek people to work hard to make both ends meet. Since 1940, this industrious and peace loving country has suffered invasion, four years of cruel enemy occupation, and bitter internal strife.

When forces of liberation entered Greece they found that the retreating Germans had destroyed virtually all the railways, roads, port facilities, communications, and merchant marine. More than a thousand villages had been burned. Eighty-five percent of the children were tubercular. Livestock, poultry, and draft animals had almost disappeared. Inflation had wiped out practically all savings.

As a result of these tragic conditions, a militant minority, exploiting human want and misery, was able to create political chaos which, until now, has made economic recovery impossible.

Greece is today without funds to finance the importation of those goods which are essential to bare subsistence. Under these circumstances the people of Greece cannot make progress in solving their problems of reconstruction. Greece is in desperate need of financial and economic assistance to enable it to resume purchases of food, clothing, fuel and seeds. These are indispensable for the subsistence of its people and are obtainable only from abroad. Greece must have help to import the goods necessary to restore internal order and security, so essential for economic and political recovery.

The Greek Government has also asked for the assistance of experienced American administrators, economists and technicians to insure that the financial and other aid given to Greece shall be used effectively in creating a stable and self-sustaining economy and in improving its public administration.

The very existence of the Greek state is today threatened by the terrorist activities of several thousand armed men, led by Communists, who defy the government's authority at a number of points, particularly along the northern boundaries. A Commission appointed by the United Nations Security Council is at present investigating disturbed conditions in northern Greece and alleged border violations along the frontier between Greece on the one hand and Albania, Bulgaria, and Yugoslavia on the other.

Meanwhile, the Greek Government is unable to cope with the situation. The Greek army is small and poorly equipped. It needs supplies and equipment if it is to restore the authority of the government throughout Greek territory. Greece must have assistance if it is to become a self-supporting and self-respecting democracy.

The United States must supply that assistance. We have already extended to Greece certain types of relief and economic aid but these are inadequate.

There is no other country to which democratic Greece can turn.

No other nation is willing and able to provide the necessary support for a democratic Greek government.

The British Government, which has been helping Greece, can give no further financial or economic aid after March 31. Great Britain finds itself under the necessity of reducing or liquidating its commitments in several parts of the world, including Greece.

We have considered how the United Nations might assist in this crisis. But the situation is an urgent one requiring immediate action and the United Nations and its related organizations are not in a position to extend help of the kind that is required.

It is important to note that the Greek Government has asked for our aid in utilizing effectively the financial and other assistance we may give to Greece, and in improving its public administration. It is of the utmost importance that we supervise the use of any funds made available to Greece; in such a manner that each dollar spent will count toward making Greece self-supporting, and will help to build an economy in which a healthy democracy can flourish.

No government is perfect. One of the chief virtues of a democracy, however, is that its defects are always visible and under democratic processes can be pointed out and corrected. The Government of Greece is not perfect. Nevertheless it represents eighty-five percent of the members of the Greek Parliament who were chosen in an election last year. Foreign observers, including 692 Americans, considered this election to be a fair expression of the views of the Greek people.

The Greek Government has been operating in an atmosphere of chaos and extremism. It has made mistakes. The extension of aid by this country does not mean that the United States condones everything that the Greek Government has done or will do. We have condemned in the past, and we condemn now, extremist measures of the right or the left. We have in the past advised tolerance, and we advise tolerance now.

Greece's neighbor, Turkey, also deserves our attention.

The future of Turkey as an independent and economically sound state is clearly no less important to the freedom-loving peoples of the world than the future of Greece. The circumstances in which Turkey finds itself today are considerably different from those of Greece. Turkey has been spared the disasters that have beset Greece. And during the war, the United States and Great Britain furnished Turkey with material aid.

Nevertheless, Turkey now needs our support.

Since the war Turkey has sought financial assistance from Great Britain and the United States for the purpose of effecting that modernization necessary for the maintenance of its national integrity.

That integrity is essential to the preservation of order in the Middle East.

The British government has informed us that, owing to its own difficulties it can no longer extend financial or economic aid to Turkey.

As in the case of Greece, if Turkey is to have the assistance it needs, the United States must supply it. We are the only country able to provide that help.

I am fully aware of the broad implications involved if the United States extends assistance to Greece and Turkey, and I shall discuss these implications with you at this time.

One of the primary objectives of the foreign policy of the United States is the creation of conditions in which we and other nations will be able to work out a way of life free from coercion. This was a fundamental issue in the war with Germany and Japan. Our victory was won over countries which sought to impose their will, and their way of life, upon other nations.

To ensure the peaceful development of nations, free from coercion, the United States has taken a leading part in establishing the United Nations. The United Nations is designed to make possible lasting freedom and independence for all its members. We shall not realize our objectives, however, unless we are willing to help free peoples to maintain their free institutions and their national integrity against aggressive movements that seek to impose upon them totalitarian regimes. This is no more than a frank recognition that totalitarian regimes imposed on free peoples, by direct or indirect aggression, undermine the foundations of international peace and hence the security of the United States.

The peoples of a number of countries of the world have recently had totalitarian regimes forced upon them against their will. The Government of the United States has made frequent protests against coercion and intimidation, in violation of the Yalta agreement, in Poland, Rumania, and Bulgaria. I must also state that in a number of other countries there have been similar developments.

At the present moment in world history nearly every nation must choose between alternative ways of life. The choice is too often not a free one.

One way of life is based upon the will of the majority, and is distinguished by free institutions, representative government, free elections, guarantees of individual liberty, freedom of speech and religion, and freedom from political oppression.

The second way of life is based upon the will of a minority forcibly imposed upon the majority. It relies upon terror and oppression, a controlled press and radio; fixed elections, and the suppression of personal freedoms.

I believe that it must be the policy of the United States to support free peoples who are resisting attempted subjugation by armed minorities or by outside pressures.

I believe that we must assist free peoples to work out their own destinies in their own way.

I believe that our help should be primarily through economic and financial aid which is essential to economic stability and orderly political processes.

The world is not static, and the status quo is not sacred. But we cannot allow changes in the status quo in violation of the Charter of the United Nations by such methods as coercion, or by such subterfuges as political infiltration. In helping free and independent nations to maintain their freedom, the United States will be giving effect to the principles of the Charter of the United Nations.

It is necessary only to glance at a map to realize that the survival and integrity of the Greek nation are of grave importance in a much wider situation. If Greece should fall under the control of an armed minority, the effect upon its neighbor, Turkey, would be immediate and serious. Confusion and disorder might well spread throughout the entire Middle East.

Moreover, the disappearance of Greece as an independent state would have a profound effect upon those countries in Europe whose peoples are struggling against great difficulties to maintain their freedoms and their independence while they repair the damages of war.

It would be an unspeakable tragedy if these countries, which have struggled so long against overwhelming odds, should lose that victory for which they sacrificed so much. Collapse of free institutions and loss of independence would be disastrous not only for them but for the world. Discouragement and possibly failure would quickly be the lot of neighboring peoples striving to maintain their freedom and independence.

Should we fail to aid Greece and Turkey in this fateful hour, the effect will be far reaching to the West as well as to the East.

We must take immediate and resolute action.

I therefore ask the Congress to provide authority for assistance to Greece and Turkey in the amount of $400,000,000 for the period ending June 30, 1948. In requesting these funds, I have taken into consideration the maximum amount of relief assistance which would be furnished to Greece out of the $350,000,000 which I recently requested that the Congress authorize for the prevention of starvation and suffering in countries devastated by the war.

In addition to funds, I ask the Congress to authorize the detail of American civilian and military personnel to Greece and Turkey, at the request of those countries, to assist in the tasks of reconstruction, and for the purpose of supervising the use of such financial and material assistance as may be furnished. I recommend that authority also be provided for the instruction and training of selected Greek and Turkish personnel.

Finally, I ask that the Congress provide authority which will permit the speediest and most effective use, in terms of needed commodities, supplies, and equipment, of such funds as may be authorized.

If further funds, or further authority, should be needed for purposes indicated in this message, I shall not hesitate to bring the situation before the Congress. On this subject the Executive and Legislative branches of the Government must work together.

This is a serious course upon which we embark.

I would not recommend it except that the alternative is much more serious. The United States contributed $341,000,000,000 toward winning World War II. This is an investment in world freedom and world peace.

The assistance that I am recommending for Greece and Turkey amounts to little more than 1 tenth of 1 percent of this investment. It is only common sense that we should safeguard this investment and make sure that it was not in vain.

The seeds of totalitarian regimes are nurtured by misery and want. They spread and grow in the evil soil of poverty and strife. They reach their full growth when the hope of a people for a better life has died. We must keep that hope alive.

The free peoples of the world look to us for support in maintaining their freedoms.

If we falter in our leadership, we may endanger the peace of the world—and we shall surely endanger the welfare of our own nation.

Great responsibilities have been placed upon us by the swift movement of events. I am confident the Congress will face these responsibilities squarely.

Sources: "The Truman Doctrine." Courtesy of the U.S. Historical Documents Archive. On-line. Available at: http://w3.one.net/ ~mweiler/ushda/trudoct.htm. Accessed January 16, 2002. *Public Papers of the Presidents of the United States: Harry S. Truman, 1947.* Washington, DC: GPO, 1948, pp. 176–180.

The Marshall Plan Speech (1947)

Secretary of State George C. Marshall presented this speech at a luncheon for honorary degree recipients following Harvard University's commencement ceremonies on June 5, 1947. The speech unveiled the most massive reconstruction project ever envisioned and encapsulated U.S. hopes of stifling Soviet expansionism in Europe. The Marshall Plan, known as the Economic Cooperation Act, was presented to the Congress and approved with much bipartisan support. President Truman signed it into law on April 3, 1948.

Mr. President, Dr. Conant, members of the Board of Overseers, Ladies and Gentlemen:

I'm profoundly grateful and touched by the great distinction and honor and great compliment accorded me by the authorities of Harvard this morning. I'm overwhelmed, as a matter of fact, and I'm rather fearful of my inability to maintain such a high rating as you've been generous enough to accord to me. In these historic and lovely surroundings, this perfect day, and this very wonderful assembly, it is a tremendously impressive thing to an individual in my position.

But to speak more seriously, I need not tell you that the world situation is very serious. That must be apparent to all intelligent people. I think one difficulty is that the problem is one of such enormous complexity that the very mass of facts presented to the public by press and radio make it exceedingly difficult for the man in the street to reach a clear appraisement of the situation. Furthermore, the people of this country are distant from the troubled areas of the earth and it is hard for them to comprehend the plight and consequent reactions of the long-suffering peoples, and the effect of those reactions on their governments in connection with our efforts to promote peace in the world.

In considering the requirements for the rehabilitation of Europe, the physical loss of life, the visible destruction of cities, factories, mines, and railroads was correctly estimated, but it has become obvious during recent months that this visible destruction was probably less serious than the dislocation of the entire fabric of European economy. For the past ten years conditions have been abnormal. The feverish preparation for war and the more feverish maintenance of the war effort engulfed all aspects of national economies. Machinery has fallen into disrepair or is entirely obsolete. Under the arbitrary and destructive Nazi rule, virtually every possible enterprise was geared into the German war machine. Long-standing commercial ties, private institutions, banks, insurance companies, and shipping companies disappeared through loss of capital, absorption through nationalization, or by simple destruction. In many countries, confidence in the local currency has been severely shaken. The breakdown of the business structure of Europe during the war was complete. Recovery has been seriously retarded by the fact that two years after the close of hostilities a peace settlement with Germany and Austria has not been agreed upon. But even given a more prompt solution of these difficult problems, the rehabilitation of the economic structure of Europe quite evidently will require a much longer time and greater effort than has been foreseen.

There is a phase of this matter which is both interesting and serious. The farmer has always produced the foodstuffs to exchange with the city dweller for the other necessities of life. This division of labor is the basis of modern civilization. At the present time it is threatened with breakdown. The town and city industries are not producing adequate goods to exchange with the food-producing farmer. Raw materials and fuel are in short supply. Machinery is lacking or worn out. The farmer or the peasant cannot find the goods for sale which he desires to purchase. So the sale of his farm produce for money which he cannot use seems to him an unprofitable transaction. He, therefore, has withdrawn many fields from crop cultivation and is using them for grazing. He feeds more grain to stock and finds for himself and his family an ample supply of food, however short he may be on clothing and the other ordinary gadgets of civilization. Meanwhile, people in the cities are short of food and fuel, and in some places approaching the starvation levels. So the governments are forced to use their foreign money and credits to procure these necessities abroad. This process exhausts funds which are urgently needed for reconstruction. Thus a very serious situation is rapidly developing which bodes no good for the world. The modern system of the division of labor upon which the exchange of products is based is in danger of breaking down.

The truth of the matter is that Europe's requirements for the next three or four years of foreign food and other essential products— principally from America—are so much greater than her present ability to pay that she must have substantial additional help or face economic, social, and political deterioration of a very grave character.

The remedy lies in breaking the vicious circle and restoring the confidence of the European people in the economic future of their own countries and of Europe as a whole. The manufacturer and the farmer throughout wide areas must be able and willing to exchange their product for currencies, the continuing value of which is not open to question.

Aside from the demoralizing effect on the world at large and the possibilities of disturbances arising as a result of the desperation of the people concerned, the consequences to the economy of the United States should be apparent to all. It is logical that the United States should do whatever it is able to do to assist in the return of normal economic health in the world, without which there can be no political stability and no assured peace. Our policy is directed not against any country or doctrine but against hunger, poverty, desperation, and chaos. Its purpose should be the revival of a working economy in the world so as to permit the emergence of political and social conditions in which free institutions can exist. Such assistance, I am convinced, must not be on a piecemeal basis as various crises develop. Any assistance that this Government may render in the future should provide a cure rather than a mere palliative. Any government that is willing to assist in the task of recovery will find full cooperation, I am sure, on the part of the United States Government. Any government which maneuvers to block the recovery of other countries cannot expect help from us. Furthermore, governments, political parties, or groups which seek to perpetuate human misery in order to profit therefrom politically or otherwise will encounter the opposition of the United States.

It is already evident that, before the United States Government can proceed much further in its efforts to alleviate the situation and help start the European world on its way to recovery, there must be some agreement among the countries of Europe as to the requirements of the situation and the part those countries themselves will take in order to give proper effect to whatever action might be undertaken by this Government. It would be neither fitting nor efficacious for this Government to undertake to draw up unilaterally a program designed to place Europe on its feet economically. This is the business of the Europeans. The initiative, I think, must come from Europe. The role of this country should consist of friendly aid in the drafting of a European program and of later support of such a program so far as it may be practical for us to do so. The program should be a joint one, agreed to by a number, if not all European nations.

An essential part of any successful action on the part of the United States is an understanding on the part of the people of America of the character of the problem and the remedies to be applied. Political passion and prejudice should have no part. With foresight, and a willingness on the part of our people to face up to the vast responsibility which history has clearly placed upon our country, the difficulties I have outlined can and will be overcome.

Thank you very much.

Source: Marshall, George C. "Against Hunger, Poverty, Desperation and Chaos." Speech at the Harvard University Commencement, June 5, 1947. Reprinted in *Foreign Affairs,* May-June 1997, 76 (no. 3): 160.

"Mr. X" Article in Foreign Affairs (1947)

"The Sources of Soviet Conduct," published in Foreign Affairs *in July, was written by George F. Kennan under a pseudonym, Mr. X, because it was considered highly controversial. The article is often cited as the basis for the U.S. "containment" strategy, which would govern U.S. relations with the Soviet Union for four decades. Kennan subsequently argued that the containment approach was too literally applied to the U.S. policy toward Moscow.*

Part 1

The political personality of Soviet power as we know it today is the product of ideology and circumstances: ideology inherited by the present Soviet leaders from the movement in which they had their political origin, and circumstances of the power that they now have exercised for nearly three decades in Russia. There can be few tasks of psychological analysis more difficult than to try to trace the interaction of these two forces and the relative role of each in the determination of official Soviet conduct. Yet the attempt must be made if that conduct is to be understood and effectively countered.

It is difficult to summarize the set of ideological concepts with which the Soviet leaders came into power. Marxian ideology, in its Russian-Communist projection, has always been in process of subtle evolution. The materials on which it bases itself are extensive and complex. But the outstanding features of Communist thought as it existed in 1916 may perhaps be summarized as follows: (a) that the central factor in the life of man, the factor which determines the character of public life and the "physiognomy of society," is the system by which material goods are produced and exchanged; (b) that the capitalist system of production is a nefarious one which inevitably leads to the exploitation of the working class by the capital-owning class and is incapable of developing adequately the economic resources of society or of distributing fairly the material goods produced by human labor; (c) that capitalism contains the seeds of its own destruction and must, in view of the inability of the capital-owning class to adjust itself to economic change, result eventually and inescapably in a revolutionary transfer of power to the working class; and (d) that imperialism, the final phase of capitalism, leads directly to war and revolution.

The rest may be outlined in Lenin's own words: "Unevenness of economic and political development is the inflexible law of capitalism. It follows from this that the victory of Socialism may come originally in a few capitalist countries or even in a single capitalist country. The victorious proletariat of that country, having expropriated the capitalists and having organized Socialist production at home, would rise against the remaining capitalist world, drawing to itself in the process the oppressed classes of other countries." It must be noted that there is no assumption that capitalism would perish without proletarian revolution. A final push was needed from a revolutionary proletariat movement in order to tip over the tottering structure.

For 50 years prior to the outbreak of the Revolution, this pattern of thought had exercised great fascination for the members of the Russian revolutionary movement. Frustrated, discontented, hopeless of finding self-expression—or too impatient to seek it—in the confining limits of the Tsarist political system, yet lacking wide popular support for their choice of bloody revolution as a means of social betterment, these revolutionists found in Marxist theory a highly convenient rationalization for their own instinctive desires. It afforded pseudoscientific justification for their impatience, for their categorical denial of all value in the Tsarist system, for their yearning for power and revenge and for their inclination to cut corners in the pursuit of it. It is therefore no wonder that they had come to believe implicitly in the truth and soundness of the Marxian-Leninist teachings, so congenial to their own impulses and emotions. Their sincerity need not be impugned. This is a phenomenon as old as human nature itself. It has never been more aptly described than by Edward Gibbon, who wrote in *The Decline and Fall of the Roman Empire:* "From enthusiasm to imposture the step is perilous and slippery; the demon of Socrates affords a memorable instance of how a wise man may deceive himself, how a good man may deceive others, how the conscience may suffer a mixed and middle state between self-illusion and voluntary fraud." And it was with this set of illusions that the Bolshevik Party entered into power.

Now it must be noted that through all the years of preparation for revolution, the attention of these men, as indeed of Marx himself, had been centered less on the future form which Socialism would take than on the necessary overthrow of rival power which, in their view, had to precede the introduction of Socialism. Their views, therefore, on the positive program to be put into effect, once power was attained, were for the most part nebulous, visionary and impractical. Beyond the nationalization of industry and the expropriation of large private capital holdings there was no agreed program. The treatment of the peasantry, which according to the Marxist formulation was not of the proletariat, had always been a vague spot in the pattern of Communist thought; and it remained an object of controversy and vacillation for the first ten years of Communist power.

The circumstances of the immediate postrevolution period—the existence in Russia of civil war and foreign intervention, together with the obvious fact that the Communists represented only a tiny minority of the Russian people—made the establishment of dictatorial power a necessity. The experiment with "war Communism" and the abrupt attempt to eliminate private production and trade had unfortunate economic consequences and caused further bitterness against the new revolutionary regime. Although the temporary relaxation of the effort to communize Russia, represented by the New Economic Policy, alleviated some of this economic distress and thereby served its purpose, it also made it evident that the "capitalistic sector of society" was still prepared to profit at once from any relaxation of governmental pressure, and would, if permitted to continue to exist, always constitute a powerful opposing element to the Soviet regime and a serious rival for influence in the country. Somewhat the same situation prevailed with respect to the individual peasant who, in his own small way, was also a private producer.

Lenin, had he lived, might have proved a great enough man to reconcile these conflicting forces to the ultimate benefit of Russian society, though this is questionable. But be that as it may, Stalin, and those whom he led in the struggle for succession to Lenin's position of leadership, were not the men to tolerate rival political forces in the sphere of power which they coveted. Their sense of insecurity was too great. Their particular brand of fanaticism, unmodified by any of the Anglo-Saxon traditions of compromise, was too fierce and too jealous to envisage any permanent sharing of power. From the Russian-Asiatic world out of which they had emerged they carried with them a skepticism as to the possibilities of permanent and peaceful coexistence of rival forces. Easily persuaded of their own doctrinaire "rightness," they insisted on the submission or destruction of all competing power. Outside of the Communist Party, Russian society was to have no rigidity. There were to be no forms of collective human activity or association which would not be dominated by the Party. No other force in Russian society was to be permitted to achieve vitality or integrity. Only the Party was to have structure. All else was to be an amorphous mass.

And within the Party the same principle was to apply. The mass of Party members might go through the motions of election, deliberation, decision and action; but in these motions they were to be animated not by their own individual wills but by the awesome breath of the Party leadership and the overbrooding presence of "the word."

Let it be stressed again that subjectively these men probably did not seek absolutism for its own sake. They doubtless believed—and found it easy to believe—that they alone knew what was good for society and that they would accomplish good once their power was secure and unchallengeable. But in seeking that security of their own rule they were prepared to recognise no restrictions, either of God or man, on the character of their methods. And until such time as that security might be achieved, they placed far down on their scale of operational priorities the comforts and happiness of the peoples entrusted to their care.

Now the outstanding circumstance concerning the Soviet regime is that down to the present day this process of political consolidation has never been completed and the men in the Kremlin have continued to be predominately absorbed with the struggle to secure and make absolute the power which they seized in 1917. They have endeavoured to secure it primarily against forces at home, within Soviet society itself. But they have also endeavoured to secure it against the outside world. For ideology, as we have seen, taught them that the outside world was hostile and that it was their duty eventually to overthrow the political forces beyond their borders. The powerful hands of Russian history and tradition reached up to sustain them in this feeling. Finally, their own aggressive intransigence with respect to the outside world began to find its own reaction; and they were soon forced, to use another Gibbonesque phrase, "to chastise the contumacy" which they themselves had provoked. It is an undeniable privilege of every man to prove himself right in the thesis that the world is his enemy; for if he reiterates it frequently enough and makes it the background of his conduct he is eventually to be right.

Now it lies in the nature of the mental world of the Soviet leaders, as well as in the character of their ideology, that no opposition to them can be officially recognized as having any merit or justification whatsoever. Such opposition can flow, in theory, only from the hostile and incorrigible forces of dying capitalism. As long as remnants of capitalism were officially recognised as existing in Russia, it was possible to place on them, as an internal element, part of the blame for the maintenance of a dictatorial form of society. But these remnants were liquidated, little by little, this justification fell away; and when it was indicated officially that they had been finally destroyed, it disappeared altogether. And this fact created one of the most basic of the compulsions which came to act upon the Soviet regime: since capitalism no longer existed in Russia and since it could not be admitted that there could be serious or widespread opposition to the Kremlin springing spontaneously from the liberated masses under its authority, it became necessary to justify the retention of the dictatorship by stressing the menace of capitalism abroad.

This began at an early date. In 1924 Stalin specifically defended the retention of the "organs of suppression," meaning, among others, the army and the secret police, on the ground that "as long as there is a capitalist encirclement there will be danger of intervention with the consequences that flow from that danger." In accordance with that theory, and from that time on, all internal opposition forces in Russia have consistently been portrayed as agents of foreign forces of reaction antagonistic to Soviet power.

By the same token, tremendous emphasis has been placed on the original communist thesis of basic antagonism between the capitalist and the Socialist worlds. It is clear, from many indications, that this emphasis is not found in reality. The real facts concerning it have been confused by the existence abroad of genuine resentment provoked by Soviet philosophy and tactics and occasionally by the existence of great centers of military power, notably the Nazi regime in Germany and the Japanese Government of the late 1930s, which did indeed have aggressive designs against the Soviet Union. But there is ample evidence that the stress laid in Moscow on the menace confronting the Soviet society from the world outside its borders is founded not in the realities of foreign antagonism but in the necessity of explaining away the maintenance of dictatorial authority at home.

Now the maintenance of this pattern of Soviet power, namely, the pursuit of unlimited authority domestically, accompanied by the cultivation of the semimyth of implacable foreign hostility, as gone far to shape the actual machinery of Soviet power as we know it today.

Internal organs of administration which did not serve this purpose became vastly swollen. The security of Soviet power came to rest on the iron discipline of the Party, on the severity and ubiquity of the secret police, and on the uncompromising economic monopolist of the state. The "organs of suppression," in which the Soviet leaders had sought security from rival forces, became in large measures the masters of those whom they were designed to serve. Today the major part of the structure of Soviet power is committed to the perfection of the dictatorship and to the maintenance of the concept of Russia as in a state of siege, with the enemy lowering beyond the walls. And the millions of human beings who form that part of the structure of power must defend at all costs this concept of Russia's position, for without it they are themselves superfluous.

As things stand today, the rulers can no longer dream of parting with these organs of suppression. The quest for absolute power, pursued now for nearly three decades with a ruthlessness unparalleled (in scope at least) in modern times, has again produced internally, as it did externally, its own reaction. The excesses of the police apparatus have fanned the potential opposition to the regime into something far greater and more dangerous than it could have been before those excesses began.

But least of all can the rulers dispense with the fiction by which the maintenance of dictatorial power has been defended. For this fiction has been canonized in Soviet philosophy by the excesses already committed in its name; and it is now anchored in the Soviet structure of thought by bonds far greater than those of mere ideology.

Part 2

So much for the historical background. What does it spell in terms of the political personality of Soviet power as we know it today?

Of the original ideology, nothing has been officially junked. Belief is maintained in the basic badness of capitalism, in the inevitability of its destruction, in the obligation of the proletariat to assist in that destruction and to take power into its own hands. But stress has come to be laid primarily on those concepts which relate most specifically to the Soviet regime itself: to its position as the sole truly Socialist regime in a dark and misguided world, and to the relationships of power within it.

The first of these concepts is that of the innate antagonism between capitalism and Socialism. We have seen how deeply that concept has become imbedded in foundations of Soviet power. It has profound implications for Russia's conduct as a member of international society. It means that there can never be on Moscow's side of the Soviet Union a sincere assumption of a community of aims between the Soviet Union and powers which are regarded as capitalist. It must invariably be assumed in Moscow that the aims of the capitalist world are antagonistic to the Soviet regime, and therefore to the interests of the peoples it controls. If the Soviet government occasionally sets its signature to documents which would indicate the contrary, this is to be regarded as a tactical maneuver permissible in dealing with the enemy (who is without honour) and should be taken in the spirit of caveat emptor. Basically, the antagonism remains. It is postulated. And from it flow many of the phenomena which we would find disturbing in the Kremlin's conduct of foreign policy: the secretiveness, the lack of frankness, the duplicity, the wary suspiciousness and the basic unfriendliness of purpose. These phenomena are there to stay, for the foreseeable future. There can be variations of degree and of emphasis. When there is something the Russians want from us, one or the other of these features of their policy may be thrust temporarily into the background; and when that happens there will always be Americans who will leap forward with gleeful announcements that "the Russians have changed," and some who will even try to take credit for having brought about such "changes." But we should not be misled by tactical maneuvers. These characteristics of Soviet policy, like the postulate from which they flow, are basic to the internal nature of Soviet power, and will be with us, whether in the foreground or in the background, until the internal nature of Soviet power is changed.

This means that we are going to continue for a long time to find the Russians difficult to deal with. It does not mean that they should be considered as embarked upon a do-or-die program to overthrow our society by a given date. The theory of the inevitability of the eventual fall of capitalism has the fortunate connotation that there is no hurry about it. The forces of progress can take their time in preparing the final coup de grace. Meanwhile, what is vital is that the "Socialist fatherland"—that oasis of power which has already been won for Socialism in the person of the Soviet Union—should be cherished and defended by all good Communists at home and abroad, its fortunes promoted, its enemies badgered and confounded. The promotion of premature, "adventuristic" revolutionary projects abroad which might embarrass Soviet power in any way would be an inexcusable, even a counterrevolutionary act. The cause of Socialism is the support and promotion of Soviet power, as defined in Moscow.

This brings us to the second of the concepts important to the contemporary Soviet outlook. That is the infallibility of the Kremlin. The Soviet concept of power, which permits no focal points of organization outside the Party itself, requires that the Party leadership remain in theory the sole repository of truth. For if truth were to be found elsewhere, there would be justification for its expression in organized activity. But it is precisely that which the Kremlin cannot and will not permit.

The leadership of the Communist Party is therefore always right, and has always been right since in 1929 Stalin formalized his personal power by announcing that decisions of the Politburo were being taken unanimously.

On the principle of infallibility there rests the iron discipline of the Communist Party. In fact, the two concepts are mutually self-supporting. Perfect discipline requires recognition of infallibility. Infallibility requires the observance of discipline. The two together go far to determine the behaviorism of the entire Soviet apparatus of power. But the effect cannot be understood unless a third factor be taken into account: namely, the fact that the leadership is at liberty to put forward for tactical purposes any particular thesis which it finds useful to the cause at any particular moment and to require the faithful and unquestioning acceptance of the thesis by the members of the movement as a whole. This means that truth is not a constant but is actually created, for all intents and purposes, by the Soviet leaders themselves. It may vary from week to week, month to month. It is nothing absolute and immutable—nothing which flows from objective reality. It is only the most recent manifestation of the wisdom of those in whom ultimate wisdom is supposed to reside, because they represent the logic of history. The accumulative effect of these factors is to give to the whole subordinate apparatus of Soviet power an unshakable stubbornness and steadfastness in its orientation. This orientation can be changed at will by the Kremlin but by no other power. Once a given party line has been laid down on a given issue of current policy, the whole Soviet governmental machine, including the mechanism of diplomacy, moves inexorably along the prescribed path, like a persistent toy automobile wound up and headed in a given direction, stopping only when it meets with some unanswerable force. The individuals who are the components of this machine are unamenable to argument or reason which comes to them from the outside world. Like the white dog before the phonograph, they only hear the "master's voice." And if they are called off from the purposes last dictated to them, it is the master who must call them off. Thus the foreign representative cannot hope that his words will make any impression on them. The most he can hope is that they will be transmitted to those at the top, who are capable of changing the party line. But even those are not likely to be swayed by any normal logic in the words of the bourgeois representative. Since there can be no appeal to common purposes, there can be no common appeal to common mental approaches. For this reason, facts speak louder than words to the ears of the Kremlin; and words carry the greatest weight when they have the ring of reflecting, or being backed up by facts of unchallengeable validity.

But we have seen that the Kremlin is under no ideological compulsion to accomplish its purposes in a hurry. Like the Church, it is dealing in ideological concepts which are of long-term validity, and it can afford to be patient. It has no right to risk the existing achievements of the revolution for the sake of vain baubles of the future. The very teachings of Lenin himself require great caution and flexibility in the pursuit of Communist purposes. Again, these precepts are fortified by the lessons of Russian history; of centuries of obscure battles between nomadic forces over stretches of vast unfortified plain. Here caution, circumspection, flexibility and deception are the valuable qualities; and their value finds natural appreciation in the Russian or the oriental mind. Thus the Kremlin has no compunction about retreating in the face of superior force. And being under the compulsion of no timetable, it does not get panicky under the necessity for such a retreat. Its political action is a fluid stream which moves constantly, wherever it is permitted to move, toward a given goal. Its main thing is that there should always be pressure, unceasing constant pressure, toward the desired goal. There is no trace of any feeling in Soviet psychology that that goal must be reached at any given time.

These considerations make Soviet diplomacy at once easier and more difficult to deal with than the diplomacy of individual aggressive leaders like Napoleon and Hitler. On the one hand it is more sensitive to contrary force, more ready to yield on individual sectors of the diplomatic front when that force is felt to be too strong, and thus more rational in the logic and rhetoric of power. On the other hand it cannot be easily defeated or discouraged by a single victory on the part of its opponents. And the patient persistence by which it is animated means that it can be effectively countered not by sporadic acts but only by intelligent long-range policies on the part of Russia's adversaries— policies no less steady in their purpose, and no less variegated and resourceful in their application, than those of the Soviet Union itself.

In these circumstances it is clear that the main element of any United States policy toward the Soviet Union must be that of a long-term, patient but firm and vigilant containment of expansive tendencies. It is important to note, however, that such a policy has nothing to do with outward histrionics: with threats or blustering or superfluous gestures of outward "toughness." Although the Kremlin is basically flexible in its reaction to political realities, it is by no means unamenable to considerations of prestige. Like almost any other government, it can be placed by tactless and threatening gestures in a position where it cannot afford to yield even though this might be dictated by its sense of realism. The Russian leaders are keen judges of human psychology, and as such they are highly conscious that loss of temper and of self-control is never a source of strength in political affairs. They are quick to exploit such evidences of weakness. For these reasons, it is a sine qua non of successful dealing with Russia that the foreign government in question should remain at all times cool and collected and that its demands on Russian policy should be put forward in such a manner as to leave the way open for a compliance not too detrimental to Russian prestige.

Part 3

In the light of the above, it will be clearly seen that the Soviet pressure against the free institutions of the Western world is something that can be contained by adroit and vigilant application of counterforce at a series of constantly shifting geographical and political points, corresponding to the shifts and maneuvers of Soviet policy, but which cannot be charmed or talked out of existence. The Russians look forward to a duel of infinite duration, and they see that already they have scored great successes. It must be borne in mind that there was a time where the Communist Party represented far more of a minority in the sphere of Russian national life than Soviet power today represents in the world community.

But if ideology convinces the rulers of Russia that truth is on their side and that they can therefore afford to wait, those of us on whom that ideology has no claim are free to examine objectively that premise. The Soviet thesis not only implies complete lack of control by the west over its own economic destiny, it likewise assumes Russian unity, discipline and patience over an infinite period. Let us bring this apocalyptic vision down to earth, and suppose that the western world finds the strength and resourcefulness to contain Soviet power over a period of ten to fifteen years. What does that spell for Russia itself?

The Soviet leaders, taking advantage of the contributions of modern technique to the arts of despotism, have solved the question of obedience within the confines of their power. Few challenge their authority; and even those who do are unable to make that challenge valid as against the organs of suppression of the state.

The Kremlin has proved able to accomplish its purpose of building up in Russia, regardless of the interests of the inhabitants, an industrial foundation of heavy metallurgy, which is, to be sure, not yet complete but is nevertheless approaching those of the other major industrial countries. All of this, however, both the maintenance of internal political security and the building of industry, has been carried out at a terrible cost in human life and in human hopes and energies. It has necessitated the use of forced labour on a scale unprecedented in modern times under conditions of peace. It has involved the neglect or abuse of other phases of Soviet economic life, particularly agriculture, consumers' goods production, housing and transportation.

To all that, the war has added its tremendous toll of destruction, death and human exhaustion. In consequence of all this, we have in Russia today a population which is physically and spiritually disillusioned. The mass of people are disillusioned, skeptical and no longer as accessible as they once were to the magical attraction which Soviet power still radiates to its followers abroad. The avidity with which people seized upon the slight respite accorded to the Church for tactical reasons during the war was eloquent testimony to the fact that their capacity for faith and devotion found little expression in the purposes of the regime.

In these circumstances, there are limits to the physical and nervous strength of the people themselves. These limits are absolute ones, and are binding even for the cruelest dictatorship, because beyond them people cannot be driven. The forced labor camps and the other agencies of constraint provide temporary means of compelling people to work longer hours than their own volition or mere economic pressure would dictate; but if people survive at all they become old before their time and must be considered as human casualties to the demands of dictatorship. In either case their best powers are no longer available to society and can no longer be enlisted in the service of the state.

Here only the younger generation can help. The younger generation, despite all vicissitudes and sufferings, is numerous and vigorous; and the Russians are talented people. But it remains to be seen what will be the effects on mature performance of the abnormal emotional strains of childhood which Soviet dictatorship created and which were enormously increased by the war. Such things as normal security and placidity of home environment have practically ceased to exist in the Soviet Union outside of the most remote farms and villages. And observers are not yet sure whether that is not going to leave its mark on the overall capacity of the generation now coming into maturity.

In addition to this, we have the fact that Soviet economic development, while it can list certain formidable achievements, has been precariously spotty and uneven. Russian Communists who speak of the "uneven development of capitalism" should blush at the contemplation of their own national economy. Here certain branches of economic life, such as the metallurgical and machine industries, have been pushed out of all proportion to other sectors of the economy. Here is a nation striving to become in a short period one of the great industrial nations of the world while it has no highway network worthy of the name and only a relatively primitive network of railways. Much has been done to increase efficiency of labor and to teach primitive peasants something about the operation of machines. But maintenance is still a crying deficiency of all Soviet economy. Construction is hasty and poor in quality. Depreciation must be enormous. And in vast sectors of economic life it has not yet been possible to instill into labor anything like that general culture of production and technical self-respect which characterizes the skilled worker of the west.

It is difficult to see how these deficiencies can be corrected at an early date by a tired and dispirited population working largely under the shadow of fear and compulsion. And as long as they are not overcome, Russia will remain economically a vulnerable, and in a certain sense an impotent, nation, capable of exporting its enthusiasm and of radiating the strange charm of its political vitality but unable to back up those articles of export by the real evidences of material power and prosperity.

Meanwhile, a great uncertainty hangs over the political life of the Soviet Union. That is the uncertainty involved in the transfer of power from one individual or a group of individuals to others.

This is, of course, outstandingly the problem of the personal position of Stalin. We must remember that his succession to Lenin's pinnacle of pre-eminence in the Communist movement was the only such transfer of individual authority which the Soviet Union has experienced. That transfer took 12 years to consolidate. It cost the lives of millions of people and shook the state to its foundations. The attendant tremors were felt all through the international revolutionary movement, to the disadvantage of the Kremlin itself.

It is always possible that another transfer of pre-eminent power may take place quietly and inconspicuously, with no repercussions anywhere. But again, it is possible that the questions may unleash, to use some of Lenin's words, one of those "incredibly swift transitions" from "delicate deceit" to "wild violence" which characterize Russian history, and may shake Soviet power to its foundations.

But this is not only a question of Stalin himself. There has been, since 1938, a dangerous concealment of political life in the higher circles of Soviet power. The All-Union Congress of Soviets, in theory the supreme body of the Party, is supposed to meet not less than once in three years. It will soon be eight full years since its last meeting. During this period membership in the Party has numerically doubled. Party mortality during the war was enormous; and today well over half of the Party members are persons who entered since the last Party congress was held. Meanwhile, the same small group of men has carried on at the top through an amazing series of national vicissitudes. Surely there is some reason why the experiences of the war brought basic political changes to every one of the great governments of the west. Surely the causes of that phenomenon are basic enough to be present somewhere in the obscurity of Soviet political life, as well. And yet no recognition has been given to these causes in Russia.

It must be surmised from this that even within so highly disciplined an organization as the Communist Party there must be a growing divergence in age, outlook and interest in between the great mass of Party members, only so recently recruited into the movement, and the little self-perpetuating clique of men at the top, whom most of these Party members have never met, with whom they have never conversed, and with whom they have no political intimacy.

Who can say whether, in these circumstances, the eventual rejuvenation of the higher spheres of authority (which can only be a matter of time) can take place smoothly and peacefully, or whether rivals in the quest for higher power will eventually reach down into these politically immature and inexperienced masses in order to find support for their respective claims? If this were to ever happen, strange consequences could flow for the Communist Party: for the membership at large has been exercised only in the practices of iron discipline and obedience and not in the arts of compromise and accommodation. And if disunity were ever to seize and paralyze the Party, the chaos and weakness of Russian society would be revealed in forms beyond description. For we have seen that Soviet power is only a crust concealing an amorphous mass of human beings among whom no independent organizational structure is tolerated. In Russia there is not even such a thing as local government. The present generation of Russians have never known spontaneity of collective action. If, consequently anything were ever to occur to disrupt the unity and efficacy of the Party as the political instrument, Soviet Russia might be changed overnight from one of the strongest to one of the weakest and most pitiable of national societies.

Thus the future of Soviet power may not be by any means as secure as Russian capacity for self-delusion would make it appear to the men in the Kremlin. That they can keep power themselves, they have demonstrated. That they can quietly and easily turn it over to others remains to be proved. Meanwhile, the hardships of their rule and the vicissitudes of international life have taken a heavy toll on the strength and hopes of the great people on whom their power rests. It is curious to note that the ideological power of Soviet authority is strongest today in areas beyond the frontiers of Russia, beyond the reach of its police power. This phenomenon brings to mind a comparison used by Thomas Mann in his great novel *Buddenbrooks.* Observing that human institutions often show the greatest outward brilliance at a moment when inner decay is in reality farthest advanced, he compared the Buddenbrook family, in the days of its greatest glamour, to one of those stars whose light shines most brightly on this world when in reality it has long ceased to exist. And who can say with assurance that the strong light still cast by the Kremlin on the dissatisfied peoples of the western world is not the powerful afterglow of a constellation which is in actuality on the wane? This cannot be proved. And it cannot be disproved. But the possibility remains (and in the opinion of this writer it is a strong one) that Soviet power, like the capitalist world of its conception, bears within it the seeds of its own decay, and that the sprouting of these seeds is well advanced.

Part 4

It is clear that the United States cannot expect in the foreseeable future to enjoy political intimacy with the Soviet regime. It must continue to regard the Soviet Union as a rival, not a partner, in the political arena. It must continue to expect that Soviet politics will reflect no abstract love of peace and stability, no real faith in the possibility of a permanent happy coexistence of the Socialist and capitalist worlds, but rather a cautious, persistent pressure toward the disruption and weakening of all rival influence and rival power.

Balanced against this are the facts that Russia, as opposed to the western world in general, is still by far the weaker party, that Soviet policy is highly flexible, and that Soviet society may well contain deficiencies which will eventually weaken its own total potential. This would of itself warrant the United States entering with reasonable confidence upon a policy of firm containment, designed to confront the Russians with unalterable counterforce at every point where they show signs of encroaching upon the interest of a peaceful and stable world.

But in actuality the possibilities for American policy are by no means limited to holding the line and hoping for the best. It is entirely possible for the United States to influence by its actions the internal developments, both within Russia and throughout the international Communist movement, by which Russian policy is largely determined. This is not only a question of the modest measure of informational activity which this government can conduct in the Soviet Union and elsewhere, although that too is important. It is rather a question of the degree to which the United States can create among the peoples of the world generally the impression of a country which knows what it wants, which is coping successfully with the problems of its internal life and with the responsibilities of a world power, and which has a spiritual vitality capable of holding its own among the major ideological currents of its time. To the extent that such an impression can be created and maintained, the aims of the Russian Communism must appear sterile and quixotic, the hopes and enthusiasm of Moscow's supporters must wane, and added strain must be imposed on the Kremlin's foreign policies. For the palsied decrepitude of the capitalist world is the keystone of Communist philosophy. Even the failure of the United States to experience the early economic depression which the ravens of Red Square have been predicting with such complacent confidence since hostilities ceased would have deep and important repercussions throughout the Communist world.

By the same token, exhibitions of indecision, disunity and internal disintegration within this country have an exhilarating effect on the whole Communist movement. At each evidence of these tendencies, a thrill of hope and excitement goes through the Communist world; a new jauntiness can be noted in the Moscow tread; new groups of foreign supporters cling onto what they can only view as the bandwagon of international politics; and Russian pressure increases all along the line in international affairs.

It would be an exaggeration to say that American behavior unassisted and alone could exercise a power of life and death over the Communist movement and bring about the early fall of Soviet power in

Russia. But the United States has it in its power to increase enormously the strains under which Soviet policy must operate, to force upon the Kremlin a far greater degree of moderation and circumspection than it has had to observe in recent years, and in this way to promote tendencies which must eventually find their outlet in either the breakup or the mellowing of Soviet power. For no mystical, messianic movement—particularly not that of the Kremlin—can face frustration indefinitely without eventually adjusting itself in one way or another to the logic of that state of affairs.

Thus the decision will fall in large measure on this country itself. The issue of Soviet-American relations is in essence a test of the overall worth of the United States as a nations among nations. To avoid destruction the United States need only measure up to its own best traditions and prove itself worthy of preservation as a great nation.

Surely, there was never a fairer test of national quality than this. In the light of these circumstances, the thoughtful observer of Russian-American relations will find no cause for complaint in the Kremlin's challenge to American society. He will rather experience a certain gratitude to a Providence which, by providing the American people with this implacable challenge, has made their entire security as a nation dependent on pulling themselves together and accepting the responsibilities of moral and political leadership that history plainly intended them to bear.

Source: Kennan, George. "The Sources of Soviet Conduct." *Foreign Affairs*, 25, no. 4 (July 1947): 566–582. Reprinted by permission of *Foreign Affairs* (Volume 25, Issue Number 4). Copyright (1947) by the Council on Foreign Relations, Inc.

The Inter-American Treaty of Reciprocal Assistance (1947)

This document, better known as the Rio Treaty, was signed on September 2, 1947, by the United States and eighteen Latin American countries (with four others signing since then) to create a Western Hemisphere defense bloc and collective security agreement. Thus, an attack on one state requires all other members to respond. The Rio Treaty is the first agreement of its type in U.S. history. The treaty makes explicit the U.S. commitment to the region but does not require that the United States pay attention to it with long-term involvement, as many in the region might wish.

The Rio Treaty is an extensive, detailed document, and so is not reprinted here. It can be located at: http://www.oas.org/juridico/english/Treaties/b-29.html.

North Atlantic Treaty Organization Charter (1949)

The North Atlantic Treaty Organization (NATO) Charter, promulgated on April 4, 1949, began the era of firm, legal U.S. connection to the defense issues in Western Europe and Canada. The
organization began with democracies in Western Europe, the
United States, and Canada, and then expanded to include West
Germany. NATO was established as a collective defense pact to
protect Europe against potential Soviet expansionism in the
region, but by the late 1990s, it had expanded far beyond its original membership to include former Communist states in Eastern
Europe. The charter can be found on-line at: http://www.
nato.int/docu/basictxt/treaty.htm.

Dean Acheson's "Perimeter" Speech (1950)

*On January 12, 1950, Secretary of State Dean Acheson gave a speech to
the National Press Club in which he identified certain areas around
which the United States would draw a security perimeter against Soviet
aggression, implying that the United States would not defend those
areas outside of the perimeter. One of the places left outside the perimeter was Korea. Six months later, the North Koreans moved forces against
South Korea, provoking Washington to intervene under UN auspices.
The speech, which Acheson gave somewhat informally, without a prepared text, and the turn of events that followed indicate how closely
leaders around the world focus on the words of U.S. policymakers, who
even today may not always appreciate the influence they wield.*

What is the situation in regard to the military security of the Pacific
area, and what is our policy in regard to it?

In the first place, the defeat and the disarmament of Japan has
placed upon the United States the necessity of assuming the military
defense of Japan so long as that is required, both in the interest of our
security and in the interests of the security of the entire Pacific area
and, in all honor, in the interest of Japanese security. We have
American—and there are Australian—troops in Japan. I am not in a
position to speak for the Australians, but I can assure you that there is
no intention of any sort of abandoning or weakening the defenses of
Japan and that whatever arrangements are to be made either through
permanent settlement or otherwise, that defense must and shall be
maintained between us.

This defensive perimeter runs along the Aleutians to Japan and then goes to the Ryukyus. We hold important defense positions in the Ryukyu Islands, and those we will continue to hold. In the interest of the population of the Ryukyu Islands, we will at an appropriate time offer to hold these islands under trusteeship of the United Nations. But they are essential parts of the defensive perimeter of the Pacific, and they must and will be held.

The defensive perimeter runs from the Ryukyus to the Philippine Islands. Our relations, our defensive relations, with the Philippines are contained in agreements between us. Those agreements are being loyally carried out and will be loyally carried out. Both peoples have learned by bitter experience the vital connections between our mutual defense requirements. We are in no doubt about that, and it is hardly necessary for me to say an attack on the Philippines could not and would not be tolerated by the United States. But, I hasten to add that no one perceives the imminence of any such attack.

So far as the military security of other areas in the Pacific is concerned, it must be clear that no person can guarantee these areas against military attack. But it must also be clear that such a guarantee is hardly sensible or necessary within the realm of practical relationship.

Should such an attack occur—one hesitates to say where such an armed attack could come from—the initial reliance must be on the people attacked to resist it and then upon the commitments of the entire civilized world under the Charter of the United Nations, which so far has not provided a weak reed to lean on by any people who are determined to protect their independence against outside aggression. But it is a mistake, I think, in considering Pacific and Far Eastern problems to become obsessed with military considerations. Important as they are, there are other problems that press, and these other problems are not capable of solution through military means. These other problems arise out of the susceptibility of many areas, and many countries in the Pacific area, to subversion and penetration. That cannot be stopped by military means. . . .

That leads me to the other thing I wanted to point out, and that is the limitation of effective American assistance. American assistance can be effective when it is the missing component in a situation which might otherwise be solved. The United States cannot furnish all these components to solve the question. It cannot furnish determination, it cannot furnish will, and it cannot furnish the loyalty of a people to its government. But if the will and if the determination exists and if the people are behind their government, then, and not always then, is there a very good chance. In that situation, American help can be effective and it can lead to an accomplishment which could not otherwise be achieved. . . .

Korea

In Korea, we have taken great steps which have ended our military occupation, and in cooperation with the United Nations, have established an independent and sovereign country recognized by nearly all the rest of the world. We have given that nation great help in getting itself established. We are asking the Congress to continue that help until it is firmly established, and that legislation is not pending before the Congress. The idea that we should scrap all of that, that we should stop half way through the achievement of the establishment of this country, seems to me to be the most utter defeatism and utter madness of our interests in Asia. . . .

So after this survey, what we conclude, I believe, is that there is a new day which has dawned in Asia. It is a day in which the Asian peoples are on their own, and know it, and intend to continue on their own. It is a day in which the old relationships between east and west are gone, relationships which at their worst were exploitation, and which at their best were paternalism. That relationship is over, and the relationship of east and west must now be in the Far East one of respect and mutual helpfulness. We are their friends. Others are their friends. We and those others are willing to help, but we can help only where we are wanted and only where the conditions of help are really sensible and possible. So what we can see is that this new day in Asia, this new day which is dawning, may go on to a glorious noon or it may darken and it may drizzle out. But that decision lies within the countries of Asia and within the power of the Asian people. It is not a decision which a friend or even an enemy from the outside can decide for them.

Source: Paterson, Thomas G. "Dean Acheson on the Defense Perimeter in Asia, 1950." In: *Major Problems in American Foreign Policy.* Vol. 2, *Since 1914.* 3rd ed. Lexington, MA: D.C. Heath, 1989, pp. 398–400.

NSC 68 (1950)

In an April 14, 1950, report to President Harry Truman entitled "United States Objectives and Programs for National Security," the National Security Council made suggestions that would have profound effects on the United States and global security for the next fifty years. Labeled by Senator Henry "Scoop" Jackson as the "first comprehensive statement of national security strategy," the study outlined a number of policy options for U.S. national security strategy, finally advocating the massive military buildup that led to the creation of the hydrogen bomb and the role of the United States as a "global policeman."

The existence of this report has long been known, but its declassification was a monumental event for scholars. This document, now in the public domain, is available on-line at: http://www.mtholyoke.edu/acad/intrel/nsc-68/nsc68-1.htm.

The Domino Theory (1954)

The domino theory, which was first expressed by President Dwight Eisenhower in a press conference on April 7, 1954, is the notion that the collapse of one government under threat of Communist oppression would lead to the collapse of neighboring states and a further progression of collapse around the world. The fear that the domino effect would become a problem facing the United States at various places around the world had a powerful influence on national security policy throughout the Cold War.

Question, Robert Richards, Copley Press: Mr. President, would you mind commenting on the strategic importance of Indochina to the free world? I think there has been, across the country, some lack of understanding on just what it means to us.

The President: You have, of course, both the specific and the general when you talk about such things.

First of all, you have the specific value of a locality in its production of materials that the world needs.

Then you have the possibility that many human beings pass under a dictatorship that is inimical to the free world.

Finally, you have broader considerations that might follow what you would call the "falling domino" principle. You have a row of dominoes set up, you knock over the first one, and what will happen to the last one is the certainty that it will go over very quickly. So you could have a beginning of a disintegration that would have the most profound influences.

Now, with respect to the first one, two of the items from this particular area that the world uses are tin and tungsten. They are very important. There are others, of course, the rubber plantations and so on.

Then with respect to more people passing under this domination, Asia, after all, has already lost some 450 million of its peoples to the Communist dictatorship, and we simply cannot afford greater losses.

But when we come to the possible sequence of events, the loss of Indochina, of Burma, of Thailand, of the Peninsula, and Indonesia following, now you begin to talk about areas that not only multiply the disadvantages that you would suffer through loss of materials, sources of materials, but now you are talking about millions and millions and millions of people.

Finally, the geographical position achieved thereby does many things. It turns the so-called island defensive chain of Japan, Formosa, of the Philippines and to the southward; it moves in to threaten Australia and New Zealand.

It takes away, in its economic aspects, that region that Japan must have as a trading area or Japan, in turn, will have only one place in the world to go—that is toward the Communist areas in order to live.

So, the possible consequences of the loss are just incalculable to the free world.

Sources: Public Papers of the Presidents of the United States: Dwight D. Eisenhower, 1954. Washington, DC: GPO, 1955, pp. 381–390. Paterson, Thomas G. "Dwight D. Eisenhower Explains the 'Domino Theory,' 1954." In: *Major Problems in American Foreign Policy.* Vol. 2, *Since 1914.* 3rd ed. Lexington, MA: D.C. Heath, 1989, pp. 453–454.

John Foster Dulles's "Massive Retaliation" Speech (1954)

On January 12, 1954, Secretary of State John Foster Dulles declared in a speech to the Council on Foreign Policy that the United States would respond with massive force "at places and with means of its own choosing" if provoked by Soviet aggression. Rather than putting the United States in a position to announce how it would answer any individual attack, Dulles's speech was intended to make certain that any potential adversary understood the range of potential responses in case of an attack on the United States or its interests. Many interpreted the speech as meaning the United States would likely make a nuclear response to such an attack.

The Soviet Communists are planning for what they call "an entire historical era," and we should do the same. They seek, through many types of maneuvers, gradually to divide and weaken the free nations by overextending them in efforts which, as Lenin put it, are "beyond their strength, so that they come to practical bankruptcy." Then, said Lenin, "our victory is assured." Then, said Stalin, will be "the moment for the decisive blow."

In the face of this strategy, measures cannot be judged adequate merely because they ward off an immediate danger. It is essential to do this, but it is also essential to do so without exhausting ourselves.

When the Eisenhower administration applied this test, we felt that some transformations were needed.

It is not sound military strategy permanently to commit U.S. land forces to Asia to a degree that leaves us no strategic reserves.

It is not sound economics, or good foreign policy, to support permanently other countries; for in the long run, that creates as much ill will as good will.

Also, it is not sound to become permanently committed to military expenditures so vast that they lead to "practical bankruptcy." . . .

We need allies and collective security. Our purpose is to make these relationships more effective, less costly. This can be done by placing more reliance on deterrent power and less dependence on local defensive power.

This is accepted practice so far as local communities are concerned. We keep locks on our doors, but we do not have an armed guard in every home. We rely principally on a community security system so well equipped to punish any who break in and steal that, in fact, would-be aggressors are generally deterred. That is the modern way of getting maximum protection at a bearable cost.

Local defense will always be important. But there is no local defense which alone will contain the mighty landpower of the Communist world. Local defenses must be reinforced by the further deterrent of massive retaliatory power. A potential aggressor must know that he cannot always prescribe battle conditions that suit him. Otherwise, for example, a potential aggressor, who is glutted with manpower, might be tempted to attack in confidence that resistance would be confined to manpower. He might be tempted to attack in places where his superiority was decisive.

The way to deter aggression is for the free community to be willing and able to respond vigorously at places and with means of its own choosing.

So long as our basic policy concepts were unclear, our military leaders could not be selective in building our military power. If an enemy could pick his time and place and method of warfare—and if our policy was to remain the traditional one of meeting aggression by direct and local opposition—then we needed to be ready to fight in the Arctic and in the Tropics; in Asia, the Near East, and in Europe; by sea, by land, and by air; with old weapons and with new weapons. . . .

But before military planning could be changed, the President and his advisers, as represented by the National Security Council, had to take some basic policy decisions. This has been done. The basic decision was to depend primarily upon a great capability to retaliate, instantly, by means and at places of our choosing. Now the Department of Defense and the Joint Chiefs of Staff can shape our military establishment to fit what is *our* policy, instead of having to try to be ready to the meet the enemy's many choices. That permits a selection of military means instead of a multiplication of means. As a result, it is now possible to get, and share, more basic security at less cost.

Source: Paterson, Thomas G, and Dennis Merrill, eds. "Secretary of State John Foster Dulles Explains Massive Retaliation, 1954." In: *Major Problems in American Foreign Policy.* Vol. 2, *Since 1914.* 4th ed. Lexington, MA: D.C. Heath, 1995, pp. 423–425.

Final Declaration of the Geneva Conference on Indochina: The Geneva Accords (1954)

After the May 1954 defeat of the French by the Viet Minh at Dien Bien Phu following a long and embarrassing siege, an international conference was called to determine a reasonable division of former French Indochina into North and South Vietnam. The conference led to an extended discussion of the types of governments and actions the two Vietnams would choose after establishing their territory. The Geneva Accords marked a decisive shift from French to U.S. involvement in the former French Indochina as the United States had the military prowess to work against Ho Chi Minh's Communist North Vietnam. One notable peripheral event at this meeting was the insult suffered by Chinese Foreign Minister Zhou Enlai when Secretary of State John Foster Dulles refused to shake his hand.

The complete text of the accords can be found on-line at: http://www.mtholyoke.edu/acad/intrel/genevacc.htm. A print source for the accords is Senate Committee on Foreign Relations, *Background Information Relating to Southeast Asia and Vietnam,* 90th Cong., 1st sess., 1967 (3rd rev. ed.), 50–62.

President Dwight Eisenhower's "Military-Industrial Complex" Speech (1961)

This speech, broadcast to the nation on January 17, 1961, was President Dwight D. Eisenhower's valedictory warning as he left office upon President John F. Kennedy's inauguration. Its concerns about an "unwarranted influence" by the military in conjunction with industry remain relevant today. President Eisenhower spoke of the probability that an unbreakable alliance between the upper echelons of the military and various defense contractors could pose a national security threat to the United States. This speech has been a marker for many who have feared that the United States is forging a policy of militarism that cannot be broken for economic reasons.

My fellow Americans:

Three days from now, after half a century in the service of our country, I shall lay down the responsibilities of office as, in traditional and solemn ceremony, the authority of the Presidency is vested in my successor.

This evening I come to you with a message of leave-taking and farewell, and to share a few final thoughts with you, my countrymen.

Like every other citizen, I wish the new President, and all who will labor with him, Godspeed. I pray that the coming years will be blessed with peace and prosperity for all.

Our people expect their President and the Congress to find essential agreement on issues of great moment, the wise resolution of which will better shape the future of the Nation.

My own relations with the Congress, which began on a remote and tenuous basis when, long ago, a member of the Senate appointed me to West Point, have since ranged to the intimate during the war and immediate postwar period, and, finally, to the mutually interdependent during these past eight years.

In this final relationship, the Congress and the Administration have, on most vital issues, cooperated well, to serve the national good rather than mere partisanship, and so have assured that the business of the Nation should go forward. So, my official relationship with the Congress ends in a feeling, on my part, of gratitude that we have been able to do so much together.

II.

We now stand ten years past the midpoint of a century that has witnessed four major wars among great nations. Three of these involved our own country. Despite these holocausts America is today the strongest, the most influential and most productive nation in the world. Understandably proud of this pre-eminence, we yet realize that America's leadership and prestige depend, not merely upon our unmatched material progress, riches and military strength, but on how we use our power in the interests of world peace and human betterment.

III.

Throughout America's adventure in free government, our basic purposes have been to keep the peace, to foster progress in human achievement, and to enhance liberty, dignity and integrity among people and among nations. To strive for less would be unworthy of a free and religious people. Any failure traceable to arrogance or our lack of comprehension or readiness to sacrifice would inflict upon us grievous hurt both at home and abroad.

Progress toward these noble goals is persistently threatened by the conflict now engulfing the world. It commands our whole attention, absorbs our very beings. We face a hostile ideology—global in scope, atheistic in character, ruthless in purpose, and insidious in method. Unhappily the danger it poses promises to be of indefinite duration. To meet it successfully, there is called for, not so much the emotional and transitory sacrifices of crisis, but rather those which enable us to carry forward steadily, surely, and without complaint the burdens of a prolonged and complex struggle—with liberty the stake. Only thus shall we remain, despite every provocation, on our charted course toward permanent peace and human betterment.

Crises there will continue to be. In meeting them, whether foreign or domestic, great or small, there is a recurring temptation to feel that some spectacular and costly action could become the miraculous solution to all current difficulties. A huge increase in newer elements of our defense; development of unrealistic programs to cure every ill in agriculture; a dramatic expansion in basic and applied research—these and many other possibilities, each possibly promising in itself, may be suggested as the only way to the road we wish to travel.

But each proposal must be weighed in the light of a broader consideration: the need to maintain balance in and among national programs—balance between the private and the public economy; balance between cost and hoped for advantage; balance between the clearly necessary and the comfortably desirable; balance between our essential requirements as a nation and the duties imposed by the nation upon the individual; balance between actions of the moment and the national welfare of the future. Good judgment seeks balance and progress; lack of it eventually finds imbalance and frustration.

The record of many decades stands as proof that our people and their government have, in the main, understood these truths and have responded to them well, in the face of stress and threat. But threats, new in kind or degree, constantly arise.

Of these, I mention two only.

IV.

A vital element in keeping the peace is our military establishment. Our arms must be mighty, ready for instant action, so that no potential aggressor may be tempted to risk his own destruction.

Our military organization today bears little relation to that known by any of my predecessors in peacetime, or indeed by the fighting men of World War II or Korea.

Until the latest of our world conflicts, the United States had no armaments industry. American makers of plowshares could, with time and as required, make swords as well. But now we can no longer risk emergency improvisation of national defense; we have been compelled to create a permanent armaments industry of vast proportions. Added to this, three and a half million men and women are directly engaged in the defense establishment. We annually spend on military security more than the net income of all United States corporations.

This conjunction of an immense military establishment and a large arms industry is new in the American experience. The total influence—economic, political, even spiritual—is felt in every city, every State house, every office of the Federal government. We recognize the imperative need for this development. Yet we must not fail to comprehend its grave implications. Our toil, resources and livelihood are all involved; so is the very structure of our society.

In the councils of government, we must guard against the acquisition of unwarranted influence, whether sought or unsought, by the military-industrial complex. The potential for the disastrous rise of misplaced power exists and will persist.

We must never let the weight of this combination endanger our liberties or democratic processes. We should take nothing for granted. Only an alert and knowledgeable citizenry can compel the proper meshing of the huge industrial and military machinery of defense with our peaceful methods and goals, so that security and liberty may prosper together.

Akin to, and largely responsible for the sweeping changes in our industrial-military posture, has been the technological revolution during recent decades.

In this revolution, research has become central; it also becomes more formalized, complex, and costly. A steadily increasing share is conducted for, by, or at the direction of, the Federal government.

Today, the solitary inventor, tinkering in his shop, has been overshadowed by task forces of scientists in laboratories and testing fields. In the same fashion, the free university, historically the fountainhead of free ideas and scientific discovery, has experienced a revolution in the conduct of research. Partly because of the huge costs involved, a government contract becomes virtually a substitute for intellectual curiosity. For every old blackboard there are now hundreds of new electronic computers.

The prospect of domination of the nation's scholars by Federal employment, project allocations, and the power of money is ever present and is gravely to be regarded.

Yet, in holding scientific research and discovery in respect, as we should, we must also be alert to the equal and opposite danger that public policy could itself become the captive of a scientific-technological elite.

It is the task of statesmanship to mold, to balance, and to integrate these and other forces, new and old, within the principles of our democratic system—ever aiming toward the supreme goals of our free society.

V.

Another factor in maintaining balance involves the element of time. As we peer into society's future, we—you and I, and our government—must avoid the impulse to live only for today, plundering, for our own ease and convenience, the precious resources of tomorrow. We cannot mortgage the material assets of our grandchildren without risking the loss also of their political and spiritual heritage. We want democracy to survive for all generations to come, not to become the insolvent phantom of tomorrow.

VI.

Down the long lane of the history yet to be written America knows that this world of ours, ever growing smaller, must avoid becoming a community of dreadful fear and hate, and be, instead, a proud confederation of mutual trust and respect.

Such a confederation must be one of equals. The weakest must come to the conference table with the same confidence as do we, protected as we are by our moral, economic, and military strength. That table, though scarred by many past frustrations, cannot be abandoned for the certain agony of the battlefield.

Disarmament, with mutual honor and confidence, is a continuing imperative. Together we must learn how to compose differences, not with arms, but with intellect and decent purpose. Because this need is so sharp and apparent I confess that I lay down my official responsibilities in this field with a definite sense of disappointment. As one who has witnessed the horror and the lingering sadness of war—as one who knows that another war could utterly destroy this civilization which has been so slowly and painfully built over thousands of years— I wish I could say tonight that a lasting peace is in sight.

Happily, I can say that war has been avoided. Steady progress toward our ultimate goal has been made. But, so much remains to be done. As a private citizen, I shall never cease to do what little I can to help the world advance along that road.

VII.

So in this my last good night to you as your President—I thank you for the many opportunities you have given me for public service in war and peace. I trust that in that service you find some things worthy; as for the rest of it, I know you will find ways to improve performance in the future.

You and I—my fellow citizens—need to be strong in our faith that all nations, under God, will reach the goal of peace with justice. May we be ever unswerving in devotion to principle, confident but humble with power, diligent in pursuit of the Nation's great goals.

To all the peoples of the world, I once more give expression to America's prayerful and continuing aspiration:

We pray that peoples of all faiths, all races, all nations, may have their great human needs satisfied; that those now denied opportunity shall come to enjoy it to the full; that all who yearn for freedom may experience its spiritual blessings; that those who have freedom will understand, also, its heavy responsibilities; that all who are insensitive to the needs of others will learn charity; that the scourges of poverty, disease and ignorance will be made to disappear from the earth, and that, in the goodness of time, all peoples will come to live together in a peace guaranteed by the binding force of mutual respect and love.

Source: Eisenhower, Dwight D. "Televised Farewell Address to the American People." In: *Public Papers of the Presidents of the United States: Dwight D. Eisenhower, 1960.* Washington, DC: GPO, 1961, pp. 1035–1040.

Gulf of Tonkin Resolution (1964)

Based on the report of an attack on U.S. ships in the Gulf of Tonkin off the Vietnamese coast, President Johnson went to Congress on August 5, 1964, to ask for a broadening of his power to combat Communist expansionism in Vietnam. As a result, on August 7 Congress passed the Gulf of Tonkin Resolution, which gave the president authority to "take all necessary measures" to secure peace in the region. Both the president's message to Congress (excerpted) and the resolution are reprinted here.

The Gulf of Tonkin Resolution has had memorable effects on U.S. national security policy. After the Vietnam conflict, serious questions arose about the real course of events that provoked this declaration, with many analysts questioning whether the United States was in fact attacked. The outcome of the conflict cast further doubt on the wisdom of intervention in such conflicts and made Congress less willing to grant wide military powers to the executive. At the time, however, only one voice in the Senate, that of Oregon maverick Wayne Morse, questioned the need for such a vast expansion of presidential powers. Subsequently, no president until George W. Bush has ever had the luxury of unquestioned support by the Congress, which has feared the type of individual power that Johnson received through this resolution.

1. President Johnson's Message to Congress, August 5, 1964

Last night I announced to the American people that the North Vietnamese regime had conducted further deliberate attacks against U.S. naval vessels operating in international waters, and I had therefore directed air action against gunboats and supporting facilities used in these hostile operations. This air action has now been carried out with substantial damage to the boats and facilities. Two U.S. aircraft were lost in the action.

After consultation with the leaders of both parties in the Congress, I further announced a decision to ask the Congress for a resolution expressing the unity and determination of the United States in supporting freedom and in protecting peace in southeast Asia.

These latest actions of the North Vietnamese regime has given a new and grave turn to the already serious situation in southeast Asia. Our commitments in that area are well known to the Congress. They were first made in 1954 by President Eisenhower. They were further defined in the Southeast Asia Collective Defense Treaty approved by the Senate in February 1955.

This treaty with its accompanying protocol obligates the United States and other members to act in accordance with their constitutional processes to meet Communist aggression against any of the parties or protocol states.

Our policy in southeast Asia has been consistent and unchanged since 1954. I summarized it on June 2 in four simple propositions:

> America keeps her word. Here as elsewhere, we must and shall honor our commitments.
>
> The issue is the future of southeast Asia as a whole. A threat to any nation in that region is a threat to all, and a threat to us.
>
> Our purpose is peace. We have no military, political, or territorial ambitions in the area.
>
> This is not just a jungle war, but a struggle for freedom on every front of human activity. Our military and economic assistance to South Vietnam and Laos in particular has the purpose of helping these countries to repel aggression and strengthen their independence.

The threat to the free nations of southeast Asia has long been clear. The North Vietnamese regime has constantly sought to take over South Vietnam and Laos. This Communist regime has violated the Geneva accords for Vietnam. It has systematically conducted a campaign of subversion, which includes the direction, training, and supply of personnel and arms for the conduct of guerrilla warfare in South Vietnamese territory. In Laos, the North Vietnamese regime has maintained military forces, used Laotian territory for infiltration into South Vietnam, and most recently carried out combat operations—all in direct violation of the Geneva Agreements of 1962.

In recent months, the actions of the North Vietnamese regime have become steadily more threatening. . . .

As President of the United States I have concluded that I should now ask the Congress, on its part, to join in affirming the national determination that all such attacks will be met, and that the United States will continue in its basic policy of assisting the free nations of the area to defend their freedom.

As I have repeatedly made clear, the United States intends no rashness, and seeks no wider war. We must make it clear to all that the United States is united in its determination to bring about the end of Communist subversion and aggression in the area. We seek the full and effective restoration of the international agreements signed in Geneva in 1954, with respect to South Vietnam, and again in Geneva in 1962, with respect to Laos. . . .

2. Joint Resolution of Congress H.J. RES 1145, August 7, 1964

Resolved by the Senate and House of Representatives of the United States of America in Congress assembled,

That the Congress approves and supports the determination of the President, as Commander in Chief, to take all necessary measures to repel any armed attack against the forces of the United States and to prevent further aggression.

Section 2. The United States regards as vital to its national interest and to world peace the maintenance of international peace and security in southeast Asia. Consonant with the Constitution of the United States and the Charter of the United Nations and in accordance with its obligations under the Southeast Asia Collective Defense Treaty, the United States is, therefore, prepared, as the President determines, to take all necessary steps, including the use of armed force, to assist any member or protocol state of the Southeast Asia Collective Defense Treaty requesting assistance in defense of its freedom.

Section 3. This resolution shall expire when the President shall determine that the peace and security of the area is reasonably assured by international conditions created by action of the United Nations or otherwise, except that it may be terminated earlier by concurrent resolution of the Congress.

Source: Public Papers of the Presidents of the United States: Lyndon Baines Johnson, 1963–1964. Washington, DC: GPO, 1965, pp. 930–932. Public Law 88-408 (78 Stat 384), 1964.

UN Security Council Resolution 242 (1967)

This is perhaps the most cited UN Security Council resolution of the post–World War II period, focusing on the Palestinian-Israeli conflict and the cessation of the Six Day War between Israel and the Arab states of Egypt, Jordan, and Syria in June 1967. Signed on November 22, 1967, the resolution required Israel to return all territories it had gained in the Six Day War and assigned a UN representative to visit the region to help with peace efforts.

As the resolution suggests, international support of Israel had diminished by 1967, and the United States became concerned that Israel's ability to survive was threatened, regardless of the decisiveness of the Israeli victory in the Six Day War. Since then, the United States has played a much more vigorous role in the Middle East than in prior decades, consistently supportive of Israeli sovereignty and generally supportive of Israel's claims to the West Bank and Gaza yet also encouraging the return of the occupied territories to the Palestinians.

The resolution is available at: http://www.un.org/documents /sc/res/1967/scres67.htm or in *Resolutions and Decisions of the Security Council* (New York: United Nations Publications, 1998).

The Nixon Doctrine (1969)

On July 25, 1969, at a press conference during a stopover in Guam en route to a visit to Southeast Asia, President Richard Nixon announced that the United States would support the efforts of other states to defend themselves against Communism and other threatening actions. This became known as "Vietnamization" because Nixon specifically spoke of the Army of the Republic of Vietnam (South Vietnam) taking a broader role in its own defense, with U.S. financial support. Unlike the Truman Doctrine, whereby the United States increased its role in combating Communist expansionism, the Nixon Doctrine was designed to decrease U.S. responsibility in conflicts around the world.

Nixon's enunciation was coincidental with initial U.S. moves to get out of Vietnam. With his election in 1968, President Nixon had indicated that he had a secret plan to end the war, but during his first year in office, no evidence of such a plan was forthcoming. These comments were some of the initial indicators that he was moving toward extricating the United States from the region with the notion that South Vietnam could fight its own war.

I believe that the time has come when the United States, in our relations with all of our Asian friends, [must] be quite emphatic on two points: One, that we will keep our treaty commitments, for example, with Thailand under SEATO [Southeast Asia Treaty Organization]; but, two, that as far as the problems of internal security are concerned, as far as the problems of military defense, except for the threat of military defense, except for the threat of a major power involving nuclear weapons, that the United States is going to encourage and has a right to expect that this problem will be increasingly handled by, and the responsibility for it taken by, the Asian nations themselves.

I believe, incidentally, from my preliminary conversations with several Asian leaders over the past few months that they are going to be willing to undertake this responsibility. It will not be easy, but if the United States just continues down the road of responding to requests for assistance, of assuming the primary responsibility for defending these countries when they have internal problems or external problems, they are never going to take care of themselves.

Source: Public Papers of the Presidents of the United States: Richard M. Nixon, 1969. Washington, DC: GPO, 1970, p. 549.

Nuclear Nonproliferation Treaty (1970)

With the French nuclear weapons tests in 1960 and the Chinese tests a mere four years later, the international community began to contemplate a world with dozens of nuclear states. In the early 1960s, several states unlikely to ever develop nuclear weapons raised the issue of creating a nuclear nonproliferation treaty. Although it took the better part of a decade to draft and ratify, the resulting treaty was hailed as an attempt to curb nuclear proliferation. It was initially signed in 1968 by 185 countries, including the United States and the Soviet Union, and came into force on March 5, 1970.

This agreement, which identified the nuclear powers and the non-nuclear powers as of the date of its implementation, has since been controversial. Although it commits the nuclear powers to move toward deemphasizing the role of nuclear weapons in their military arsenals, those provisions were long ignored by the superpowers. The treaty has also been rejected by some of the states most important in articulating its original intent—Israel, India, and Pakistan—which now see it as an infringement of their rights to independent domestic development and national security. The treaty is available on-line at: http://www.state.gov/www/global/arms/treaties/npt1.html#2.

The Pentagon Papers (1971)

The Pentagon Papers is a vast, multivolume collection of analyses of U.S. involvement in Vietnam from the 1950s through the early 1970s. It discusses the wide array of concerns about, alternatives to, and ramifications of the various U.S. actions in Vietnam. The existence of *The Pentagon Papers* was made public in the early 1970s, generating a Supreme Court case about the needs of national security versus the public's right to know—one of the original scrimmages in the civil-military transformation that has occurred in the United States over the past thirty years.

This work gives such a broad view of the many different perspectives on the Vietnam conflict within the U.S. government that an entire volume would be insufficient to examine its scope. The *Papers* are available in full but are most often read in the abridged form. One abridged version is *The Pentagon Papers,* abridged edition, edited by George Herring (New York: McGraw Hill Educational Publishers, 1993).

Strategic Arms Limitation Treaty I (1972)

The governments of Richard Nixon and Leonid Brezhnev began tentative negotiations on limiting strategic weapons (long-range nuclear weapons that could hit the U.S. or Soviet homelands, often defined as having a range of over 5,000 kilometers) in the late 1960s. The SALT I talks culminated in a 1972 treaty that actually increased the amount of arms that each side could have. Tied to the SALT I talks was the Antiballistic Missile (ABM) Treaty (see below), which limits the deployment of defensive systems. These were the initial bilateral arms control discussions that tried to curb strategic proliferation. Until President George W. Bush withdrew from the treaty in 2001, they remained the bedrock of the arms control regime.

The SALT I is available on-line at: http://fas.org/ nuke/control/salt1/text/salt1.htm.

Antiballistic Missile Treaty (1972)

The Antiballistic Missile Treaty, signed by the United States and the Soviet Union on May 26, 1972, prohibited either side from establishing more than two antiballistic missile sites. A protocol to the ABM Treaty four years later reduced this further to a single site. The United States deployed its site in North Dakota, and the Soviet Union chose to defend its capital city, Moscow.

The point of the agreement was that both sides considered such defensive systems to be destabilizing because they might embolden a government, convincing it that it could act aggressively without the threat of retaliation if the defensive systems prohibited by this agreement were in place. The ABM Treaty is now considered obsolete by many, and in December 2001 the United States officially withdrew from the treaty in favor of developing and deploying a missile defense system. However, others around the world still consider the treaty crucial, fearing its abdication would result in a global arms race. The treaty can be found on-line at: http://www.state.gov/www/global/arms/treaties/abm/abm2.html.

The Shanghai Communiqué (1972)

When President Nixon made the initial U.S. foray to the People's Republic of China in February 1972, much depended on the outcome. Eager to end the animosity which had for a quarter-century characterized relations between the United States and Communist China, Nixon and his national security advisor, Henry Kissinger, had carefully laid the groundwork for the trip to China, where they hoped to restore diplomatic relations between the two countries. The major sticking point was Taiwan; for years the United States had supported the GMD, the Nationalist government of Chiang Kai-shek in Taiwan.

Nixon's trip and his meetings with Communist Party Chairman Mao Zedong and Foreign Minister Zhou Enlai required that the United States and China address the issue of which China—Taiwan or the People's Republic—the United States would recognize. Because Mao's China was still Communist, the United States was not yet willing to abandon its GMD allies on Taiwan. (That move, in the form of recognition of the People's Republic of China as the government of China, did not occur until 1979.) However, the United States needed to make some concession to China in order to create a thaw between the two powers. This carefully crafted communiqué of February 28, 1972, satisfied the public in each country without reaching a complete agreement.

President Nixon went to China not only in an attempt to change the U.S. relationship with Mao's China but also to show the Soviet

Union that the United States was capable of forming an alliance with another Communist power. It was "balance of power" or "Realpolitik" in action. The Soviets got the message, and in May of that same year Nixon was invited to Moscow to sign the SALT I and the ABM Treaties.

1. President Richard Nixon of the United States of America visited the People's Republic of China at the invitation of Premier Chou En-lai of the People's Republic of China from February 21 to February 28, 1972. Accompanying the President were Mrs. Nixon, U.S. Secretary of State William Rogers, Assistant to the President Dr. Henry Kissinger, and other American officials.

2. President Nixon met with Chairman Mao Tsetung of the Communist Party of China on February 21. The two leaders had a serious and frank exchange of views on Sino-U.S. relations and world affairs.

3. During the visit, extensive, earnest and frank discussions were held between President Nixon and Premier Chou En-lai on the normalization of relations between the United States of America and the People's Republic of China, as well as on other matters of interest to both sides. In addition, Secretary of State William Rogers and Foreign Minister Chi Peng-fei held talks in the same spirit.

4. President Nixon and his party visited Peking and viewed cultural, industrial and agricultural sites, and they also toured Hangchow and Shanghai where, continuing discussions with Chinese leaders, they viewed similar places of interest.

5. The leaders of the People's Republic of China and the United States of America found it beneficial to have this opportunity, after so many years without contact, to present candidly to one another their views on a variety of issues. They reviewed the international situation in which important changes and great upheavals are taking place and expounded their respective positions and attitudes.

6. The Chinese side stated: Wherever there is oppression there is resistance. Countries want independence, nations want liberation and the people want revolution—this has become the irresistible trend of history. All nations, big or small, should be equal; big nations should not bully the small and strong nations should not bully the weak. China will never be a superpower and it opposes hegemony and power politics of any kind. The Chinese side stated that it firmly supports the struggles of all the oppressed people and nations for freedom and liberation and that the people of all countries have the right to choose their social systems according to their own wishes and the right to safeguard the independence, sovereignty and territorial integrity of their own countries and oppose foreign aggression, interference, control and subversion. All foreign troops should be withdrawn to their own countries. The Chinese side expressed its firm support to the peoples of

Viet Nam, Laos and Cambodia in their efforts for the attainment of their goal and its firm support to the seven-point proposal of the Provisional Revolutionary Government of the Republic of South Viet Nam and the elaboration of February this year on the two key problems in the proposal, and to the Joint Declaration of the Summit Conference of the Indochinese Peoples. It firmly supports the eight-point program for the peaceful unification of Korea put forward by the Government of the Democratic People's Republic of Korea on April 12, 1971, and the stand for the abolition of the "U.N. Commission for the Unification and Rehabilitation of Korea." It firmly opposes the revival and outward expansion of Japanese militarism and firmly supports the Japanese people's desire to build an independent, democratic, peaceful and neutral Japan. It firmly maintains that India and Pakistan should, in accordance with the United Nations resolutions on the India-Pakistan question, immediately withdraw all their forces to their respective territories and to their own sides of the ceasefire line in Jammu and Kashmir and firmly supports the Pakistan Government and people in their struggle to preserve their independence and sovereignty and the people of Jammu and Kashmir in their struggle for the right of self-determination.

7. The U.S. side stated: Peace in Asia and peace in the world requires efforts both to reduce immediate tensions and to eliminate the basic causes of conflict. The United States will work for a just and secure peace; just, because it fulfills the aspirations of peoples and nations for freedom and progress; secure, because it removes the danger of foreign aggression. The United States supports individual freedom and social progress for all the peoples of the world, free of outside pressure or intervention. The United States believes that the effort to reduce tensions is served by improving communication between countries that have different ideologies so as to lessen the risks of confrontation through accident, miscalculation or misunderstanding. Countries should treat each other with mutual respect and be willing to compete peacefully, letting performance be the ultimate judge. No country should claim infallibility and each country should be prepared to reexamine its own attitudes for the common good. The United States stressed that the peoples of Indochina should be allowed to determine their destiny without outside intervention; its constant primary objective has been a negotiated solution; the eight-point proposal put forward by the Republic of Viet Nam and the United States on January 27, 1972 represents a basis for the attainment of that objective; in the absence of a negotiated settlement, the United States envisages the ultimate withdrawal of all U.S. forces from the region consistent with the aim of self-determination for each country of Indochina. The United States will maintain its close ties with and support for the Republic of Korea; the United States will support efforts of the Republic of Korea to seek a relaxation of tension and increased communication in the Korean

peninsula. The United States places the highest value on its friendly relations with Japan; it will continue to develop the existing close bonds. Consistent with the United Nations Security Council Resolution of December 21, 1971, the United States favors the continuation of the ceasefire between India and Pakistan and the withdrawal of all military forces to within their own territories and to their own sides of the ceasefire line in Jammu and Kashmir; the United States supports the right of the peoples of South Asia to shape their own future in peace, free of military threat, and without having the area become the subject of great power rivalry.

8. There are essential differences between China and the United States in their social systems and foreign policies. However, the two sides agreed that countries, regardless of their social systems, should conduct their relations on the principles of respect for the sovereignty and territorial integrity of all states, nonaggression against other states, noninterference in the internal affairs of other states, equality and mutual benefit, and peaceful coexistence. International disputes should be settled on this basis, without resorting to the use or threat of force. The United States and the People's Republic of China are prepared to apply these principles to their mutual relations.

9. With these principles of international relations in mind the two sides stated that:

- progress toward the normalization of relations between China and the United States is in the interests of all countries
- both wish to reduce the danger of international military conflict
- neither should seek hegemony in the Asia-Pacific region and each is opposed to efforts by any other country or group of countries to establish such hegemony
- neither is prepared to negotiate on behalf of any third party or to enter into agreements or understandings with the other directed at other states.

10. Both sides are of the view that it would be against the interests of the peoples of the world for any major country to collude with another against other countries, or for major countries to divide up the world into spheres of interest.

11. The two sides reviewed the long-standing serious disputes between China and the United States. The Chinese side reaffirmed its position: The Taiwan question is the crucial question obstructing the normalization of relations between China and the United States; the Government of the People's Republic of China is the sole legal government of China; Taiwan is a province of China which has long been returned to the motherland; the liberation of Taiwan is China's internal affair in which no other country has the right to interfere; and

all U.S. forces and military installations must be withdrawn from Taiwan. The Chinese Government firmly opposes any activities which aim at the creation of "one China, one Taiwan", "one China two governments", "two Chinas", an "independent Taiwan" or advocate that "the status of Taiwan remains to be determined."

12. The U.S. side declared: The United States acknowledges that all Chinese on either side of the Taiwan Strait maintain there is but one China and that Taiwan is a part of China. The United States Government does not challenge that position. It reaffirms its interest in a peaceful settlement of the Taiwan question by the Chinese themselves. With this prospect in mind, it affirms the ultimate objective of the withdrawal of all U.S. forces and military installations from Taiwan. In the meantime, it will progressively reduce its forces and military installations on Taiwan as the tension in the area diminishes. The two sides agreed that it is desirable to broaden the understanding between the two peoples. To this end, they discussed specific areas in such fields as science, technology, culture, sports and journalism, in which people-to-people contacts and exchanges would be mutually beneficial. Each side undertakes to facilitate the further development of such contacts and exchanges.

13. Both sides view bilateral trade as another area from which mutual benefit can be derived, and agreed that economic relations based on equality and mutual benefit are in the interest of the peoples of the two countries. They agree to facilitate the progressive development of trade between their two countries.

14. The two sides agreed that they will stay in contact through various channels, including the sending of a senior U.S. representative to Peking from time to time for concrete consultations to further the normalization of relations between the two countries and continue to exchange views on issues of common interest.

15. The two sides expressed the hope that the gains achieved during this visit would open up new prospects for the relations between the two countries. They believe that the normalization of relations between the two countries is not only in the interest of the Chinese and American peoples but also contributes to the relaxation of tension in Asia and the world.

16. President Nixon, Mrs. Nixon and the American party expressed their appreciation for the gracious hospitality shown them by the Government and people of the People's Republic of China.

Source: "Joint Communique of the United States of America and the People's Republic of China." Taiwan Documents Project Web site. On-line. Available at: http://newtaiwan.virtualave.net/communique01. htm. Accessed January 17, 2002.

War Powers Resolution (1973)

Passed by the Senate over President Nixon's veto on November 7, 1973, the War Powers Act remains one of the more contentious edicts of the Cold War period. In an attempt to limit the ability of future presidents to act without constitutional authority, it requires congressional consultation before the U.S. military is involved in any hostilities, limiting the president's ability to in effect declare war unilaterally. The resolution reflects the accumulation of frustration on Capitol Hill over the seemingly unfettered presidential power of Presidents Johnson and Nixon after the Gulf of Tonkin Resolution in 1964.

The War Powers Resolution has never been challenged before the Supreme Court, and presidents have sought to adhere to the sense of the resolution, if not the letter, to prevent a possible loss before the court. It is available on-line at: http://www4.law.cornell.edu/uscode/50/1541.html and in print as U.S. Public Law 93-148. 93rd Cong., H. J. Res. 542. November 7, 1973.

Camp David Accords (1978)

In intensive, round-the-clock negotiations at Camp David, Maryland, President Jimmy Carter negotiated with Israeli Prime Minister Menachem Begin and Egyptian President Anwar el-Sadat through the first part of September 1978 to broker this agreement, which brought an end to hostilities between Egypt and Israel. The peace between Egypt and Israel, which the United States guarantees through peacekeepers in the region, is one of the most enduring events of this region's long and tempestuous diplomatic effort.

The pivotal U.S. role as the only "honest broker" acceptable to both sides in the conflict dates to this agreement. Each president since 1978 has attempted to further the process, but often significant disappointment has been the only tangible result. Although peace has never been achieved, the United States continues to view Israel as its firm strategic ally in the region. The Clinton administration's commitment to Israel, which many Arabs saw as unreasonable, is cited as a reason for the September 2001 attacks on the United States.

The Camp David Framework for Peace, 1978

Muhammad Anwar al-Sadat, President of the Arab Republic of Egypt, and Menachem Begin, Prime Minister of Israel, met with Jimmy Carter, President of the United States of America, at Camp David from September 5 to September 17, 1978, and have agreed on the following framework for peace in the Middle East. They invite other parties to the Arab-Israel conflict to adhere to it.

Preamble

The search for peace in the Middle East must be guided by the following:

- The agreed basis for a peaceful settlement of the conflict between Israel and its neighbors is United Nations Security Council Resolution 242, in all its parts.
- After four wars during thirty years, despite intensive human efforts, the Middle East, which is the cradle of civilization and the birthplace of three great religions, does not yet enjoy the blessings of peace. The people of the Middle East yearn for peace so that the vast human and natural resources of the region can be turned to the pursuits of peace and so that this area can become a model for coexistence and cooperation among nations.
- The historic initiative of President Sadat in visiting Jerusalem and the reception accorded to him by the Parliament, government and people of Israel, and the reciprocal visit of Prime Minister Begin to Ismailia [Egypt], the peace proposals made by both leaders, as well as the warm reception of these missions by the people of both countries, have created an unprecedented opportunity for peace which must not be lost if this generation and future generations are to be spared the tragedies of war.
- The provisions of the Charter of the United Nations and other accepted norms of international law and legitimacy now provide accepted standards for the conduct of relations among the states.
- To achieve a relationship of peace, in the spirit of Article 2 of the United Nations Charter, future negotiations between Israel and any neighbor prepared to negotiate peace and security with it are necessary for the purpose of carrying out all the provisions and principles of Resolutions 242 and 338. [UN Security Council Resolution 338, adopted on October 22, 1973, secured a cease-fire in the October War between Israel and Egypt/Syria and called for direct negotiations between the parties on the basis of Resolution 242.]

- Peace requires respect for the sovereignty, territorial integrity and political independence of every state in the area and their right to live in peace within secure and recognized boundaries free from threats or acts of force. Progress toward that goal can accelerate movement toward a new era of reconciliation in the Middle East marked by cooperation in promoting economic development, in maintaining stability, and in assuring security.
- Security is enhanced by a relationship of peace and by cooperation between nations which enjoy normal relations. In addition, under the terms of peace treaties, the parties can, on the basis of reciprocity, agree to special security arrangements such as demilitarized zones, limited armaments, early warning stations, the presence of international forces, liaison, agreed measures for monitoring, and other arrangements that they agree are useful.

Framework

Taking these factors into account, the parties are determined to reach a just, comprehensive, and durable settlement of the Middle East conflict through the conclusion of peace treaties based on Security Council Resolutions 242 and 338 in all their parts. Their purpose is to achieve peace and good neighborly relations. They recognize that, for peace to endure, it must involve all those who have been most deeply affected by the conflict. They therefore agree that this framework, as appropriate, is intended by them to constitute a basis for peace not only between Egypt and Israel, but also between Israel and each of its other neighbors which is prepared to negotiate peace with Israel on this basis. . . .

Sources: Public Papers of the Presidents of the United States: James E. Carter, 1979. Vol. 2. Washington, DC: GPO, 1980, pp. 1523–1528. Paterson, Thomas G., and Dennis Merrill. Major Problems in American Foreign Relations. Vol. 2, Since 1914. 4th ed. Lexington, MA: Houghton Mifflin, 1995, pp. 665–668.

Strategic Arms Limitation Treaty II (1979)

The Strategic Arms Limitation Treaty of 1979, better known as SALT II, was signed by the United States under the Carter administration and Leonid Brezhnev's Soviet Union on June 18, 1979. It attracted considerable opposition in the United States because the conservative wing of the Republican Party believed that the limits imposed by the treaty, which allowed the Soviets to increase their stockpile while the United States had to reduce its already larger numbers, left the United States open to attack. This "window of vulnerability" became a major campaign plank for candidate Ronald Reagan as he opposed Carter for the presidency in 1980. The treaty can be viewed on-line at: http://www.state.gov/www/global/arms/treaties/salt2-2.html.

Taiwan Relations Act (1979)

The Taiwan Relations Act (TRA) is the only U.S. law that exists on U.S.-Chinese-Taiwan relations. The TRA was passed on April 10, 1979, after President Jimmy Carter normalized relations with Beijing at the expense of the traditional U.S. ally, Taiwan. Initially several members of Congress attempted to file suit to reverse the abdication of the U.S.-Taiwan Defense Treaty, but the Supreme Court refused to hear the case, ending the judicial options for opposing it. The TRA was passed by Congress in a bipartisan attempt to remedy the abandonment of the nation's traditional ally.

In the TRA, the United States affirms its expectation that the future of Taiwan will be determined by peaceful means, stating that it will consider any effort to do otherwise as a matter a grave concern and that it will provide Taiwan with defensive arms. Unlike the presidential communiqués with China signed by Presidents Richard Nixon, Jimmy Carter, and Ronald Reagan, the TRA is a law, which is binding upon the U.S. government. Because the TRA is a lengthy document, only the first four sections are presented here.

Taiwan Relations Act. Public Law 96-8. April 10, 1979.

To help maintain peace, security, and stability in the Western Pacific and to promote the foreign policy of the United States by authorizing the continuation of commercial, cultural, and other relations between the people of the United States and the people on Taiwan, and for other purposes.

Be it enacted by the Senate and the House of Representatives of the United States of America in Congress assembled,

Section 1: Short Title
This Act may be cited as the "Taiwan Relations Act."

Section 2: Findings and Declaration of Policy
    (a) The President having terminated governmental relations between the United States and the governing authorities on Taiwan recognized by the United States as the Republic of

China prior to January 1, 1979, the Congress finds that the enactment of this Act is necessary—

(1) to help maintain peace, security, and stability in the Western Pacific; and

(2) to promote the foreign policy of the United States by authorizing the continuation of commercial, cultural, and other relations between the people of the United States and the people on Taiwan.

(b) It is the policy of the United States—

(1) to preserve and promote extensive, close, and friendly commercial, cultural, and other relations between the people of the United States and the people on Taiwan, as well as the people on the China mainland and all other peoples of the Western Pacific area;

(2) to declare that peace and stability in the area are in the political, security, and economic interests of the United States, and are matters of international concern;

(3) to make clear that the United States decision to establish diplomatic relations with the People's Republic of China rests upon the expectation that the future of Taiwan will be determined by peaceful means;

(4) to consider any effort to determine the future of Taiwan by other than peaceful means, including by boycotts or embargoes, a threat to the peace and security of the Western Pacific area and of grave concern to the United States;

(5) to provide Taiwan with arms of a defensive character; and

(6) to maintain the capacity of the United States to resist any resort to force or other forms of coercion that would jeopardize the security, or the social or economic system, of the people on Taiwan.

(c) Nothing contained in this Act shall contravene the interest of the United States in human rights, especially with respect to the human rights of all the approximately eighteen million inhabitants of Taiwan. The preservation and enhancement of the human rights of the people on Taiwan are hereby reaffirmed as objectives of the United Sates.

Section 3: Implementation of United States Policy With Regard to Taiwan

(a) In furtherance of the policy set forth in section 2 of this Act, the United States will make available to Taiwan such defense articles and defense services in such quantity as may be necessary to enable Taiwan to maintain a sufficient self-defense capability.

(b) The President and the Congress shall determine the nature and quantity of such defense articles and services based solely upon their judgment of the needs of Taiwan, in accordance with procedures established by law. Such determination of Taiwan's defense needs shall include review by United States military authorities in connection with recommendations to the President and the Congress.

(c) The President is directed to inform the Congress promptly of any threat to the security or the social or economic system of the people on Taiwan and any danger to the interests of the United States arising therefrom. The President and the Congress shall determine, in accordance with constitutional processes, appropriate action by the United States in response to any such danger.

Section 4: Application of Laws; International Agreements

(a) The absence of diplomatic relations or recognition shall not affect the application of the laws of the United States with respect to Taiwan, and the laws of the United States shall apply with respect to Taiwan in the manner that the laws of the United States applied with respect to Taiwan prior to January 1, 1979.

(b) The application of subsection (a) of this section shall include, but shall not be limited to, the following:

(1) Whenever the laws of the United States refer or relate to foreign countries, nations, states, governments, or similar entities, such terms shall include and such laws shall apply with respect to Taiwan.

(2) Whenever authorized by or pursuant to the laws of the United States to conduct or carry out programs, transactions, or other relations with respect to foreign countries, nations, states, governments, or similar entities, the President or any agency of the United States Government is authorized to conduct and carry out . . . such programs, transactions, and other relations with respect to Taiwan (including but not limited to, the performance of services for the United States through contracts with commercial entities on Taiwan), in accordance with the applicable laws of the United States.

(3) (A) The absence of diplomatic relations and recognition with respect to Taiwan shall not abrogate, infringe, modify, deny, or otherwise affect in any way any rights or obligations (including but not limited to those involving contracts, debts, or property interests of any kind) under the laws of the United States heretofore or hereafter acquired by or with respect to Taiwan.

(B) For all purposes under the laws of the United States, including actions in any court in the United States, recognition of the People's Republic of China shall not affect in any way the ownership of or other rights or interests in properties, tangible and intangible, and other things of value, owned or held on or prior to December 31, 1978, or thereafter acquired or earned by the governing authorities on Taiwan.

(4) Whenever the application of the laws of the United States depends upon the law that is or was applicable on Taiwan or compliance therewith, the law applied by the people on Taiwan shall be considered the applicable law for that purpose.

(5) Nothing in this Act, nor the facts of the President's action in extending diplomatic recognition to the People's Republic of China, the absence of diplomatic relations between the people on Taiwan and the United States, or the lack of recognition by the United States, and attendant circumstances thereto, shall be construed in any administrative or judicial proceeding as a basis for any United States Government agency, commission, or department to make a finding of fact or determination of law, under the Atomic Energy Act of 1954 and the Nuclear Non-Proliferation Act of 1978, to deny an export license application or to revoke an existing export license for nuclear exports to Taiwan.

(6) For purposes of the Immigration and Nationality Act, Taiwan may be treated in the manner specified in the first sentence of section 202(b) of that Act.

(7) The capacity of Taiwan to sue and be sued in courts in the United States, in accordance with the laws of the United States, shall not be abrogated, infringed, modified, denied or otherwise affected in any way by the absence of diplomatic relations or recognition.

(8) No requirement, whether expressed or implied, under the laws of the United States with respect to maintenance of diplomatic relations or recognition shall be applicable with respect to Taiwan.

(c) For all purposes, including actions in any court in the United States, the Congress approves the continuation in force of all treaties and other international agreements, including multilateral conventions, entered into by the United States and the governing authorities on Taiwan recognized by the United States as the Republic of China prior to January 1, 1979, and in force between them on December 31, 1978, unless and until terminated in accordance with law.

(d) Nothing in this Act may be construed as a basis for supporting the exclusion or expulsion of Taiwan from continued membership in any international financial institution or any other international organization. . . .

Source: Public Law 96-8. 96th Cong., April 10, 1979. *Taiwan Relations Act.*

President Ronald Reagan's SDI/Grenada Speech (1983)

In a nationally televised speech from the Oval Office on March 23, 1983, President Reagan announced his support for the Strategic Defense Initiative (SDI). Although the speech remains famous for that reason, President Reagan also indicated major and growing U.S. concerns about military links between the Caribbean island state of Grenada and Fidel Castro Ruz's Cuba, foreshadowing U.S. intervention in Grenada seven months later. (The photographs mentioned in the speech are not reproduced here.) This was one of the more memorable speeches of the Reagan presidency because it portrayed a future in which the countries of the world would be sharing higher-technology defensive systems.

The SDI program became known almost immediately as Star Wars. The U.S. technological base, vastly stronger than that of the Soviet Union, reinforced the country's negotiating position at various arms control fora and summits. The program also drove the less able Soviets to spend money they could not afford in an attempt to keep up, contributing to the collapse of the Soviet Union. During the Clinton and second Bush administrations, SDI has evolved into the Ballistic Missile Defense program.

My fellow Americans, thank you for sharing your time with me tonight.

The subject I want to discuss with you, peace and national security, is both timely and important. Timely, because I've reached a decision which offers a new hope for our children in the 21st century, a decision I'll tell you about in a few minutes. And important because there's a very big decision that you must make for yourselves. This subject involves the most basic duty that any President and any people share, the duty to protect and strengthen the peace.

At the beginning of this year, I submitted to the Congress a defense budget which reflects my best judgment of the best understanding of the experts and specialists who advise me about what we and our allies must do to protect our people in the years ahead. That budget is much more than a long list of numbers, for behind all the numbers lies America's ability to prevent the greatest of human tragedies and preserve our free way of life in a sometimes dangerous world. It is part of a careful, long-term plan to make America strong again after too many years of neglect and mistakes.

Our efforts to rebuild America's defenses and strengthen the peace began 2 years ago when we requested a major increase in the defense program. Since then, the amount of those increases we first proposed has been reduced by half, through improvements in management and procurement and other savings.

The budget request that is now before the Congress has been trimmed to the limits of safety. Further deep cuts cannot be made without seriously endangering the security of the Nation. The choice is up to the men and women you've elected to the Congress, and that means the choice is up to you.

Tonight, I want to explain to you what this defense debate is all about and why I'm convinced that the budget now before the Congress is necessary, responsible, and deserving of your support. And I want to offer hope for the future.

But first, let me say what the defense debate is not about. It is not about spending arithmetic. I know that in the last few weeks you've been bombarded with numbers and percentages. Some say we need only a 5-percent increase in defense spending. The so-called alternate budget backed by liberals in the House of Representatives would lower the figure to 2 to 3 percent, cutting our defense spending by $163 billion over the next 5 years. The trouble with all these numbers is that they tell us little about the kind of defense program America needs or the benefits and security and freedom that our defense effort buys for us.

What seems to have been lost in all this debate is the simple truth of how a defense budget is arrived at. It isn't done by deciding to spend a certain number of dollars. Those loud voices that are occasionally heard charging that the Government is trying to solve a security problem by throwing money at it are nothing more than noise based on ignorance. We start by considering what must be done to maintain peace and review all the possible threats against our security. Then a strategy for strengthening peace and defending against those threats must be agreed upon. And, finally, our defense establishment must be evaluated to see what is necessary to protect against any or all of the potential threats. The cost of achieving these ends is totaled up, and the result is the budget for national defense.

There is no logical way that you can say, let's spend x billion dollars less. You can only say, which part of our defense measures do we believe we can do without and still have security against all contingencies? Anyone in the Congress who advocates a percentage or a specific dollar cut in defense spending should be made to say what part of our defenses he would eliminate and he should be candid enough to acknowledge that his cuts mean cutting our commitments to allies or inviting greater risk or both.

The defense policy of the United States is based on a simple premise: The United States does not start fights. We will never be an aggressor. We maintain our strength in order to deter and defend against aggression—to preserve freedom and peace.

Since the dawn of the atomic age, we've sought to reduce the risk of war by maintaining a strong deterrent and by seeking genuine arms control. "Deterrence" means simply this: making sure any adversary who thinks about attacking the United States, or our allies, or our vital interests, concludes that the risks to him outweigh any potential gains. Once he understands that, he won't attack. We maintain the peace through our strength; weakness only invites aggression.

This strategy of deterrence has not changed. It still works. But what it takes to maintain deterrence has changed. It took one kind of military force to deter an attack when we had far more nuclear weapons than any other power; it takes another kind now that the Soviets, for example, have enough accurate and powerful nuclear weapons to destroy virtually all of our missiles on the ground. Now, this is not to say that the Soviet Union is planning to make war on us. Nor do I believe a war is inevitable—quite the contrary. But what must be recognized is that our security is based on being prepared to meet all threats.

There was a time when we depended on coastal forts and artillery batteries, because, with the weaponry of that day, any attack would have had to come by sea. Well, this is a different world, and our defenses must be based on recognition and awareness of the weaponry possessed by other nations in the nuclear age.

We can't afford to believe that we will never be threatened. There have been two world wars in my lifetime. We didn't start them and, indeed, did everything we could to avoid being drawn into them. But we were ill-prepared for both. Had we been better prepared, peace might have been preserved.

For 20 years the Soviet Union has been accumulating enormous military might. They didn't stop when their forces exceeded all requirements of a legitimate defensive capability. And they haven't stopped now. During the past decade and a half, the Soviets have built up a massive arsenal of new strategic nuclear weapons—weapons that can strike directly at the United States.

As an example, the United States introduced its last new intercontinental ballistic missile, the Minute Man III, in 1969, and we're now dismantling our even older Titan missiles. But what has the Soviet Union done in these intervening years? Well, since 1969 the Soviet Union has built five new classes of ICBM's, and upgraded these eight times. As a result, their missiles are much more powerful and accurate than they were several years ago, and they continue to develop more, while ours are increasingly obsolete.

The same thing has happened in other areas. Over the same period, the Soviet Union built 4 new classes of submarine-launched ballistic missiles and over 60 new missile submarines. We built 2 new types of submarine missiles and actually withdrew 10 submarines from strategic missions. The Soviet Union built over 200 new Backfire bombers, and their brand new Blackjack bomber is now under development. We haven't built a new long-range bomber since our B-52's were deployed about a quarter of a century ago, and we've already retired several hundred of those because of old age. Indeed, despite what many people think, our strategic forces only cost about 15 percent of the defense budget.

Another example of what's happened: in 1978 the Soviets had 600 intermediate-range nuclear missiles based on land and were beginning to add the SS-20—a new, highly accurate, mobile missile with 3 warheads. We had none. Since then the Soviets have strengthened their lead. By the end of 1979, when Soviet leader Brezhnev declared "a balance now exists," the Soviets had over 800 warheads. We still had none. A year ago this month, Mr. Brezhnev pledged a moratorium, or freeze, on SS-20 deployment. But by last August, their 800 warheads had become more than 1,200. We still had none. Some freeze. At this time Soviet Defense Minister Ustinov announced "approximate parity of forces continues to exist." But the Soviets are still adding an average of 3 new warheads a week, and now have 1,300. These warheads can reach their targets in a matter of a few minutes. We still have none. So far, it seems that the Soviet definition of parity is a box score of 1,300 to nothing, in their favor.

So, together with our NATO allies, we decided in 1979 to deploy new weapons, beginning this year, as a deterrent to their SS-20s and as an incentive to the Soviet Union to meet us in serious arms control negotiations. We will begin that deployment late this year. At the same time, however, we're willing to cancel our program if the Soviets will dismantle theirs. This is what we've called a zero-zero plan. The Soviets are now at the negotiating table—and I think it's fair to say that without our planned deployments, they wouldn't be there.

Now let's consider conventional forces. Since 1974 the United States has produced 3,050 tactical combat aircraft. By contrast, the Soviet Union has produced twice as many. When we look at attack submarines, the United States has produced 27 while the Soviet Union has produced 61. For armored vehicles, including tanks, we have produced 11,200. The Soviet Union has produced 54,000—nearly 5 to 1 in their favor. Finally, with artillery, we've produced 950 artillery and rocket launchers while the Soviets have produced more than 13,000—a staggering 14-to-1 ratio.

There was a time when we were able to offset superior Soviet numbers with higher quality, but today they are building weapons as sophisticated and modern as our own.

As the Soviets have increased their military power, they've been emboldened to extend that power. They're spreading their military influence in ways that can directly challenge our vital interests and those of our allies.

The following aerial photographs, most of them secret until now, illustrate this point in a crucial area very close to home: Central America and the Caribbean Basin. They're not dramatic photographs. But I think they help give you a better understanding of what I'm talking about.

This Soviet intelligence collection facility, less than a hundred miles from our coast, is the largest of its kind in the world. The acres and acres of antennae fields and intelligence monitors are targeted on key U.S. military installations and sensitive activities. The installation in Lourdes, Cuba, is manned by 1,500 Soviet technicians. And the satellite ground station allows instant communications with Moscow. This 28 square-mile facility has grown by more than 60 percent in size and capability during the past decade.

In western Cuba, we see this military airfield and it complement of modern, Soviet-built Mig-23 aircraft. The Soviet Union uses this Cuban airfield for its own long-range reconnaissance missions. And earlier this month, two modern Soviet antisubmarine warfare aircraft began operating from it. During the past 2 years, the level of Soviet arms exports to Cuba can only be compared to the levels reached during the Cuban missile crisis 20 years ago.

This third photo, which is the only one in this series that has been previously made public, shows Soviet military hardware that has made its way to Central America. This airfield with its M18 helicopters, antiaircraft guns, and protected fighter sites is one of a number of military facilities in Nicaragua which has received Soviet equipment funneled through Cuba, and reflects the massive military buildup going on in that country.

On the small island of Grenada, at the southern end of the Caribbean chain, the Cubans, with Soviet financing and backing, are in the process of building an airfield with a 10,000-foot runway. Grenada doesn't even have an air force. Who is it intended for? The Caribbean is a very important passageway for our international commerce and military lines of communication. More than half of all American oil imports now pass through the Caribbean. The rapid buildup of Grenada's military potential is unrelated to any conceivable threat to this island country of under 110,000 people and totally at odds with the pattern of other eastern Caribbean States, most of which are unarmed.

The Soviet-Cuban militarization of Grenada, in short, can only be seen as power projection into the region. And it is in this important economic and strategic area that we're trying to help the Governments of El Salvador, Costa Rica, Honduras, and others in their struggles for democracy against guerrillas supported through Cuba and Nicaragua.

These pictures only tell a small part of the story. I wish I could show you more without compromising our most sensitive intelligence sources and methods. But the Soviet Union is also supporting Cuban military forces in Angola and Ethiopia. They have bases in Ethiopia and South Yemen, near the Persian Gulf oil fields. They've taken over the port that we built at Cam Ranh Bay in Vietnam. And now for the first time in history, the Soviet Navy is a force to be reckoned with in the South Pacific.

Some people may still ask: Would the Soviets ever use their formidable military power? Well, again, can we afford to believe they won't? There is Afghanistan. And in Poland, the Soviets denied the will of the people and in so doing demonstrated to the world how their military power could also be used to intimidate.

The final fact is that the Soviet Union is acquiring what can only be considered an offensive military force. They have continued to build far more intercontinental ballistic missiles than they could possibly need simply to deter an attack. Their conventional forces are trained and equipped not so much to defend against an attack as they are to permit sudden, surprise offensives of their own.

Our NATO allies have assumed a great defense burden, including the military draft in most countries. We're working with them and our other friends around the world to do more. Our defensive strategy means we need military forces that can move very quickly, forces that are trained and ready to respond to any emergency.

Every item in our defense program—our ships, our tanks, our planes, our funds for training and spare parts—is intended for one all-important purpose: to keep the peace. Unfortunately, a decade of neglecting our military forces had called into question our ability to do that.

When I took office in January 1981, I was appalled by what I found: American planes that couldn't fly and American ships that couldn't sail for lack of spare parts and trained personnel and insufficient fuel and ammunition for essential training. The inevitable result of all this was poor morale in our Armed Forces, difficulty in recruiting the brightest young Americans to wear the uniform, and difficulty in convincing our most experienced military personnel to stay on.

There was a real question then about how well we could meet a crisis. And it was obvious that we had to begin a major modernization program to ensure we could deter aggression and preserve the peace in the years ahead.

We had to move immediately to improve the basic readiness and staying power of our conventional forces, so they could meet—and therefore help deter—a crisis. We had to make up for lost years of investment by moving forward with a long-term plan to prepare our forces to counter the military capabilities our adversaries were developing for the future.

I know that all of you want peace, and so do I. I know too that many of you seriously believe that a nuclear freeze would further the cause of peace. But a freeze now would make us less, not more, secure and would raise, not reduce, the risks of war. It would be largely unverifiable and would seriously undercut our negotiations on arms reduction. It would reward the Soviets for their massive military buildup while preventing us from modernizing our aging and increasingly vulnerable forces. With their present margin of superiority, why should they agree to arms reductions knowing that we were prohibited from catching up?

Believe me, it wasn't pleasant for someone who had come to Washington determined to reduce government spending, but we had to move forward with the task of repairing our defenses or we would lose our ability to deter conflict now and in the future. We had to demonstrate to any adversary that aggression could not succeed, and that the only real solution was substantial, equitable, and effectively verifiable arms reduction—the kind we're working for right now in Geneva.

Thanks to your strong support, and bipartisan support from the Congress, we began to turn things around. Already, we're seeing some very encouraging results. Quality recruitment and retention are up dramatically—more high school graduates are choosing military careers, and more experienced career personnel are choosing to stay. Our men and women in uniform at last are getting the tools and training they need to do their jobs.

Ask around today, especially among our young people, and I think you will find a whole new attitude toward serving their country. This reflects more than just better pay, equipment, and leadership. You the American people have sent a signal to these young people that it is once again an honor to wear the uniform. That's not something you measure in a budget, but it's a very real part of our nation's strength.

It'll take us longer to build the kind of equipment we need to keep peace in the future, but we've made a good start.

We haven't built a new long-range bomber for 21 years. Now we're building the B-1. We hadn't launched one new strategic submarine for 17 years. Now we're building one Trident submarine a year. Our land-based missiles are increasingly threatened by the many huge, new Soviet ICBM's. We're determining how to solve that problem. At the same time, we're working in the START and INF negotiations with the goal of achieving deep reductions in the strategic and intermediate nuclear arsenals of both sides.

We have also begun the long-needed modernization of our conventional forces. The Army is getting its first new tank in 20 years. The Air Force is modernizing. We're rebuilding our Navy, which shrank from about a thousand ships in the late 1960s to 453 during the 1970s. Our nation needs a superior navy to support our military forces and vital interests overseas. We're now on the road to achieving a 600-ship navy and increasing the amphibious capabilities of our marines, who are now serving the cause of peace in Lebanon. And we're building a real capability to assist our friends in the vitally important Indian Ocean and Persian Gulf region.

This adds up to a major effort, and it isn't cheap. It comes at a time when there are many other pressures on our budget and when the American people have already had to make major sacrifices during the recession. But we must not be misled by those who would make defense once again the scapegoat of the Federal budget.

The fact is that in the past few decades we have seen a dramatic shift in how we spend the taxpayer's dollar. Back in 1955, payments to individuals took up only about 20 percent of the Federal budget. For nearly three decades, these payments steadily increased and, this year, will account for 49 percent of the budget. By contrast, in 1955 defense took up more than half of the Federal budget. By 1980 this spending had fallen to a low of 23 percent. Even with the increase that I am requesting this year, defense will still amount to only 28 percent of the budget.

The calls for cutting back the defense budget come in nice, simple arithmetic. They're the same kind of talk that led the democracies to neglect their defenses in the 1930s and invited the tragedy of World War II. We must not let that grim chapter of history repeat itself through apathy or neglect.

This is why I'm speaking to you tonight to urge you to tell your Senators and Congressmen that you know we must continue to restore our military strength. If we stop in midstream, we will send a signal of decline, of lessened will, to friends and adversaries alike. Free people must voluntarily through open debate and democratic means, meet the challenge that totalitarians pose by compulsion. It's up to us, in our time, to choose and choose wisely between the hard but necessary task of preserving peace and freedom and the temptation to ignore our duty and blindly hope for the best while the enemies of freedom grow stronger day by day.

The solution is well within our grasp. But to reach it, there is simply no alternative but to continue this year, in this budget, to provide the resources we need to preserve the peace and guarantee our freedom.

Now, thus far tonight I've shared with you my thoughts on the problems of national security we must face together. My predecessors in the Oval Office have appeared before you on other occasions to describe the threat posed by Soviet power and have proposed steps to address that threat. But since the advent of nuclear weapons, those steps have been increasingly directed toward deterrence of aggression through the promise of retaliation.

This approach to stability through offensive threat has worked. We and our allies have succeeded in preventing nuclear war for more than three decades. In recent months, however, my advisers, including in particular the Joint Chiefs of Staff, have underscored the necessity to break out of a future that relies solely on offensive retaliation for our security.

Over the course of these discussions, I've become more and more deeply convinced that the human spirit must be capable of rising above dealing with other nations and human beings by threatening their existence. Feeling this way, I believe we must thoroughly examine every opportunity for reducing tensions and for introducing greater stability into the strategic calculus on both sides.

One of the most important contributions we can make is, of course, to lower the level of all arms, and particularly nuclear arms. We're engaged right now in several negotiations with the Soviet Union to bring about a mutual reduction of weapons. I will report to you a week from tomorrow my thoughts on that score. But let me just say, I'm totally committed to this course.

If the Soviet Union will join with us in our effort to achieve major arms reduction we will have succeeded in stabilizing the nuclear balance. Nevertheless, it will still be necessary to rely on the specter of retaliation, on mutual threat. And that's a sad commentary on the human condition. Wouldn't it be better to save lives than to avenge them? Are we not capable of demonstrating our peaceful intentions by applying all our abilities and our ingenuity to achieving a truly lasting stability? I think we are. Indeed, we must.

After careful consultation with my advisers, including the Joint Chiefs of Staff, I believe there is a way. Let me share with you a vision of the future which offers hope. It is that we embark on a program to counter the awesome Soviet missile threat with measures that are defensive. Let us turn to the very strengths in technology that spawned our great industrial base and that have given us the quality of life we enjoy today.

What if free people could live secure in the knowledge that their security did not rest upon the threat of instant U.S. retaliation to deter a Soviet attack, that we could intercept and destroy strategic ballistic missiles before they reached our own soil or that of our allies?

I know this is a formidable, technical task, one that may not be accomplished before the end of this century. Yet, current technology has attained a level of sophistication where it's reasonable for us to begin this effort. It will take years, probably decades of effort on many fronts. There will be failures and setbacks, just as there will be successes and breakthroughs. And as we proceed, we must remain constant in preserving the nuclear deterrent and maintaining a solid capability for flexible response. But isn't it worth every investment necessary to free the world from the threat of nuclear war? We know it is.

In the meantime, we will continue to pursue real reductions in nuclear arms, negotiating from a position of strength that can be ensured only by modernizing our strategic forces. At the same time, we must take steps to reduce the risk of a conventional military conflict escalating to nuclear war by improving our nonnuclear capabilities.

America does possess now the technologies to attain very significant improvements in the effectiveness of our conventional, nonnuclear forces. Proceeding boldly with these new technologies, we can significantly reduce any incentive that the Soviet Union may have to threaten attack against the United States or its allies.

As we pursue our goal of defensive technologies, we recognize that our allies rely upon our strategic offensive power to deter attacks against them. Their vital interests and ours are inextricably linked. Their safety and ours are one. And no change in technology can or will alter that reality. We must and shall continue to honor our commitments.

I clearly recognize that defensive systems have limitations and raise certain problems and ambiguities. If paired with offensive systems, they can be viewed as fostering an aggressive policy, and no one wants that. But with these considerations firmly in mind, I call upon the scientific community in our country, those who gave us nuclear weapons, to turn their great talents now to the cause of mankind and world peace, to give us the means of rendering these nuclear weapons impotent and obsolete.

Tonight, consistent with our obligations of the ABM treaty and recognizing the need for closer consultation with our allies, I'm taking an important first step. I am directing a comprehensive and intensive effort to define a long-term research and development program to begin to achieve our ultimate goal of eliminating the threat posed by strategic nuclear missiles. This could pave the way for arms control measures to eliminate the weapons themselves. We seek neither military superiority nor political advantage. Our only purpose—one all people share—is to search for ways to reduce the danger of nuclear war.

My fellow Americans, tonight we're launching an effort which holds the promise of changing the course of human history. There will be risks, and results take time. But I believe we can do it. As we cross this threshold, I ask for your prayers and your support.

Thank you, good night, and God bless you.

Source: Public Papers of the Presidents of the United States: Ronald W. Reagan, 1983. Vol. 1. Washington, DC: GPO, 1984, pp. 437–443.

Tower Report on the Iran-Contra Scandal (1987)

With the October 1986 discovery of the two-pronged deception carried out in the White House (arms in return for hostages in the Middle East and illegal funding for *contrarevolucionarios* in

Nicaragua), the Congress called for an investigation of the Reagan White House. One of the reports was issued on February 26, 1987, by former Senator John Tower, former National Security Advisor Brent Scowcroft (who held the same position later under President George H. W. Bush), and others. It became known as the Tower Report. An extensive summary of events in the scandal, the report is far too lengthy to reprint here. The best source for its findings, however, is the National Security Archive at George Washington University, encapsulated in Peter Kornbluh, Malcolm Byrne, and Theodore Draper, eds., *The Iran-Contra Scandal: The Declassified History* (Washington, DC: The New Press, 1993). An executive summary of the report can be found on-line at: http://www.webcom.com/pinknoiz/covert/icsummary.html.

Strategic Arms Reduction Treaty (1991)

The Strategic Arms Reduction Treaty, better known as START I, was signed by the Soviet Union and the United States on July 31, 1991, not long before the Soviet Union dissolved into sixteen republics. It was far less controversial than the earlier arms control treaties because the Soviet threat was clearly nowhere near as important as it had been for the last forty years. START I was the final treaty to be signed by these two adversaries, as the Soviet Union ceased to exist on September 31, 1991. It was the triumph of Western, democratic, capitalism against a bloated ideological system, but it was not the end of national security issues for the United States. The text of the agreement is available on-line at: http://fas.org/nuke/control/start1/text/index.htm

North American Free Trade Association (1994)

The original movement toward free trade in North America was built upon the friendship between U.S. President Ronald Reagan and Canadian Prime Minister Brian Mulroney, who in the late 1980s reduced the trade barriers between these two states. In 1990 President George H. W. Bush proclaimed the desire for a free trade zone of the Americas, reaching between Alaska and Tierra del Fuego in Argentina. Finally, the NAFTA agreement of January

1, 1994, between Mexico, Canada, and the United States was designed to build on the earlier bilateral agreement, as an intermediate step before including the entire region in a free trade organization. Treaty provisions are available on-line at: http://www-tech.mit.edu/Bulletins/nafta.html.

World Trade Organization (1994)

The World Trade Organization (WTO) was formally established on April 15, 1994, when it replaced its parent body, the General Agreement on Tariffs and Trade (GATT), which began in the first years after World War II. The WTO is still evolving as the primary international body to promote international free trade.

Through the WTO, the United States strives to include potential aggressor states in the international system, hence encouraging them to participate in the international community as reasonable, nonaggressive actors. One example of this strategy is China, which was formally accepted into the WTO on December 11, 2001. The founding texts for the WTO appear on-line at: http://www.wto.org/english/docs_e/legal_e/13-mprot. wpf.

Comprehensive Test Ban Treaty (1996)

The Comprehensive Test Ban Treaty (CTBT), originally discussed as early as the 1960s, would prohibit testing of nuclear devices at any time as a deterrent to nuclear weapons development. It took thirty years for the CTBT to be negotiated and put before the world community for signature, which occurred on September 10, 1996. It was exceptionally controversial for the United States and did not achieve ratification by the U.S. Senate, on the grounds that it was dangerous to prohibit the United States from testing new weapons. The international community condemned this omission, chalking it up to U.S. hegemony and arrogance, rather than serious apprehensions about security threats resulting from the treaty. This raised further questions about U.S. reliability as a partner. The treaty text is located on-line at: http://fas.org/nuke/control/ctbt/text/ramaker.htm.

President George W. Bush's War on Terrorism Speech (2001)

In the sadness and bewilderment of the aftermath of the terrorist attacks on Washington and New York on September 11, 2001, President George W. Bush issued a charge to the country to begin a new and enduring war on terrorism. These remarks, made on September 20 to a joint session of Congress, indicated the administration's evolving views of the new international conflict and the national security concerns it raised.

Mr. Speaker, Mr. President Pro-Tempore, members of Congress, and fellow Americans:

In the normal course of events, presidents come to this chamber to report the State of the nation. Tonight, no such report is needed. It has already been delivered by the American people.

We have seen it in the courage of passengers, who rushed terrorists to save others on the ground—passengers like an exceptional man named Todd Beamer. And would you please help me to welcome his wife, Lisa Beamer, here tonight.

We have seen the state of our Union in the endurance of rescuers, working past exhaustion. We have seen the unfurling of flags, the lighting of candles, the giving of blood, the saying of prayers—in English, Hebrew, and Arabic. We have seen the decency of a loving and giving people who have made the grief of strangers their own.

My fellow citizens, for the last nine days, the entire world has seen for itself the state of our Union—and it is strong.

Tonight we are a country awakened to danger and called to defend freedom. Our grief has turned to anger, and anger to resolution. Whether we bring our enemies to justice, or bring justice to our enemies, justice will be done.

I thank the Congress for its leadership at such an important time. All of America was touched on the evening of the tragedy to see Republicans and Democrats joined together on the steps of this Capitol, singing "God Bless America." And you did more than sing; you acted, by delivering $40 billion to rebuild our communities and meet the needs of our military.

Speaker Hastert, Minority Leader Gephardt, Majority Leader Daschle and Senator Lott, I thank you for your friendship, for your leadership and for your service to our country.

And on behalf of the American people, I thank the world for its outpouring of support. America will never forget the sounds of our National Anthem playing at Buckingham Palace, on the streets of Paris, and at Berlin's Brandenburg Gate.

We will not forget South Korean children gathering to pray outside our embassy in Seoul, or the prayers of sympathy offered at a mosque in Cairo. We will not forget moments of silence and days of mourning in Australia and Africa and Latin America. Nor will we forget the citizens of 80 other nations who died with our own: dozens of Pakistanis; more than 130 Israelis; more than 250 citizens of India; men and women from El Salvador, Iran, Mexico and Japan; and hundreds of British citizens. America has no truer friend than Great Britain. Once again, we are joined together in a great cause—so honored the British Prime Minister has crossed an ocean to show his unity of purpose with America. Thank you for coming, friend.

On September the 11th, enemies of freedom committed an act of war against our country. Americans have known wars—but for the past 136 years, they have been wars on foreign soil, except for one Sunday in 1941. Americans have known the casualties of war—but not at the center of a great city on a peaceful morning. Americans have known surprise attacks—but never before on thousands of civilians. All of this was brought upon us in a single day—and night fell on a different world, a world where freedom itself is under attack.

Americans have many questions tonight. Americans are asking: Who attacked our country? The evidence we have gathered all points to a collection of loosely affiliated terrorist organizations known as al Qaeda. They are the same murderers indicted for bombing American embassies in Tanzania and Kenya, and responsible for bombing the USS *Cole*.

Al Qaeda is to terror what the Mafia is to crime. But its goal is not making money; its goal is remaking the world—and imposing its radical beliefs on people everywhere.

The terrorists practice a fringe form of Islamic extremism that has been rejected by Muslim scholars and the vast majority of Muslim clerics—a fringe movement that perverts the peaceful teachings of Islam. The terrorists' directive commands them to kill Christians and Jews, to kill all Americans, and make no distinction among military and civilians, including women and children.

This group and its leader—a person named Osama bin Laden—are linked to many other organizations in different countries, including the Egyptian Islamic Jihad and the Islamic Movement of Uzbekistan. There are thousands of these terrorists in more than 60 countries. They are recruited from their own nations and neighborhoods and brought to camps in places like Afghanistan, where they are trained in the tactics of terror. They are sent back to their homes or sent to hide in countries around the world to plot evil and destruction.

The leadership of al Qaeda has great influence in Afghanistan and supports the Taliban regime in controlling most of that country. In Afghanistan, we see al Qaeda's vision for the world.

Afghanistan's people have been brutalized—many are starving and many have fled. Women are not allowed to attend school. You can be jailed for owning a television. Religion can be practiced only as their leaders dictate. A man can be jailed in Afghanistan if his beard is not long enough.

The United States respects the people of Afghanistan—after all, we are currently its largest source of humanitarian aid—but we condemn the Taliban regime. It is not only repressing its own people, it is threatening people everywhere by sponsoring and sheltering and supplying terrorists. By aiding and abetting murder, the Taliban regime is committing murder.

And tonight, the United States of America makes the following demands on the Taliban: Deliver to United States authorities all the leaders of al Qaeda who hide in your land. Release all foreign nationals, including American citizens, you have unjustly imprisoned. Protect foreign journalists, diplomats and aid workers in your country. Close immediately and permanently every terrorist training camp in Afghanistan, and hand over every terrorist, and every person in their support structure, to appropriate authorities. Give the United States full access to terrorist training camps, so we can make sure they are no longer operating.

These demands are not open to negotiation or discussion. The Taliban must act, and act immediately. They will hand over the terrorists, or they will share in their fate.

I also want to speak tonight directly to Muslims throughout the world. We respect your faith. It's practiced freely by many millions of Americans, and by millions more in countries that America counts as friends. Its teachings are good and peaceful, and those who commit evil in the name of Allah blaspheme the name of Allah. The terrorists are traitors to their own faith, trying, in effect, to hijack Islam itself. The enemy of America is not our many Muslim friends; it is not our many Arab friends. Our enemy is a radical network of terrorists, and every government that supports them.

Our war on terror begins with al Qaeda, but it does not end there. It will not end until every terrorist group of global reach has been found, stopped and defeated.

Americans are asking, why do they hate us? They hate what we see right here in this chamber—a democratically elected government. Their leaders are self-appointed. They hate our freedoms—our freedom of religion, our freedom of speech, our freedom to vote and assemble and disagree with each other.

They want to overthrow existing governments in many Muslim countries, such as Egypt, Saudi Arabia, and Jordan. They want to drive Israel out of the Middle East. They want to drive Christians and Jews out of vast regions of Asia and Africa.

These terrorists kill not merely to end lives, but to disrupt and end a way of life. With every atrocity, they hope that America grows fearful, retreating from the world and forsaking our friends. They stand against us, because we stand in their way.

We are not deceived by their pretenses to piety. We have seen their kind before. They are the heirs of all the murderous ideologies of the 20th century. By sacrificing human life to serve their radical visions—by abandoning every value except the will to power—they follow in the path of fascism, and Nazism, and totalitarianism. And they will follow that path all the way, to where it ends: in history's unmarked grave of discarded lies.

Americans are asking: How will we fight and win this war? We will direct every resource at our command—every means of diplomacy, every tool of intelligence, every instrument of law enforcement, every financial influence, and every necessary weapon of war—to the disruption and to the defeat of the global terror network.

This war will not be like the war against Iraq a decade ago, with a decisive liberation of territory and a swift conclusion. It will not look like the air war above Kosovo two years ago, where no ground troops were used and not a single American was lost in combat.

Our response involves far more than instant retaliation and isolated strikes. Americans should not expect one battle, but a lengthy campaign, unlike any other we have ever seen. It may include dramatic strikes, visible on TV, and covert operations, secret even in success. We will starve terrorists of funding, turn them one against another, drive them from place to place, until there is no refuge or no rest. And we will pursue nations that provide aid or safe haven to terrorism. Every nation, in every region, now has a decision to make. Either you are with us, or you are with the terrorists. From this day forward, any nation that continues to harbor or support terrorism will be regarded by the United States as a hostile regime.

Our nation has been put on notice: We are not immune from attack. We will take defensive measures against terrorism to protect Americans. Today, dozens of federal departments and agencies, as well as state and local governments, have responsibilities affecting homeland security. These efforts must be coordinated at the highest level. So tonight I announce the creation of a Cabinet-level position reporting directly to me—the Office of Homeland Security.

And tonight I also announce a distinguished American to lead this effort, to strengthen American security: a military veteran, an effective governor, a true patriot, a trusted friend—Pennsylvania's Tom Ridge. He will lead, oversee and coordinate a comprehensive national strategy to safeguard our country against terrorism, and respond to any attacks that may come.

These measures are essential. But the only way to defeat terrorism as a threat to our way of life is to stop it, eliminate it, and destroy it where it grows.

Many will be involved in this effort, from FBI agents to intelligence operatives to the reservists we have called to active duty. All deserve our thanks, and all have our prayers. And tonight, a few miles from the damaged Pentagon, I have a message for our military: Be ready. I've called the Armed Forces to alert, and there is a reason. The hour is coming when America will act, and you will make us proud.

This is not, however, just America's fight. And what is at stake is not just America's freedom. This is the world's fight. This is civilization's fight. This is the fight of all who believe in progress and pluralism, tolerance and freedom.

We ask every nation to join us. We will ask, and we will need, the help of police forces, intelligence services, and banking systems around the world. The United States is grateful that many nations and many international organizations have already responded—with sympathy and with support. Nations from Latin America, to Asia, to Africa, to Europe, to the Islamic world. Perhaps the NATO Charter reflects best the attitude of the world: An attack on one is an attack on all.

The civilized world is rallying to America's side. They understand that if this terror goes unpunished, their own cities, their own citizens may be next. Terror, unanswered, can not only bring down buildings, it can threaten the stability of legitimate governments. And you know what—we're not going to allow it.

Americans are asking: What is expected of us? I ask you to live your lives, and hug your children. I know many citizens have fears tonight, and I ask you to be calm and resolute, even in the face of a continuing threat.

I ask you to uphold the values of America, and remember why so many have come here. We are in a fight for our principles, and our first responsibility is to live by them. No one should be singled out for unfair treatment or unkind words because of their ethnic background or religious faith.

I ask you to continue to support the victims of this tragedy with your contributions. Those who want to give can go to a central source of information, libertyunites.org, to find the names of groups providing direct help in New York, Pennsylvania, and Virginia.

The thousands of FBI agents who are now at work in this investigation may need your cooperation, and I ask you to give it.

I ask for your patience, with the delays and inconveniences that may accompany tighter security; and for your patience in what will be a long struggle.

I ask your continued participation and confidence in the American economy. Terrorists attacked a symbol of American prosperity. They did not touch its source. America is successful because of the hard work, and creativity, and enterprise of our people. These were the true strengths of our economy before September 11th, and they are our strengths today.

And, finally, please continue praying for the victims of terror and their families, for those in uniform, and for our great country. Prayer has comforted us in sorrow, and will help strengthen us for the journey ahead.

Tonight I thank my fellow Americans for what you have already done and for what you will do. And ladies and gentlemen of the Congress, I thank you, their representatives, for what you have already done and for what we will do together.

Tonight, we face new and sudden national challenges. We will come together to improve air safety, to dramatically expand the number of air marshals on domestic flights, and take new measures to prevent hijacking. We will come together to promote stability and keep our airlines flying, with direct assistance during this emergency.

We will come together to give law enforcement the additional tools it needs to track down terror here at home. We will come together to strengthen our intelligence capabilities to know the plans of terrorists before they act, and find them before they strike.

We will come together to take active steps that strengthen America's economy, and put our people back to work.

Tonight we welcome two leaders who embody the extraordinary spirit of all New Yorkers: Governor George Pataki, and Mayor Rudolph Giuliani. As a symbol of America's resolve, my administration will work with Congress, and these two leaders, to show the world that we will rebuild New York City.

After all that has just passed—all the lives taken, and all the possibilities and hopes that died with them—it is natural to wonder if America's future is one of fear. Some speak of an age of terror. I know there are struggles ahead, and dangers to face. But this country will define our times, not be defined by them. As long as the United States of America is determined and strong, this will not be an age of terror; this will be an age of liberty, here and across the world.

Great harm has been done to us. We have suffered great loss. And in our grief and anger we have found our mission and our moment. Freedom and fear are at war. The advance of human freedom—the great achievement of our time, and the great hope of every time—now depends on us. Our nation—this generation—will lift a dark threat of violence from our people and our future. We will rally the world to this cause by our efforts, by our courage. We will not tire, we will not falter, and we will not fail.

It is my hope that in the months and years ahead, life will return almost to normal. We'll go back to our lives and routines, and that is good. Even grief recedes with time and grace. But our resolve must not pass. Each of us will remember what happened that day, and to whom it happened. We'll remember the moment the news came—where we were and what we were doing. Some will remember an image of a fire, or a story of rescue. Some will carry memories of a face and a voice gone forever.

And I will carry this: It is the police shield of a man named George

Howard, who died at the World Trade Center trying to save others. It was given to me by his mom, Arlene, as a proud memorial to her son. This is my reminder of lives that ended, and a task that does not end.

I will not forget this wound to our country or those who inflicted it. I will not yield; I will not rest; I will not relent in waging this struggle for freedom and security for the American people.

The course of this conflict is not known, yet its outcome is certain. Freedom and fear, justice and cruelty, have always been at war, and we know that God is not neutral between them.

Fellow citizens, we'll meet violence with patient justice—assured of the rightness of our cause, and confident of the victories to come. In all that lies before us, may God grant us wisdom, and may He watch over the United States of America.

Thank you.

Source: "A Nation Challenged: President Bush's Address on Terrorism Before a Joint Meeting of Congress," *New York Times,* September 21, 2001, sec. B, p. 4.

6

Directory of Organizations

This chapter provides information about organizations that aim to educate about or affect national security policy. The organizations discussed here represent an array of national security issues, from direct military threats to terrorism and rogue state activities, from human rights concerns to economic, health, and environmental problems. The chapter includes a few organizations headquartered outside of the United States because they may influence U.S. decision makers, but most of the groups are U.S.-based. This is not intended to be a complete list of all groups interested in national security. The organizations are categorized into two groups: nongovernmental organizations (called NGOs) and governmental organizations. This illustrates how many groups outside of government have an impact on the national security policymaking process.

One particular type of NGO relevant to this volume are those carrying the 501(c)(3) designation under the U.S. Tax Code. These groups must spend the majority of their time in educational activities rather than in lobbying or other fund-raising. The result is that 501(c)(3) groups tend to have broader outreach to the whole community. In this chapter, some of these organizations are identified as "Educational Affiliates" to the main organizations listed here.

Tax status is a relevant issue for organizations seeking to influence the national security debate in the United States. A "corporation" (the designation under which such entities are established under the Tax Code) is considered to have "not for profit" status under Section 501(c)(3) of the U.S. Tax Code if it has an insubstantial amount of legislative activity and absolutely no political lobbying. Under such a designation, it is assumed that the corporation (organization) engages primarily in charitable, educational, religious, or scientific activities, allowing contributors to make tax deductible contributions to the corporation while allowing the corporation to be considered tax exempt for federal purposes. Other organizations in the national security field occasionally have different tax designations, such as 501(c)(6), meaning it can engage in political activities but will be taxed for such and the contributions it receives from individuals are not tax deductible to those contributors. Still a third type of organization in this chapter is the strict lobbying group, whose primary purpose is to influence the outcome of legislation or public policy by the Congress or executive branch.

Because this volume covers the period since World War II, a few organizations no longer functioning are discussed here. These are identifiable by the absence of any contact information after the title. They are included because they had a profound impact on the public policy debate and because they illustrate the transient nature of national security interests. Their role in transforming the debate has often been assumed by other organizations that are still operating.

Nongovernmental Organizations

Air Force Association
1501 Lee Highway
Arlington, VA 22209-1198
(800) 727-3337
Web site: http://www.afa.org

The Air Force Association strengthens public support for the role of the Air Force in the U.S. national security calculus. The association was established in 1946 to carry out the commitment of Colonel William "Billy" Mitchell, a father of the U.S. Air Force, to strengthening the role of air power in the military. The association has chapters across the country that enlist public support for attaining the most technologically sophisticated air force possible. The association aims to provide information that will mold public and Congressional opinion on issues related to a strong U.S. Air Force.

Publication: The association's *Air Force Magazine* appears monthly. It advertises products related to the aerospace industry, and its articles appeal to the patriotism of its members, concerned that other forces around the world may gain advantage over U.S. air power.

Educational Affiliate: The Aerospace Education Foundation is a 501(c)(3) group that works to educate youth and citizens about transformations in the aerospace field.

American Enterprise Institute for Public Policy Research
1150 Seventeenth Street, N.W.
Washington, DC 20036
(202) 862-5800
FAX: (202) 862-7178
Web site: http://www.aei.org

The American Enterprise Institute (AEI) is one of the most wide-ranging policy think tanks in the United States. Since its creation in 1943, AEI has largely focused on nurturing free markets, but its concerns also include all aspects of national security, from the role of U.S. foreign assistance to changing the trajectory of U.S. policy on China and Taiwan. AEI receives significant funding from private donors, and its membership includes many former and current practitioners of national security, particularly from the Reagan and first Bush administrations, such as Vice President Richard B. Cheney and former UN Ambassador Jeane J. Kirkpatrick. AEI has about four dozen adjunct scholars in economic and tax policy studies, international affairs, and social and political policy studies, and it holds many conferences, seminars, and meetings on national security and other concerns.

Publications: The monthly publication of the institute is the journal *American Enterprise.* AEI also produces a number of reports on various topics.

American Foreign Policy Council
1521 Sixteenth Street, N.W.
Washington, DC 20036
E-mail: afpc@afpc.org
Web site: http://www.afpc.org

The American Foreign Policy Council (AFPC) is a Washington, DC, think tank with significant interest in events in Russia, the Middle East, Central Asia, and China, as former and evolving Communist societies, that may impact U.S. national security. The AFPC's list of issues include international organized crime, chemical weapons, Sino-U.S. relations, reform in Russia, aid to the former Soviet Union, and espionage. The council makes internships available to college students and tries to connect as many people as possible to its interests.

Publications: Two major print and electronic publications from the council are the *Russia Reform Monitor* and the *China Reform Monitor,* both current assessments of events going on in these countries. AFPC also publishes the English text of major foreign affairs declarations from Russia and China. It recently began producing the *Missile Defense Briefing Report* to discuss the evolution of missile defense concerns.

American Friends Service Committee
1501 Cherry Street
Philadelphia, PA 19102
(215) 241-7500
FAX: (215) 241-7275
E-mail: afscinfo@afsc.org
Web site: http://www.afsc.org

The American Friends Service Committee (AFSC), originally a Quaker group, promotes nonviolent solutions to national security concerns. Founded as a conscientious objector organization during World War I (1917), AFSC has advocated nonviolent solutions to conflicts. The committee sponsors a variety of grassroots activities that aim to prevent the militarization of society—working both to provide conflict resolution and to prevent the need for such resolution. The committee was especially visible during the 1980s, when it was active in promoting public awareness of U.S. involvement in the Central American "dirty wars." In the post–Cold War period, AFSC has focused on ending sanctions on Iraq, since the committee finds these restrictions too hard on children, and on lessening the lure of Junior Reserve Officer Training Corps (JROTC) for youth in the United States.

Publications: AFSC publishes periodic news releases and opinion pieces in newspapers across the nation.

Amnesty International
322 Eighth Avenue
New York, NY 10001
(202) 807-8400
FAX: (202) 463-9193 or (202) 463-9292 or (202) 627-1451

E-mail: admin-us@aiusa.org
Web site: http://www.aiusa.org

Amnesty International (AI) is a worldwide organization that raises consciousness about the plight of political prisoners, based on compliance with the Universal Declaration of Human Rights. Founded in the United Kingdom in 1961, AI has local groups throughout the United States and around the world—anywhere that citizens can protest the illegal sequester of prisoners of conscience.

AI works to affect U.S. national security policy by examining existing relationships between the United States and countries in which people are held against their will and/or are tortured because of their political views. AI is also particularly critical of the death penalty in the United States. AI is a grassroots organization, supported by tax deductible donations from individuals rather than generally relying on corporate sponsorship. AI is able to exert intense international pressure on individual governments, including the United States, when they detain their citizens for political views and commit violence against civilians.

ANSER Corporation
Headquarters
2900 South Quincy Street, Suite 800
Arlington, VA 22206
(703) 416-4000 or (866) 226-5697
Web site: http://www.homelandsecurity.org

Colorado Springs Office
1250 Academy Park Loop, Suite 119
Colorado Springs, CO 80910-3707
(719) 570-4660

Fairmont Office
1000 Green River Drive, Suite 202
Fairmont, WV 26554
(304) 534-5332

Tidewater Region Office
Hampton Roads Business Center II
303 Butler Farm Road, Suite 114
Hampton, VA 23666
(757) 865-3014

ANSER, also known as Analytical Services, is a public service research institute (a federally funded research center, originally with strong Air Force ties) that has been researching relevant national and transnational topics in the security field since 1958. It has been the most forward-reaching organization in seeking to study questions of homeland security. Its separate project on that topic preceded that of the White House. ANSER holds conferences and sponsors research volumes on relevant topic areas. Along with homeland security, ANSER concentrates its efforts on studying acquisition issues in the U.S. government.

Publications: ANSER publishes books, papers, and reports, specializing in chemical warfare and homeland security, e.g., the Homeland Security Newsletter, available on-line.

Armed Forces Communications and Electronics Association
4400 Fair Lakes Court
Fairfax, VA 22033-3899
(800) 336-4583 or (703) 631-6100
E-mail: webmaster@afcea.org
Web site: http://www.afcea.org

AFCEA Educational Foundation
(703) 631-6149
E-mail: scholarship@afcea.org

The Armed Forces Communications and Electronics Association (AFCEA) is technically oriented with an increasingly important link to the intelligence community and the armed forces. It is a national and an international organization, with chapters throughout the United States and in several other countries, and it has major ties to the communications, intelligence, and defense industries. A major function of the group is to promote educational activities that will link the new practitioner, such as a college graduate, with the existing professional community in either communications or intelligence. AFCEA holds an annual conference together with the Naval Institute of the United States.

Publications: AFCEA produces studies on various issues in intelligence, cyberwar, and national defense applications. These are published either as reports or as monographs. *SIGNAL* is the association's primary publication, focusing on the links with and the issues relating to intelligence, electronics, and the armed forces.

Educational Affiliate: The educational arm of AFCEA is the

AFCEA Educational Foundation, which provides educational materials and scholarships to potential professionals in fields relating to communications, electronics, and intelligence.

Arms Control Association
1726 M Street, N.W., Suite 201
Washington, DC 20036
(202) 463-8270
FAX: (202) 463-8273
E-mail: aca@armscontrol.org

The Arms Control Association (ACA) is an outgrowth of grassroots concerns about nuclear arms proliferation in the early 1970s. ACA has long had a significant public outreach/educational function, aimed at clarifying the role of arms control in enhancing U.S. national security, and it holds press conferences, meetings, and public policy debates to raise public awareness of the problems facing arms control efforts and to question the existing public policy trajectory. The Herbert Scoville Fellowship is a particularly prestigious opportunity for graduate students to work in the arms control field under the financial auspices of ACA.

Publications: ACA publishes *Arms Control Today,* a monthly journal discussing issues of concern to the membership. The association has also published a number of monographs on arms control topics.

Atlantic Council of the United States
910 17th Street, N.W., Suite 1000
Washington, DC 20006
(202) 778-4961
FAX: (202) 463-7241
E-mail: info@acus.org
Web site: http://www.acus.org

The Atlantic Council of the United States (AC) began in the 1950s as an educational organization aiming to enhance public understanding of the ties between NATO member states. Although it has broadened its interests over five decades to include issues of national security in Asia (particularly China), Cuba, and elsewhere, the AC retains its primary focus on European concerns and most people on its board of directors are experienced in European affairs. The AC holds many conferences, symposia, and studies on relevant concerns. For example, it was one of the first groups to evaluate what would be necessary to normalize relations with Cuba once the United States decided to do so.

Publications: The council publishes the *Atlantic Council News* and *Atlantic Council Policy Papers* to highlight policy recommendations and options available to the United States.

British American Security Information Council
1012 Fourteenth Street, N.W., Suite 900
Washington, DC 20005
(202) 347-8340
FAX: (202) 347-4688
E-mail: basicus@basicint.org
Web site: http://www.basicint.org

The British American Security Information Council (BASIC), with offices in Washington and London, serves as a repository for information on weapons systems and other major issues relating to the international security environment. In particular, BASIC has had a major role in promoting international examination of "light arms" sales and the questions that surround the transparency of these sales. BASIC holds conferences and promotes linkages across the Atlantic among activists in this field.

Brookings Institution
1775 Massachusetts Avenue, N.W.
Washington, DC 20036
(202) 797-6000
FAX: (202) 797-6004
E-mail: brookinfo@brook.edu
Web site: http://www.brook.edu

The Brookings Institution was founded during World War I and is most often associated with Democratic administrations in Washington. It is one of the widest-ranging and most inclusive think tanks in the United States, with a significant portion of its work dedicated to national security issues from a variety of perspectives. Brookings has a wide array of policy analysts who consider questions in economics, political science, international relations, and other social science fields from a variety of perspectives. Programs at the Brookings Institution that concentrate on national security issues include the National Security Council Project, the Center for Northeast Asian Policy Studies, and the

Center on the United States and France, along with dedicated research projects on the Balkans, the Middle East, internally displaced persons (domestic political refugees), world health issues, and national missile defense. Brookings also has large research concentrations in governmental studies and economic studies.

Publications: The Brookings Institution has one of the most prestigious public policy presses in the world. It produces high-quality, up-to-date, and easily accessible work in a number of fields. The Brookings Press publishes several books each month; they can be ordered by phone, mail, or the Internet.

Business Executives for National Security
1717 Pennsylvania Avenue, N.W., Suite 350
Washington, DC   20006-4620
(202) 296-2125
FAX: (202) 296-2490
Web site: http://www.bens.org

The mission of Business Executives for National Security (BENS) is to bring the streamlining practices of business to the complex activities of national security. BENS attempts to raise public policy issues that relate to overall defense rather than some sort of partisan view of one budget allocation or another. Its members are some of the most prominent individuals in the business field, such as Jeff Bezos of Amazon.com, as well as in the defense industries, such as Norman Augustine of Martin-Marietta.

Recent BENS publications have focused on the budget process within the Pentagon along with the future of intelligence and the business community. BENS produces studies through its internal committees and other member groups. Its work ties the professions of its members directly to the group's overall mission of improving understanding between the national security and business fields.

Carnegie Endowment for International Peace
1779 Massachusetts Avenue, N.W.
Washington, DC 20036-2103
(202) 483-7600
FAX: (202) 483-1840
E-mail: info@ceip.org
Web site: http://www.ceip.org

The Carnegie Endowment for International Peace (CEIP) is one of the largest and wealthiest research organizations in the world.

Started at the beginning of the twentieth century by steel magnate Andrew Carnegie, the endowment has become one of the best-funded research facilities in the world. Founded with the noble goal of ending war, CEIP was challenged by the conflagration of World War I, which both undercut its goals and revealed its ultimate purpose: "advancing cooperation between nations and promoting active international engagement by the United States." Its founding coincided with the expansion of and hope for the role of international law in conflict resolution—hence the endowment's historic commitment to that field of study. The CEIP has expanded its concerns into other areas of national security, including a long-term project on nuclear nonproliferation and other discussions of current and emerging issues.

Publications: The CEIP has been the originator and publisher of the influential public policy journal *Foreign Policy,* founded in 1970 as the counter to the "establishment" journal *Foreign Affairs.* The endowment also produces a number of policy statements.

CATO Institute
1000 Massachusetts Avenue, N.W.
Washington, DC 20001-5403
(202) 842-0200
FAX: (202) 842-3490
E-mail: cklein@CATO.org
Web site: http://www.CATO.org

The CATO Institute is one of the most distinctive think tanks in the national security field because of its decidedly minimalist approach. Simply put, as an avowedly libertarian body, CATO believes in doing less; CATO's position is that the United States should take on as few national security commitments as possible and should act to protect national security only when U.S. territory is directly threatened. Thus, in CATO's view, most concern about protecting allies or credibility and expanding alliances or international commitments is misguided and unnecessary. CATO instead prefers extremely limited, defined national security responsibilities. The United States does not really require superpower status, in the organization's view. In evaluating national security concerns, CATO looks at a range of issues such as missile defense, military procurement and preparedness, and terrorism, all under the rubric of defense studies, and also focuses on various areas of the world in its foreign studies program.

Publications: CATO produces a wide range of print and online publications in book and shorter forms, such as its widely read *Policy Analysis* series. It also has audio and video cassettes on certain issues. The *CATO Journal* is a periodic journal.

Center for Defense Information
1779 Massachusetts Avenue, N.W.
Washington, DC 20036
(202) 332-0600
FAX: (202) 462-4559
E-mail: Info@cdi.org
Web site: http://www.cdi.org

The Center for Defense Information (CDI) has had a noteworthy position among groups dedicated to national security studies because it has questioned the basic assumptions used in the national security calculation and because many of the people on the CDI staff have extensive military backgrounds. The two directors of CDI for the turbulent 1970s and 1980s, for example, were retired U.S. Navy rear admirals. The current president is a highly respected academician, and the vice president and director of research are former high-ranking navy and army officers.

The CDI does not take federal contract money but is completely supported by private citizen subscriptions. The center's areas of concern include Russia, China, military reform, national missile defense, and other timely concerns.

Publications: The CDI produces the weekly publication *Defense Monitor*, a four-page assessment on pressing defense topics, and it also publishes the *CDI Military Almanac*. The center produces a weekly television program, *America's Defense Monitor*, transcripts of which are published on-line. The CDI also produces an extensive list of policy briefings on-line and offers a long list of video products.

Center for Economic Conversion
222 View Street
Mountain View, CA 94041
(650) 968-8798
FAX: (650) 968-1126
E-mail: cec@igc.org
Web site: http://www.conversion.org

The Center for Economic Conversion (CEC) started in 1975 as part of the American Friends Service Committee (see p. 209), but it became independent as a not-for-profit educational institution three years later. The CEC seeks to educate the public about strategies for meeting social needs and protecting the environment by pulling national resources away from military uses. It holds a wide array of presentations and programs to support sustainable environmental practices while deemphasizing military threats to the world community. It has a large on-line list of related links, and its internships serve to augment its Green Base Conversion program, which attempts to influence military base conversion, and its Sustainable Economics Curriculum, which introduces the concept of sustainability into high school economics courses.

Center for International Policy
1775 Massachusetts Avenue, N.W.
Suite 550
Washington, DC 20036
(202) 232-3317
FAX: (202) 232-3440
E-mail: cip@ciponline.org
Web site: http://www.us.net/cip

The Center for International Policy began in 1975 as an organization aiming to research and discuss the international security horizon within a framework of basic human rights. Its work today focuses on Colombia, Haiti, Latin American demilitarization, African demilitarization, and changing policy on Cuba. It is harshly critical of policies that it believes continue the exploitation of citizens around the world. It engages in the public policy debate through editorial writing and internships for college and graduate students.

Publications: The *International Policy Report* is the center's primary publication for encouraging public policy debate. Most issues are available in hard copy or on-line.

Center for International Security and Cooperation
Encina Hall
Stanford, CA 94305-6165
(605) 723-9635
FAX: (605) 724-5683
E-mail: aevdemon@stanford.edu
Web site: cisac.stanford.edu/global

Formerly known as the Center for International Security and Arms Control, the Center for International Security and Cooperation is part of Stanford University's Institute for International Security, which considers various areas of international concern. The center has eleven areas of focus, including Asia, nuclear weapons, Russia, and ethnic conflict. The center publishes its results and offers scholars the opportunity to work on their projects at the Stanford campus.

Publications: The center produces the on-line *CISAC Monitor* three times a year and publishes the work of scholars sponsored by the center.

Center for Naval Analyses
4825 Mark Center Drive
Alexandria, VA 22311-1850
(703) 824-2000
FAX: (703) 824-2949
E-mail: inquiries@cna.org
Web site: http://www.cna.org

The Center for Naval Analyses (CNA) was founded in 1942, along with the Rand Corporation. It is a federally funded research and development facility (FFRDC), but it conducts independent research and analysis for the Department of the Navy. The CNA focuses on Navy and Marine issues, but it is also able to look at a wide range of subjects for other organizations because of the strong analytical skills of its staff. For example, CNA is presently looking at all the options available to the U.S. Navy when it fulfills President George W. Bush's commitment to close the Vieques bombing site in Puerto Rico. Although much of the center's focus is on naval activities, in the 1990s it established the Center for Strategic Studies to consider evolving threats from various regions of the world that might not have been the focus of the Department of the Navy's concerns in the past.

Publications: Because of its wide-ranging interests, CNA is a particularly active publisher of works on national security issues. Most of these publications are short, timely reports issued to stimulate discussion on a particular issue, but the center also publishes extended reports resulting from its many conferences and seminars. Most of its public, unclassified research is available through the National Technical Information Service (see p. 273) or the Defense Technical Information Center (see p. 266).

Center for Security Policy
1920 L Street, N.W., Suite 210
Washington, DC 20036
(202) 835-9077
FAX: (202) 835-9066
E-mail: info@security-policy.org
Web site: http://www.security-policy.org

Founded in 1988 by Frank Gaffney, a prominent figure in the Reagan administration's strategy on arms control and stopping Soviet expansionism in the 1980s, the Center for Security Policy (CSP) is an active forum for discussing the trade, technology, defense, and security issues that confront the United States because of changes in the international community. The CSP has a small internship program to complement its small staff, but for the most part it relies on the exceptionally prominent conservative members of its Board of Advisors, such as Gaffney, who bring notoriety to the center because of their passionate views, which are similar to those held by the Reagan administration in the 1980s.

The most pressing issues of interest to CSP include the enduring threat posed by Russia, the need for missile defense, the role of the Palestinians in promoting world terrorism and violence, the threats posed by conditions in Panama, Cuba, and Haiti, and various other special concerns. The William Casey Institute is a recent creation within CSP that brings business and international policymakers together to understand the complexity of the evolving international environment. Under its auspices, two international symposia are held annually (in New York and Washington, DC) to discuss the "nexus" of interests between the business and policy communities on these topics.

Publications: The CSP specializes in real-time press releases on the issues it considers to be ignored by the mainstream think tanks and media outlets. Decision briefs, press releases, and *Casey Institute Perspectives* are the main mediums by which CSP disperses its policy positions.

Center for Strategic and International Studies
1800 K Street, N.W.
Washington, DC 20006
(202) 887-0200
FAX: (202) 775-3199

E-mail: webmaster@csis.org
Web site: http://www.csis.org

The Center for Strategic and International Studies (CSIS) is probably the most visible international affairs think tank in the United States today. Its programs are extensive, and the center has rich resources for pursuing new work. Begun in the mid-1960s as a research arm of the American Enterprise Institute for Public Policy Research (see p. 209), CSIS has long since outpaced the other "younger" think tanks in the nation's capital. It has one of the most prestigious boards of directors of any think tank in the nation, with all the former presidential administrations represented at some point in its history. The work of CSIS reaches not only former public officials, but also academics, retired military officers, and a variety of other professionals. CSIS may be the most widely quoted think tank in the national security community.

Additionally, CSIS involves many individuals in advisory capacities as counselors to the organization and to individual projects. CSIS conducts regional studies in Africa, Latin America, Western Europe, the former Soviet Union, and Asia, and it focuses on various functional topics, such as energy, the environment, the effects of the 1973–1974 petroleum embargo, which it was the first group to examine, and the debate on arms control and weapons proliferation. Additionally, CSIS provides a large number of public analysts to policy-related talk shows and for public outreach. It produces a *Directory of Specialists*, which is unparalleled in its coverage of all of these areas, and it makes certain its speakers are widely utilized.

Publications: The CSIS has an exhaustive list of publications. Its most prestigious product is the *Washington Quarterly*, a journal with a wide public-policy reach that has long been one of the two or three most important journals in the public U.S. national security debate, especially on the Middle East and on terrorism.

Centre for Counterintelligence and Security Studies
5650 General Washington Drive
Alexandria, VA 22312
(703) 642-6340
FAX: (703) 642-7451
E-mail: ci@cicentre.com
Web site: http://cicentre.com

The Centre for Counterintelligence and Security Studies (CI Centre) is dedicated to educating U.S. citizens about the role of counterintelligence and its value to various private and public sector activities. The CI Centre is more active than scholarly, with a significant portion of its work done through classes and short seminars on security issues. It offers eighteen courses, examining issues such as "Targeting of America by Adversaries" and "Overview of Chinese Intelligence Targeting of America."

Publications: The CI Centre produces course materials for its educational work but does not publish many individual monographs or periodic reports. Its Web site, however, does have extensive and impressive links to other national security sites, particularly those related to intelligence.

Chicago Council on Foreign Relations
116 South Michigan Avenue, 10th Floor
Chicago, IL 60603-6097
(312) 726-3860
FAX: (312) 726-4491
Web site: http://www.ccfr.org

The Chicago Council on Foreign Relations (CCFR) is part of a U.S. network of organizations known as the Foreign Policy Association (see p. 229), and it is by the far the largest and most prestigious, dating back to 1922. It conducts many educational programs, some directed at specialists, others at educators in the Midwest, and still others at interested citizens. It tries to make access to the national security debate as open as possible to all citizens who may want to know about a particular issue. Most of CCFR's work is done through public addresses, and its Web site includes a page that carries speeches and addresses offered by CCFR-sponsored specialists. The list of activities hosted by CCFR is as vast as any in the country, with several major events each week by speakers such as former Secretary of State Madeleine Albright, former Chancellor of West Germany Helmut Schmidt, prominent academics, and other knowledgeable speakers.

Publications: CCFR's publications include a series of analyses of U.S. public opinion authored by John Reilly and based on CCFR polling information.

Coalition to Reduce Nuclear Danger
110 Maryland Avenue, N.E., Suite 505

Washington, DC 20002
(202) 546-0795
FAX: (202) 546-7970
E-mail: coalition@clw.org
Web site: http://www.clw.org/coalition

The Coalition to Reduce Nuclear Danger (CRND) began in 1995 as a coalition of fourteen antinuclear groups that worked to diminish the number of nuclear weapons and to oppose antiballistic missile defenses. These organizations include 20/20 Vision, the Natural Resources Defense Council (see p. 248), the Arms Control Association (see p. 213), the British American Security Information Council (see p. 214), the Council for a Livable World Education Fund (see p. 225), the Federation of American Scientists (see p. 228), the Institute for Science and International Security (see p. 239), the International Center, Lawyers Alliance for Nuclear Security, Physicians for Social Responsibility (see p. 243), the Union of Concerned Scientists (see p. 256), the Public Education Center, and Women's Actions for New Directions (see p. 261). The coalition uses the expertise of its members to develop a national program and an international coalition to eliminate nuclear threats.

Publications: The CRND maintains an Internet library on issues relating to its concerns. Its activities in promoting the Comprehensive Test Ban Treaty are an excellent example of its work (see the Comprehensive Test Ban Treaty Web site at http://www.clw.org/coalition/ctbindex.htm).

Cold War International History Project
The Woodrow Wilson Center
One Woodrow Wilson Plaza
1300 Pennsylvania Avenue, N.W.
Washington, DC 20004-3027
(202) 691-4110
FAX: (202) 691-4184
E-mail: coldwar1@wwic.si.edu
Web site: http://cwihp.si.edu/default.htm

The Cold War International History Project, begun with a John and Catherine T. MacArthur Foundation grant in 1991, has been a crucial source of information about the Soviet Union and the entire period of the Cold War. The project gathers, translates, and provides commentary on the huge amount of Cold War documentation that has become available in recent years. Its work is available in both print and electronic versions.

Committee in Solidarity with the People of El Salvador

During the 1980s, as the conflict in Central America became a more heated topic in the United States, one of the most vocal grassroots organizations to oppose U.S. involvement was the Committee in Solidarity with the People of El Salvador (CISPES). This group, with chapters at many university and college campuses, had support in communities across the country and argued vociferously that the United States was only exacerbating the conflict. During the Reagan and George H. W. Bush administrations, CISPES was seen by those who supported administration policies as being a "front" organization for Communist subversion in the United States. CISPES conducted rallies, sit-ins, and other activities to protest the U.S. militarization of the conflict, but the organization began to lose its steam in the early 1990s, when the conflict began to subside and the U.S. role was diminished.

Committee on the Present Danger

An organization called the Committee on the Present Danger (CPD) existed as early as 1950, when several individuals believed that the United States inadequately understood the Soviet threat against the West after World War II. A second organization with the same name but no formal links to the 1950s group became prominent during the 1970s and 1980s. This group voiced views that had been identified with the CPD in the 1950s, but it became more public and prominent than its namesake, charging that President Carter's defense plans were inadequate in the face of the escalating Soviet threat. Former arms control negotiator Paul Nitze, editor of *Commentary* magazine Norman Podhoretz, author Midge Decter, and former U.S. Ambassador to the United Nations Jeane J. Kirkpatrick have all been identified with CPD. The committee was influential in creating the "Team B" analytical approach to the Soviet Union in the late 1970s, arguing that the CIA was too soft in its evaluation of the Soviet threat.

Council for a Livable World
110 Maryland Avenue, N.E.
Washington, DC 20002
(202) 546-0795
FAX: (202) 546-5142
E-mail: clw@clw.org
Web site: http://www.clw.org

The Council for a Livable World (CLW) and its two components, the Council for a Livable World Education Fund and PeacePac, are interested in stemming the spread and possible use of weapons of mass destruction (WMD) against people around the world. The CLW and PeacePac actively lobby to promote arms control and to prevent ballistic missile defense development and other activities that may increase the likelihood of WMD use. The CLW began in 1962.

Publications: CLW publications, most of which are available at no cost, cover a wide range of national security questions such as ballistic missile defense, military spending, arms control options, and spent fuel disposal. Much of the council's work is available on-line at its Web site.

Educational Affiliate: The 501(c)(3) organization associated with the CLW is the Council for a Livable World Education Fund. This fund attempts to raise consciousness in schools and community organizations about arms control and ballistic missile issues.

Council on Foreign Relations
Washington Office
1779 Massachusetts Avenue, N.W.
Washington, DC 20036
(202) 518-3400
FAX: (202) 986-2984
E-mail: communications@cfr.org
Web site: http://www.cfr.org

New York Office
The Harold Pratt House
58 East 68th Street
New York, NY 10021
(212) 434-9400
FAX: (212) 434-9800

Created after World War I (in 1921), in the period of greatest optimism regarding the use of education to stem international conflict, the Council on Foreign Relations (CFR) is considered by many groups, on both the political right and left, to be the "establishment" organization in national security affairs. It differs significantly from the Foreign Policy Association (see p. 229) and many other groups discussed in this chapter in that CFR membership requires nomination and acceptance rather than voluntary subscription. Its membership, as a result, is more selective and tends to be wealthier. However, CFR proudly notes that it does not have any particular policy orientation or partisan role in any debate, seeking instead to promote solid, open, wide-ranging discussion of the national security concerns of the nation today and into the future.

The council holds meetings nearly every day in either New York or Washington, DC. These events may be lectures by prominent academics or policymakers from the United States or by former chiefs of state from other countries. The CFR has internships for younger individuals and fellowships for professionals interested in reorienting their career paths, including military officers.

Publications: The most prominent journal on national security over the past seven decades has been the CFR-published *Foreign Affairs,* which now includes a Spanish-language edition. The CFR also publishes reports of its meetings in a shorter form, and produces monographs on prominent topics by its members.

Council on Hemispheric Affairs
1444 I Street, N.W., Suite 211
Washington, DC 20005
(202) 216-9261
FAX: (202) 216-9193
E-mail: coha@coha.org
Web site: http://www.coha.org

The Council on Hemispheric Affairs (COHA) was established in 1975 to educate the public about the U.S. role in Latin American affairs, a focus that was broadened seven years later to include Caribbean and Canadian issues. With its extensive links to the religious community, trade unions, and other groups concerned about living conditions and labor issues in the region, COHA is actively involved in the same issues today that concerned it a quarter century ago. Its staff speaks at major media outlets and public events to raise attention to violence and to socioeconomic conditions in the region. COHA has argued against the expansion of conflict in Colombia and the use of neoliberal economic reforms to alter Latin American societies, and it has other policy suggestions particular to this region and the U.S. role. Its Web site links users to other organizations around the country and the world. COHA also offers Washington, DC, internships to students.

Defense Orientation Conference Association
9271 Old Keene Mill Drive
Burke, VA 22015-4202
(703) 451-1200
E-mail: info@doca.org
Web site: www.doca.org

The Defense Orientation Conference Association (DOCA) began in 1952, aiming for greater nationwide coordination among people who are interested in defense issues. To educate interested people about national security issues and improve links between the defense community and private citizens, DOCA holds national/ regional conferences and creates opportunities to see military installations and talk to defense experts across the country.

East-West Center
1601 East-West Road
Honolulu, HI 96849-1601
(808) 944-7111
FAX: (808) 944-7376
E-mail: ewcinfo@EastWestCenter.org
Web sites: http://www.EastWestCenter.org;
http://www.ewc.hawaii.edu

The East-West Center, housed at the Manoa campus of the University of Hawaii, is a major research facility created by the U.S. Congress in 1960 that receives funding from both the U.S. government and Asian governments, as well as private agencies, corporations, and individuals. Its mission is to inquire into issues of interest to the United States as it looks across the Pacific Ocean. The center takes three major approaches to its task. First, it has a large number of research areas, largely in "transnational issues" that affect the whole area, such as population, the environment, and economic issues. Second, it educates teachers working in the area. Finally, the center holds many public seminars on varied topics relating to the Pacific basin. The result is a well-balanced, broad approach to the East-West relationship.

Ethics and Public Policy Center
1015 Fifteenth Street, N.W., Suite 900
Washington, DC 20005
(202) 682-1200
FAX: (202) 408-0632
E-mail: ethics@eppc.org
Web site: http://www.eppc.org

The Ethics and Public Policy Center (EPPC) was established under Dr. Ernest LeFever in 1976 to link domestic issues with foreign policy concerns in light of an ethical and religious orientation. The organization has an explicit concern for the "Judeo-Christian values of Western culture." The EPPC identifies three primary interests: law and religion; religion, culture, and society; and foreign affairs. It seeks to promote less government intervention in the United States while promoting greater access to human rights and freedoms in other areas of the world. EPPC originally concerned itself with the former Soviet Union, but it has become increasingly concerned about religious freedom in China and other countries under dictatorial regimes.

  Publications: The center publishes a number of books and a quarterly newsletter. It also publishes the "Center Conversations" series, which are transcripts of various seminars, and it issues periodic commentaries on interesting topics under the title "American Purpose."

Federation of American Scientists
1717 K Street, N.W., Suite 209
Washington, DC 20036
(202) 546-3300
FAX: (202) 675-1010
E-mail: fas@fas.org
Web site: http://www.fas.org

The Federation of American Scientists (FAS), one of the older organizations listed in this chapter, was begun by engineers, mathematicians, and other participants in the Manhattan Project, which created the first atomic weapon in 1945. The FAS has been concerned with the use of atomic weapons, lobbying strongly against their use as a "normal" weapon in war. Many of the Nobel Prize winners of the post–World War II period, such as Hans Bethe, Linus Pauling, and social scientist Kenneth Arrow, have been affiliated with FAS. Indeed, the FAS remains somewhat unique among the organizations in this chapter because of the high percentage of "pure scientists" in its membership.

More recently, FAS has worked fervently against the Strategic Defense Initiative of the Reagan administration and the subsequent Ballistic Missile Defense proposal. It has long had ties to the "antimilitary" wing of the Democratic Party.

Foreign Policy Association
470 Park Avenue
New York, NY 10016
(212) 481-8100
Web site: http://www.fpa.org

The Foreign Policy Association (FPA), one of the largest national security interest groups in the United States, aims to educate the public about the complexity and variety of issues in national security and foreign affairs. The FPA began in 1918 as an educational voice during the period of debate over President Woodrow Wilson's Fourteen Points. Originally named the Committee on Nothing at All, it evolved to the League of Free Nations in November 1918, assuming its current title five years later. The association is headquartered in New York, and it has smaller subgroups in nearly all medium and large cities in the United States.

Publications: The FPA is renowned for its Great Decisions Series, which introduces many high school and undergraduate students to some of the pressing national security issues of the day. Written in a most accessible style with attractive, easily understood graphics, the series presents a balanced summary of these topics.

Foreign Policy Research Institute
1528 Walnut Street, Suite 610
Philadelphia, PA 19102
(215) 732-3774
FAX: (215) 732-4401
E-mail: FPRI@fpri.org
Web site: http://www.fpri.org

Created in 1955 as an educational, nonpartisan institute focused on international affairs, the Foreign Policy Research Institute (FPRI) offers wide-ranging publications on foreign affairs, conferences focusing on particular topics, student internships, and opportunities for teachers to learn much more about complex issues. FPRI is best known for its projects on East Asia (particularly China), South Asia, the Middle East, defense questions, and the broad question of U.S. responsibility to uphold our culture in the world.

Publications: FPRI has published the journal *Orbis* since its inauguration in 1957. About once a week it also publishes *FPRI Bulletins* on timely questions.

Fund for Peace
Washington Office
1701 K Street, N.W., 11th Floor
Washington, DC 20006
(202) 223-7940
FAX: (202) 223-7947
E-mail: comments@fundforpeace.org
Web site: http://www.fundforpeace.org

San Francisco Office
500 Howard Street, Suite 206
San Francisco, CA 94105
(415) 974-1898
FAX: (415) 543-8311

The Fund for Peace (FP) has a relatively simple mission: "to prevent war and to alleviate the conditions that cause war" through education and research that provides practical research that incorporates the principles of constitutional democracy. FP programs center on arms control, conflict resolution, internal war, and human rights. Among its programs is the Institute for the Study of World Politics, which since 1972 has allowed senior fellows to work on particular topics relevant to the fund's core interests. FP has internships and offers a range of programs providing public education on alternate approaches to resolving and preventing conflict. One notable aspect of the fund is the prominent representation by women on its governing board. The FP Web site provides numerous links to other national security Web sites.

Globalsecurity.org
300 North Washington Street, B-100
Alexandria, VA 22314
(703) 548-2700
FAX: (703) 548-2424
E-mail: info@globalsecurity.org
Web site: http://www.globalsecurity.org

Globalsecurity.org is a small, relatively new organization, established by former Federation of American Scientists (see p. 228) expert John Pike, that seeks to find new approaches to the international security environment, with an emphasis on reducing the number of nuclear weapons. Globalsecurity.org uses the Internet to make its concerns and policy suggestions accessible to policymakers, scholars, the public, and others who may be willing to endorse and encourage its positions. These positions include preventing the development of antimissile systems, curbing nuclear proliferation, deemphasizing nuclear weapons, and examining other means of achieving cooperative international security. Globalsecurity.org does this through analysis and Web-based products.

Publications: Globalsecurity.org provides on-line analysis and publishes various reports that analyze relevant, narrow topics that are not covered elsewhere but that relate to the organization's overall agenda. It also tries to disseminate primary documentation and other original materials, but much of the library section of the Web site is still under construction.

Greenpeace USA
702 H Street, N.W., Suite 300
Washington, DC 20001
(800) 326-0959
FAX: (202) 462-4507
E-mail: info@greenpeace.org
Web site: http://www.greenpeaceusa.org

Greenpeace USA is a small component of the international organization Greenpeace, which seeks to change the orientation of global affairs in a significant way. Greenpeace is probably best known as the environmental group that made headlines in the 1980s, when its vessel *Rainbow Warrior* appeared at South Pacific nuclear test sites to prevent tests. Greenpeace retains a strong focus on environmental warming and destruction but is also concerned about what it believes are threats to democracy and other public policy questions. It tries to retain a grassroots connection by recruiting activists and obtaining funding through the subscription method.

Publications: Greenpeace publishes many reports and fact sheets, most of which are available on-line. These focus on the group's environmental concerns rather than on the traditional national security concerns of most groups listed in this chapter.

Heritage Foundation
214 Massachusetts Avenue, N.W.
Washington, DC 20002
(202) 546-4400
FAX: (202) 546-8328
Web site: http://www.heritage.org

The Heritage Foundation, founded in 1973, is one of the best-funded, most prominent national security groups in the United States. It does not accept governmental funding, but it does have financial bases in corporate sponsorship and public subscriptions. The foundation identifies its core international issues as Africa, arms control/missile defense issues, Asia and the Pacific, Europe, international organizations, Latin America, the Middle East, national security, and trade/foreign aid. Although its interests are wide ranging, the Heritage Foundation is best known for its national security focus and for its support of positions that enhance U.S. power projection in the world.

Each program is well developed and is organized to promote education as well as general outreach. Several particular divisions within the foundation focus on national security from different angles. The Kathryn and Shelby Cullom Davis Institute for International Studies includes the Center for International Trade and Economics, the Asian Studies Center, and the Washington Roundtable for Asia-Pacific Press. The B. Kenneth Simons Center for Latin American Affairs is another national security group within the Heritage Foundation. Almost every day, one can find a program sponsored by the foundation, ranging from timely speeches by prominent figures in the policy debate to panel discussions, longer seminars, and other types of research and exchanges of ideas.

Publications: The Heritage Foundation publishes monographs on issues such as national missile defense and economic change in Latin America. It also issues "Backgrounders," "Heritage Reports," "Heritage Memoranda," and "Heritage Lectures," each presented in a slightly different format to reach a different target audience. These publications include summaries of speeches, analyses of pressing national security questions, and information that prepares the public for public policy debate. The foundation also publishes *Policy Review,* a bimonthly consideration of timely concerns.

High Frontier
2800 Shirlington Road, Suite 405
Arlington, VA 22206
(703) 671-4111
FAX: (703) 931-6432
E-mail: high.frontier@verizon.net
Web site: http://www.highfrontier.org

Since President Ronald Reagan first advocated space-based weapons in March 1983, High Frontier (HF) has been actively encouraging the United States to select a ballistic missile defense system and to develop weapons in outer space rather than on Earth. The organization, headed by retired General Daniel Graham, advocates this approach as a far more realistic method for keeping any U.S. adversaries from hurting the U.S. population or threatening the U.S. homeland.

Hoover Institution on War, Revolution and Peace
Stanford University
Stanford, CA 94305-6010
(650) 723-1754 or (877) 466-8374
FAX: (650) 723-1687
E-mail: horaney@hoover.stanford.edu
Web site: www-hoover.stanford.edu

The Hoover Institution on War, Revolution and Peace was founded in 1919 by Stanford benefactor and eventual President of the United States Herbert Hoover to study the issues that had led to World War I. The institution eventually became part of Stanford University, where it continues to provide education to the general public in issues relating to free societies where national security is considered a traditional notion, particularly through the National Security Forum (with a special focus on China), the Transition to Democratic Capitalism program, and the International Rivalries and Global Cooperation program. With its rich endowment, the Hoover Institution is able to invite some of the finest scholars to work at the Palo Alto facility.

Publications: Hoover scholars produce dozens of books and articles, along with hundreds of opinion essays, for public debate each year. Additionally, Hoover produces the *Hoover Digest* and *Weekly Essays* on germane and current topics of public debate. Many of the institute's publications are available on its Web site.

Hudson Institute
Indianapolis Office
5395 Emerson Way
Indianapolis, IN 46226-1475
(317) 545-1000
FAX: (317) 545-9639
Web site: http://www.hudson.org

Washington Office
1015 Eighteenth Street, N.W., Suite 300
Washington, DC 20036
(202) 223-7770
FAX: (202) 223-8537

The Hudson Institute began in New York City in 1961 with the unorthodox views of Herman Kahn, Max Singer, and Oscar Ruebhausen on how to solve long-term problems of national security and international relations. The institute moved its headquarters to Indianapolis in 1984, and it maintains numerous satellite offices across the country. It concerns itself with every aspect of public policy, including military strategy and national security, Russian/European studies, and trade. To conduct ongoing studies on specific issues, the Hudson Institute maintains two centers, one on Central Europe and Eurasian affairs and one on global food issues. It holds many long, in-depth conferences that allow specialists to get beyond superficial discussion into more substance. The institute offers internships to students and tries to engage the community in its work as much as possible.

Publications: The Hudson Institute produces a variety of materials. *Hudson Reflections* are editorials on specific issues. *Foresight,* formerly known as *Hudson Policy Bulletins,* collects op-eds on one topic into a single volume. Each issue of *Outlook* is a sixteen-page analysis of a subject. *Visions* is a quarterly piece on the institute and its scholars, and *American Outlook* is a bimonthly publication providing in-depth coverage of a couple of topics by Hudson scholars. Hudson authors also write many monographs.

Human Rights Watch
New York Office
350 Fifth Avenue, 34th floor
New York, NY 10118-3299
(212) 290-4700
FAX: (212) 736-1300
E-mail: hrwnyc@hrw.org

Washington Office
1630 Connecticut Avenue, N.W., Suite 500
Washington, DC 20009
(202) 612-4321
FAX: (202) 612-4333
E-mail: hrwdc@hrw.org

Los Angeles Office
11500 West Olympic Boulevard, Suite 445
Los Angeles, CA 90064
(310) 477-5540
FAX: (310) 477-4622
E-mail: hrwla@hrw.org

San Francisco Office
312 Sutter Street, Suite 407
San Francisco, CA 94108
(415) 362-3250
FAX: (415) 362-3255
E-mail: hrwsf@hrw.org
Web site: http://www.hrw.org

Human Rights Watch (HRW) is a global campaign to focus attention on human rights and to increase respect for these rights throughout the world. With four offices in the United States, HRW is an important presence, raising concern about the proliferation of violence and about inequalities in economic and social rights. Its activities include educational events, programs to motivate people to work with their elected governments to improve conditions around the world, and support for global justice in whatever ways are possible. HRW conducts campaigns in all areas of the world, as well as specific campaigns aimed at specific issues, such as refugees, prison reform, and arms proliferation.

Publications: In both print and electronic formats, HRW publishes reports on its area and subject campaigns (e.g., Colombia, land mines, children as soldiers). Additionally, it holds an annual international film festival to call attention to human rights conditions. Its *Human Rights Annual Report* always receives much attention for its nonpartisan, comprehensive treatment of this issue around the world.

Institute for Contemporary Studies
Latham Square
1611 Telegraph Avenue, Suite 902
Oakland, CA 94612
(510) 238-5010
FAX: (510) 238-8440
E-mail: mail@icspress.com
Web site: http://www.icspress.com/

The Institute for Contemporary Studies (ICS) was established in 1974 to promote entrepreneurship and self-governance. It espouses reduced government involvement in national security. Many of the individuals involved in the creation of the ICS were important figures in the Reagan administration and mistrust government involvement in domestic affairs but believe in the need for U.S. power projection overseas. The ICS seeks to convince the public that vast increases in national security spending and aggressive action overseas are required if the United States is to protect its capitalist lifestyle and democratic way of life. They accomplish this by publishing books and analyses on issues including education, self-governance, entrepreneurship, and social, political, and economic issues.

Institute for Defense Analyses
4850 Mark Center Drive
Alexandria, VA 22311-1882
(703) 845-2000
E-mail: webmaster@ida.org
Web site: http://www.ida.org

The first U.S. secretary of defense, James Forrestal, started the Weapons Systems Evaluation Group in 1947 to investigate the effectiveness of various weapons systems. A decade later, the Joint Chiefs of Staff worked with the Massachusetts Institute for Technology to transform the Weapons Group into an independent research organization, which has since been known as the Institute for Defense Analyses (IDA).

Like the RAND Corporation (see p. 251), the IDA is a nonprofit corporation that functions as a federally funded research and development corporation (FFRDC). It works for the Office of the Secretary of Defense, the Joint Chiefs of Staff, and other unified commands and defense groups needing expertise in security concerns. Its four core competencies are force and strategy assessment, systems evaluation, resource and support analyses, and technology assessment. Much of its work is classified, but some of its analysis is available through either the IDA itself or two sources of military information from the U.S. government: the Defense Technical Information Center and the National Technical Information Service (see p. 266 and p. 273, respectively).

Institute for Defense and Disarmament Studies
675 Massachusetts Avenue
Cambridge, MA 02139
(617) 354-4337
FAX: (617) 354-1450
E-mail: info@idds.org
Web site: http://www.idds.org

The Institute for Defense and Disarmament Studies (IDDS) was established by one of the most prominent antinuclear protesters of the 1980s, Randall Forsberg. It is an educational, nonpartisan think tank and research organization focusing on arms control, disarmament, and general defense studies. Begun in 1980, the Institute for Defense and Disarmament Studies remains a primary center for information on arms sales and proliferation issues. The educational work of IDDS is centered on Global Action to Prevent War, a Web site that represents a coalition of individuals, groups, and governments working to minimize the duration and frequency of human conflict.

Publications: Publishing forms the majority of IDDS's work. Publications include reference works, policy studies, reports on arms production and control, and the *Arms Control Reporter,* an update of arms proliferation around the world. On-line publications include articles on special topics, such as "China's Military

Capabilities" and "Arms Production and Arms Control." Additionally, IDDS maintains the extensive Database of World Arms Holdings, Production, and Trade.

Institute for Foreign Policy Analysis
Cambridge, Massachusetts, Office
Central Plaza Building, 10th Floor
675 Massachusetts Avenue
Cambridge, MA 02139
(617) 492-2116
FAX: (617) 492-8242
E-mail: mail@ifpa.org

Washington Office
1725 DeSales Street, N.W., Suite 402
Washington, DC 20036
(202) 463-7942
FAX: (202) 785-2785
E-mail: cdmail@ifpa.org
Web site: http://www.ifpa.org

The Institute for Foreign Policy Analysis (IFPA) is associated with the Fletcher School of Law and Diplomacy at Tufts University in Medford, Massachusetts. It was established in 1976 to support nonpartisan, independent research and strategic planning in national security, political economics, and foreign policy. It is not only an educational enterprise but also provides briefings, public fora, reports, and major conferences and simulations on the pressing issues of the day for policymakers and business executives. Areas of emphasis include Asian security, the Middle East, military modernization, and other questions about national security needs.

Publications: The institute produces monographs and essays, conference reports, studies, and other summaries of its activities. These are accessible through its Web site.

Institute for Policy Studies
733 15th Street, N.W., Suite 1020
Washington, DC 20005
(202) 234-9382
FAX: (202) 387-7915
Web site: http://www.ips-dc.org/index.htm

During the 1970s and 1980s, the Institute for Policy Studies was a liberal think tank that sought to prevent the United States from subjugating foreign states to its conditions. It had important ties to the international liberal community engaged in the Allende Gossens government in Chile, and it received much attention when the former Chilean official Orlando Letelier and his assistant Ronni Moffitt were killed in Washington, DC, by an assassin hired by the Chilean intelligence community. (Letelier was working at the IPS while in exile from Chile.) With the end of the Cold War, the star of the IPS set. It still produces studies and reports on U.S. involvement overseas but it is not as prominent today.

Institute for Science and International Security
236 Massachusetts Avenue, N.E., Suite 500
Washington, DC 20002
(202) 547-3633
FAX: (202) 547-3637
E-mail: isis@isis-online.org
Web site: http://www.isis-online.org

The Institute for Science and International Security (ISIS), begun in 1993, is a nonpartisan, not-for-profit organization that focuses on educating the public about policy issues in international security that are particularly related to science. Its two primary activities are the Nuclear Nonproliferation Project, which works to provide comprehensive information about nuclear programs around the world, and the Nuclear Weapons Production Project, which closely examines the U.S. Department of Energy's work with nuclear weapons research, production, and testing. ISIS is also concerned with keeping the U.S. government accountable for its nuclear programs, so it closely monitors government activities.

Publications: ISIS publishes fact sheets and reports. Two specific items, *Challenges of Fissile Material Control* and *Plutonium Watch,* appeared in 1999 as studies from ISIS. Its work is available, for the most part, at its Web site. The organization is also represented through the work of its staff published in various popular journals.

Inter-American Dialogue
1211 Connecticut Avenue, Suite 510
Washington, DC 20036
(202) 822-9002

FAX: (202) 822-9553
E-mail: iad@thedialogue.org
Web site: http://www.thedialogue.org

The Inter-American Dialogue (IAD) has been a driving force for discussion and debate on Western Hemisphere concerns since 1982. Founded during the height of national debate on the Central America policy of the Reagan administration, the IAD is able to reach across partisan lines because its membership includes people of the highest ranks of the U.S. and other Western Hemisphere governments. Membership is by invitation and is relatively limited.

IAD has four programs that study and generate public debate on specific topics: Democratic Governance, Inter-American Institutions, Trade and Economics, and Social Equity/Education. It also conducts country studies. However, much of IAD's work is done through networking, which it conducts in four distinct arenas: the Women's Leadership Conference of the Americas, the Group of Fifty, the Congressional Members Working Group, and the Network of Legislative Leaders of the Americas. In the same outreach and educational vein, IAD has extensive programs for educating students about the hemisphere.

Publications: IAD publishes its many studies in both electronic and print editions. Most are available in English and Spanish. Its periodic newsletter is the *Dialogue/Dialogo,* and IAD also produces an annual report of its many activities. Other reports are listed on the Web site.

International Institute for Strategic Studies
Arundel House
13-15 Arundel Street
London, WC2R3DX (United Kingdom)
44 (0) 20 7379-7676
FAX: 44 (0) 20 7836-3108
E-mail: iiss@iiss.org
Web site: http://www.iiss.org

U.S. Office
1749 Pennsylvania Avenue, NW, Seventh Floor
Washington, DC 20006
(202) 659-1490
FAX: (202) 296-1134
E-mail: taylor@iiss.org

The International Institute for Strategic Studies (IISS), headquartered in London since its inception in 1958, is perhaps the world's most respected analytical body on national security. Created without government funding to ensure nonpartisan credentials, IISS is primarily a research organization, but it does limited outreach through conferences, which are held around the world. In general, IISS retains a fairly traditional definition of security issues and remains centrist in analysis. Its members are nominated by peers and represent a wide slice of the international community in the security field. In 2001 it opened a Washington office.

Publications: A number of IISS items are standard references—including *Strategic Comments,* a monthly update on current security issues, such as the threat of terrorism spreading from Afghanistan; the *Adelphi Papers* series of periodic analyses that look at issues such as the competing claims to the South China Sea; the bimonthly periodical, *Survival,* a prestigious, refereed journal; and *Military Balance* and *Strategic Balance,* two of the most popular reference annuals in the world, covering arms balances, strategic developments, and world political conditions.

Inter-University Seminar on Armed Forces and Society
University of Maryland
College Park, MD
(301) 405-6013
FAX: (301) 314-1314
E-mail: isu@socy.umd.edu
Web site: http://www.bsos.umd.edu/ius

In 1960, students of Morris Janowitz at the University of Chicago began the Inter-University Seminar on Armed Forces and Society (IUS) as a seminar on civil-military relations. Eventually it became a Chicago-wide seminar and then expanded to an international constituency of specialists. Some thirty years after its founding, the seminar retains a number of its original approaches to the scholarship of civil-military issues: it uses conference-paper summaries that are written by a single, independent reader instead of by the paper authors; its meetings are very tightly run; its members must be nominated; and its work has a distinctly sociological basis. The IUS has biennial meetings for its full membership as well as occasional meetings for selected geographical areas, held somewhere outside of the United States. Along with civil-military relations, IUS fellows are concerned with strategic issues facing the United States and its allies.

Publication: The journal sponsored by the IUS is *Armed Forces and Society,* a refereed quarterly published by Transaction Books.

Jamestown Foundation
2122 P Street, N.W.
Washington, DC 20036
(202) 483-8888
FAX: (202) 483-8337
E-mail: webmaster@jamestown.org
Web site: http://www.jamestown.org

The Jamestown Foundation (JF) was created in 1983 to concentrate public attention on free-market evolution and other issues inside the Soviet Union. Today, JF has projects relating to Russia, Chechnya, and China. JF prides itself on having a realistic understanding of the changes taking place in the various parts of the former Soviet Union. It claims that this area of the national security environment has been neglected since before the Soviet Union disappeared and seeks to remedy that situation.

Publications: JF has four major publications: The *Fortnight in Review* considers trends in the former Soviet Union, with a long essay on a particular topic in each edition. The weekly *Russia's Week* briefly considers the week's developments in Russia and the former Soviet Union with a general audience in mind. *Prism* contains pieces by scholars, journalists, and other experts on economic, cultural, and political conditions in Russia. The most well-known publication, however, is *Monitor,* a daily appraisal of events in the former Soviet Union.

Johns Hopkins University Foreign Policy Institute
The Johns Hopkins University
Paul Nitze School of Advanced International Studies
1619 Massachusetts Avenue, N.W.
Washington, DC 20036
(202) 663-5773
FAX: (202) 663-5769
E-mail: fpi@mail.jhuwash.jhu.edu
Web site: http://www.sais-jhu.edu/centers/fpi

The Foreign Policy Institute (FRI), established in 1980, is a part of the Paul Nitze School of Advanced International Studies at the Johns Hopkins University. It is different than most research institutes tied to universities in that it was established with an avowed goal of crossing the gap between practical public discussion and the research community. It does this by sponsoring as visiting scholars people from a wide range of professions, including journalists. Additionally, the institute holds a number of seminars and discussion groups and promotes research events for Washington area universities and colleges. Its programs have focused on civil-military relations, South Asia, the protection of women and children, and the prevention of their trafficking by the international criminal community.

Publication: FPI publishes the *SAIS Review,* a quarterly that aims to broaden the public policy debate on national security by making publication accessible not only to established scholars but also to graduate students.

Lawyers Alliance for World Security
1901 Pennsylvania Avenue, N.W., Suite 201
Washington, DC 20006
(202) 745-2450
FAX: (202) 667-0444
E-mail: info@lawscns.org
Web site: http://www.lawscns.org

In 1992 the Lawyers Alliance for World Security (LAWS) was established out of the Lawyers Alliance for Nuclear Arms Control, founded in 1980. The prominent leaders who created LAWS, including Ambassador Thomas Graham and Erwin Griswold of Harvard, wanted to make certain that the United States considered the implications of nuclear weapons and nuclear arms races, as well as broader defense considerations. LAWS continues to educate the public and lawmakers about options in national security, adopting a more action-oriented program in recent years. It is dedicated to studying the Comprehensive Test Ban Treaty, maintaining the Nuclear Nonproliferation Treaty, stopping antimissile systems, and other activities related to ending U.S. reliance on nuclear weapons. It has chapters in Boston, New York, Chicago, and Philadelphia, and it maintains an office at the United Nations.

Publications: Most of LAWS work is made public through speeches and op-ed articles by its members. It does produce reports, which are available on-line at its Web site.

Meridian International Center
1630 Crescent Place, N.W.
Washington, DC 20009
(202) 667-6800
FAX: (202) 667-1475
E-mail: info@meridian.org
Web site: http://www.Meridian.org

The Meridian International Center (MIC) offers a nexus between people from around the world, providing the opportunity for discussion of international issues. It holds seminars, conferences, and educational programs across the country. It is especially focused on bringing foreigners to the United States to exchange ideas with U.S. citizens. MIC holds day and evening events, some aimed at high-level participants within the U.S. government and many for the average citizen. There are cultural exchanges as well as more formal academic exchanges.

Mershon Center of The Ohio State University
1501 Neil Avenue
Columbus, OH 43201
(614) 292-1681
FAX: (614) 292-2407
E-mail: herrmann.l@osu.edu
Web site: http://www.mershon.ohio-state.edu

The Mershon Center of The Ohio State University is an interdisciplinary research center dedicated to the study of international security questions. Founded through a bequest from a retired army officer, the Mershon Center seeks to promote as much interdisciplinary research and collaboration as possible across the Ohio State campus as well as with international scholars. The Mershon Center has an endowed chair named for former football coach Woodrow "Woody" Hayes and the Mason Endowed Professorship in Military History. The center also holds conferences and other activities to widen the public policy discussion as far as possible and to encourage nontraditional strategies as much as more orthodox ones.

Monterey Institute of International Studies
425 Van Buren Street
Monterey, CA 93940

(831) 647-4100
FAX: (831) 647-4199
E-mail: president@miis.edu
Web site: http://www.miis.edu

The Monterey Institute of International Studies (MIIS) is a graduate school and research facility dedicated to creating a practical link between understanding the global community and conducting the business and nonprofit activities that link the United States with the rest of the world. Because of the institute's location in Monterey, California, MIIS offers a decidedly Asian focus, offering language studies in Chinese, Japanese, and Russian in addition to programs in Spanish, French, German, and Arabic. MIIS also has a commitment to business, economic, and trade issues.

MIIS has three research centers: the Center for Nonproliferation Studies, which is one of the strongest programs in the world on nonproliferation in the largest nongovernmental body studying this topic; the Center for East Asia and Pacific Affairs, and the Center for Russian and Eurasian Studies. The work conducted by the centers includes not only Russian studies, but strong Japanese and Chinese expertise as well. Each center conducts ongoing projects and also takes on current issues when appropriate. Each holds major international conferences that then produce reports used around the world.

Publications: The *Nonproliferation Review* is a refereed journal on nonproliferation concerns. The conferences held by the centers at MIIS also publish reports, and the institute publishes an annual report. These are listed on the Web site.

National Institute for Public Policy
3031 Javier Road, Suite 300
Fairfax, VA 22031
(703) 698-0563
FAX: (703) 698-0566
E-mail: Amy.joseph@nipp.org
Web site: http://www.nipp.org

The National Institute for Public Policy (NIPP) was formed in 1981 to bring public attention to the changing military balance. In the post–Cold War era, NIPP continues to raise public awareness of the threats to the United States. Among its primary issues for concern are nonproliferation, with information about the spread of ballistic missiles available on the "NIPP Proliferation Webpage" (http://www.nipp.org/programarchive.php); ballistic missile defense, with a recent project explaining the need for this emerging technology; and the Comprehensive Test Ban Treaty, arguing that the Senate was correct to defeat it. NIPP has a small staff that engages in serious research on the issues and circulates their findings to the research and policy communities in the Washington, DC, area. Its Web site has helpful links to other security Web sites.

Publications: NIPP publishes *Comparative Strategy,* a quarterly journal on current strategy questions. NIPP also makes its reports available on-line.

National Security Archive
Gelman Library, Suite 701
The George Washington University
2130 H Street, N.W.
Washington, DC 20037
(202) 994-7000
FAX: (202) 994-7005
E-mail: nsarchiv@gwu.edu
Web site: http://www.gwu.edu/~nsarchiv/

The National Security Archive (NSA) was founded in 1985 as an offshoot of the Central American Papers Project. Its initial purpose was to gain access, through the 1967 Freedom of Information Act (FOIA), to the public papers on the Reagan involvement with Nicaraguan contras. NSA receives no funding from the federal government. It moved to its current home at George Washington University in 1995, where its public papers are available for general use. The archive retains its goal of seeking out national security papers rather than promoting any particular policy perspective.

The NSA's ongoing projects include work on Chile, China, China and the bomb, Cuba, Guatemala, Honduras, Israel, Iran, intelligence policy, Mexico, India-Pakistan, Japan, and openness in Russia and the former Soviet Union. Two extremely large projects are the Parallel History Project, on NATO and the Warsaw Pact, and the Cold War International History Project. The archive also has links to other projects working to open decision-making materials elsewhere in the world, including efforts to open the archives of the East German intelligence services and the

Tiananmen Papers on China. The archive offers internships to college students and is involved in filing FOIA requests for information-seekers unfamiliar with this process.

Publications: NSA provides public access to its collection of declassified documents, the Digital National Security Archive, as well as twenty different microfiche collections. It also produces a series of Electronic Briefing Books, which present documents on specific issues, and publishes monographs by its staff on topics such as intelligence, South Africa, the Iran-Contra scandal, and other areas germane to NSA's work. The archive has more than two dozen published collections of U.S. national security policy papers that were classified until FOIA requests opened them.

National Strategy Forum
53 West Jackson Boulevard, Suite 516
Chicago, IL 60604
(312) 697-1286
FAX: (312) 697-1296
E-mail: nsf@nsf.org
Web site: http://www.nationalstrategy.com

The National Strategy Forum is a national security organization located in Chicago. Founded by attorney Morris Leibman in 1983 as the Midwest Advisory Council, it has hosted major figures to discuss pressing issues in national security. A membership organization, the forum sponsors luncheons and occasional conferences for discussion and encourages research on international affairs.

Publication: The forum publishes a quarterly, the *National Strategy Review,* which is written in an accessible style by major scholars and practitioners in the security field.

National Strategy Information Center

The National Strategy Information Center was a particularly vigorous research group during the 1970s and 1980s, discussing the threats that the center believed were being underestimated elsewhere. Created in 1962, the center had a major role in educational activities in the national security and general international affairs field. The center also established a number of organizations with particularly strong relevance to the intelligence field, such as the National Strategy Forum in Chicago (see separate entry above).

Natural Resources Defense Council
New York Office
40 West 20th Street
New York, NY 10011
(212) 727-2700
FAX: (212) 727-1773

Washington Office
1200 New York Avenue, N.W., Suite 400
Washington, DC 20005
(202) 289-6868

San Francisco Office
71 Stevenson Street, #1825
San Francisco, CA 94105
(415) 777-0220

Los Angeles Office
6310 San Vicente Boulevard, #250
Los Angeles, CA 90048
(323) 934-6900
E-mail: nrdcinfo@nrdc.org
Web site: http://www.nrdc.org

The Natural Resources Defense Council (NRDC) was established during the first stage of the environmental movement in 1970, with assistance from the Ford Foundation. It then evolved into a membership organization, tapping into grassroots concerns in the United States about the protection of the environment. The NRDC has campaigned against defense spending (as opposed to environmental spending) and against some of the exemptions that military facilities across the country have been granted from environmental protection legislation. The council has had a major role in opposing nuclear weapons because many of the scientists who concern themselves with environmental and resource issues also understand the effects that the use of nuclear weapons would have on the environment and the citizenry. NRDC remains open to discussing arms control, nuclear proliferation, and weapons inventories, but it retains the primary goal of eliminating nuclear weapons.

Publications: The NRDC publishes the *Nuclear Weapons Databook* series, which shows the capabilities of various weapons. This long-term series presents a great deal of information basic to military balance assessments. The NRDC also publishes a series of reports on weapons and environmental issues. Many of its publications are available on-line.

Navy League of the United States
2300 Wilson Boulevard
Arlington, VA 22201-3308
(703) 528-1775
FAX: (703) 528-2333
E-mail: execdirector@navyleague.org
Web site: http://www.navyleague.org

President Theodore Roosevelt encouraged the creation of the Navy League of the United States in 1902, and today it is still an influential organization, aiming to educate the public about naval and maritime forces. The league's primary goal is to protect and assist service personnel while protecting U.S. national security in the process. The league has many programs for its members throughout the country, including educational programs for youth and Reserve Officer Training Corps (ROTC) units, and it remains involved in raising consciousness in Congress and among the public about the Navy, the Marine Corps, the Coast Guard, and the Merchant Marines. The league sponsors the annual Sea-Air-Space Systems and Technology Exposition in the nation's capital as a place for the defense community to contemplate the future.

Publications: The Navy League's primary publication is *Seapower,* a monthly magazine on topics relating to the Navy. Additionally, each January the *Almanac of SeaPower* covers data on ships, weapons, aircraft, communications, and support equipment, helping to explain how they are an important resource for national security.

Nuclear Control Institute
1000 Connecticut Avenue, Suite 410
Washington, DC 20036
(202) 822-8444
FAX: (202) 452-0892
E-mail: nci@nci.org
Web site: http://www.nci.org

The Nuclear Control Institute (NCI) started in 1981 as a nonpartisan research center interested in raising public awareness of nuclear issues. It has retained that goal, expanding its focus to include nuclear terrorism, nuclear waste disposal, nuclear non-proliferation, nuclear weapons disposal, and other issues concerning nuclear threats in the United States and abroad. NCI research is well respected and often cited in discussions of nuclear issues because of its blend of scientific and policy expertise.

Publications: NCI has conducted many studies on a wide variety of nuclear issues, which are available on the NCI Web site. Additionally, NCI makes available on-line the congressional testimony of its specialists.

Peace Action
1819 H Street, N.W.
Washington, DC 20006
(202) 862-9740
FAX: (202) 862-9762
E-mail: slynch@peace-action.org
Web site: http://www.peace-action.org

Peace Action was originally founded in 1957 as SANE (the Committee for a Sane Nuclear Policy), evolving in the 1980s into SANE/FREEZE, and taking on its current name in 1993. Peace Action retains its original goal of persuading the U.S. Congress and executive branch to abandon nuclear weapons and other weapons of mass destruction in order to protect the United States and ensure global peace. Peace Action remains committed to pushing for nonproliferation policies, arms control, and fewer conventional arms sales around the world. Its current projects focus on human rights, abolishing nuclear weapons, and developing a peace economy. Its three major campaigns in 2002 were Justice Not War, Stop Star Wars, and Abolish Nuclear Weapons. The Peace Action Education Fund is a not-for-profit organization that supports activities around the country on peaceful options in conflict resolution, including the Student Peace Action Network.

Peace Brigades International
428 8th Street, S.E., 2nd floor
Washington, DC 20003
(202) 544-3765
FAX: (202) 544-3766
E-mail: pbiusa@igc.org
Web site: http://www.peacebrigades.org

Peace Brigades International (PBI) is a grassroots organization, founded in 1981 in Canada, that engages in nonviolent intervention in conflict zones. Teams of volunteers are sent to areas of conflict in order to create a "breathing zone" between combatants, in the hopes that this will allow them time to find peaceful solutions to their disputes. PBI's first action was in 1983, when it sent peace forces to the Guatemalan civil war. More recently, PBI has been involved in trying to remedy problems in Mexico, East Timor, Colombia, and Indonesia. Its members serve as volunteers in these countries and also try to discourage U.S. government involvement in these conflicts through public education and participation in the U.S. political process.

Physicians for Social Responsibility
1875 Connecticut Avenue, N.W., Suite 1012
Washington, DC 20009
(202) 667-4260
FAX: (202) 667-4201
E-mail: psmatl@psr.org
Web site: http://www.psr.org

For almost forty years, Physicians for Social Responsibility (PSR) has been trying to engage the public in the process of understanding the environment and various health issues. In 1985, the organization won the Nobel Peace Prize. PSR attempts to raise social, political, and medical awareness, particularly in the field of nuclear nonproliferation. It is adamantly opposed to the abrogation of the Antiballistic Missile Treaty and seeks to rally the public in support of the treaty. PSR is currently engaged in several projects, including the Nuclear Security Project. Its work is publicized through the Media Center at its Web site.

RAND Corporation
Santa Monica Office
1700 Main Street
P.O. Box 2138
Santa Monica, CA 90407-2138
(310) 393-0411
FAX: (310) 393-4818

Washington Office
1200 South Hayes Street

Arlington, VA 22202-5050
(703) 413-1100
FAX: (703) 413-8111

Pittsburgh Office
201 North Craig Street, Suite 102
Pittsburgh, PA 15213
(412) 683-2300
FAX: (412) 683-2800
Web site: http://www.rand.org

The RAND Corporation (RAND) was created in 1947 as the research and development arm of the newly formed U.S. Air Force. It has long since broadened its studies beyond the traditional national security realm into "newer" definitions of security, such as health care and drug policy, but its core work remains related to all aspects of traditional national security. In both its Santa Monica headquarters and its Washington, DC, offices, RAND has a large research staff to cover national security concerns.

RAND's National Security Program has five major research emphases: the global security environment; military acquisition and technology; military force structure and employment; military logistics and infrastructure; and military personnel, training, and health. Within these programs, RAND is addressing the questions posed by its various sponsors, including the U.S. Air Force, the U.S. Army, the Office of the Secretary of Defense and various defense agencies, the Joint Staff, the Unified Commands, the intelligence community, and the Department of the Navy. Occasionally RAND does work for foreign governments as well.

Publications: RAND's publications list is exhaustive, even in the national security area alone. As a result of its multidisciplinary approach, RAND publishes of a variety of reports for any given research topic. First, it publishes Issue Papers that outline the early research efforts in each project, followed by Research Briefs, which are more substantive efforts. Further analysis on most topics is also published. The RAND Web site provides comprehensive descriptions of the materials available. Hard copies of many reports are also available for nominal fees.

Ridgway Center for International Security Studies
3J01 Posvar Hall
University of Pittsburgh
Pittsburgh, PA 15260

(412) 648-7408
FAX: (412) 624-7291
E-mail: goldy@pitt.edu
Web site: http://www.pitt.edu/~rcss

The Ridgway Center for International Security Studies at the Graduate School of Public and International Affairs at the University of Pittsburgh was established in 1988 as a dedication to Korean War hero General Matthew B. Ridgway. The multidisciplinary center examines a range of both old and new issues in the international security calculation, including transnational criminal activity, weapons of mass destruction, and regional conflicts relating to issues of state legitimacy. The center publishes reports and studies, and it offers specializations in intelligence analysis and in security and intelligence studies to graduate students at the University of Pittsburgh.

Publications: The Ridgway Center has a detailed, extensive Web site with links to government offices and sites focusing on "new" security issues, such as terrorism, transnational organized crime, information warfare, and arms control. The Ridgway Center also publishes the journal *Ridgway Viewpoints* and houses the editorial offices for the journal *Transnational Organized Crime.*

SANE/FREEZE (*See* Peace Action)

The Stanley Foundation
209 Iowa Avenue
Muscatine, IA 52761
(563) 264-1500
FAX: (563) 264-0864
E-mail: info@stanleyfoundation.org
Web site: http://www.stanleyfoundation.org/

C. Maxwell and Elizabeth Stanley created the Stanley Foundation in 1956 to find management solutions for the world's problems. To generate these solutions, the foundation has assembled thousands of world leaders and experts in conferences and meetings over the years. The Stanley Foundation focuses on four major areas of education and policy inquiry: global education, U.S. foreign policy, global governance, and media. Each of these programs brings a specific focus to the annual conferences, facilitating dialogue. After each conference, the foundation publishes extensive conference reports, including policy proposals.

Publications: The Stanley Foundation publishes its conference reports and its newsletter, *Courier.* Additionally, the foundation has a weekly radio program, *Common Ground,* to encourage debate, explore the issues, and find solutions. Most of these materials are available on-line at the Stanley Foundation Web site.

Henry L. Stimson Center
11 DuPont Circle, N.W., Ninth Floor
Washington, DC 20036
(202) 223-5956
FAX: (202) 238-9604
E-mail: info@stimson.org
Web site: http://www.stimson.org

The Henry L. Stimson Center describes itself as a "community of analysts" working toward realistic, applicable solutions to international problems. The center has several current areas of emphasis, with different projects under way in each area: The Determinants of Global Security emphasis includes the Institute for Global Democracy and work on technology, international security, and UN peace operations. Building Regional Security emphasis includes confidence-building measures for South Asia, the new China Program, which accompanies the program for Japan, and a visiting fellows program. The Weapons of Mass Destruction emphasis includes work on chemical weapons along with the New Nuclear Directions Dialogue. The curiously titled Enhancing Our Field area has projects entitled Imagine Work, Security for a New Century, and Rethinking Influence. Professionals are assigned to each area to promote realistic, substantive thinking along new lines.

Publications: The Stimson Center publishes a newsletter, press releases, and various other materials specific to region and/or topic. Printed copies of all materials are available for a fee, and an increasing number are also available on-line free of charge.

Stockholm International Peace Research Institute
Signalistgatan 9
SE 169-70 SOLNA
Sweden
46 (8) 655-97-00
FAX: 46 (8) 655-97-33
E-mail: sipri@sipri.org

Web site: http://www.sipri.org

One of the most prestigious and often-cited national security organizations in the world is the Stockholm International Peace Research Institute (SIPRI), located in the Swedish capital. SIPRI began in 1966 as an independent foundation to commemorate the century and a half of unbroken peace that Sweden had enjoyed. Its original and enduring charter has been to examine sources of conflict throughout the world and to find remedies to prevent further turmoil.

SIPRI engages in its work through conferences and workshops, scholarly assessments, and public lectures. The issues it considers are not limited to Europe, although it does emphasize issues relating to peace and conflict-avoidance with the former Soviet Union. SIPRI's activities span the globe; it holds several major international conferences annually and many lectures, often in the Olaf Palme Memorial Lecture Series, to bring attention to various concerns. SIPRI has roughly a dozen ongoing major projects, ranging from issues in the Caspian Sea Basin to arms transfers to arms control, and it has conducted many other projects over the course of its history.

Publications: Because SIPRI's mission is to find practical answers to international conflict, publications are a crucial part of its work. Its most prominent product is the annual *SIPRI Yearbook*, a comprehensive look at arms proliferation and transfers, armed conflict, attempts at resolution, military expenditures, and other aspects of the international security environment. The *Yearbook* has been published since 1969. Additionally, SIPRI produces a large number of research reports on various topics and fact sheets on discrete concerns. All SIPRI publications are considered to be impartial and authoritative in the field. SIPRI is increasingly making its work available on-line as well.

Trilateral Commission
1156 Fifteenth Street, N.W.
Washington, DC 20005
(202) 467-5410
FAX: (202) 467-5415
E-mail: admin@trilateral.org
Web site: http://www.trilateral.org

The Trilateral Commission, established in 1973 by prominent citizens from the industrialized areas of Europe, Japan, and North

America to improve national security, has long been considered a nefarious enterprise by some skeptics, who fear it amounts to a form of "world government" or some attempt by the elites in these societies to control the global context. The commission plans its work in three-year increments, noting that it currently foresees no work past the date of 2003 to which it is chartered. The commission approaches its goal of facilitating better cooperation between governments and societies around the world through group activities among relevant states. At present, the work of the commission is divided into the North America Group, the Pacific Asian Group (which only recently evolved from the Japan Group), and the European Group. The groups are each responsible for their own funding. They each hold annual meetings, as does the commission as a whole, on a rotating basis in different capitals of states where members reside. The commission's membership is comprised of 350 scholars, businesspeople, former government officials, and generally prominent individuals. Those who currently serve in government cannot hold commission membership until their government service has ended.

Publications: After each annual meeting, the Trilateral Commission publishes a report, entitled *Trialogue.* Reports on various task forces or regional projects, such as that on Central Asian stability or advancing peace prospects in the Middle East, are referred to as *Triangle Papers.* These reports are available from the commission.

Union of Concerned Scientists
Headquarters
2 Brattle Square
Cambridge, MA 02238
(617) 547-5552
E-mail: ucs@ussusa.org
Web site: http://www.ucs.org

Washington Office
1717 H Street, N.W., Suite 600
Washington, DC 20006-3919
(202) 223-6133
FAX: (202) 223-6162

West Coast Office
2397 Shattuck Avenue, Suite 203

Berkeley, CA 94704-1567
(510) 843-1872
FAX: (510) 843-3785

The Union of Concerned Scientists (UCS) grew from environmental and security concerns voiced by scientists and engineers at the Massachusetts Institute of Technology in 1969. Building on their concern that science not be misused in society, the UCS is now a large grassroots group, with fifty thousand members nationally. Although much of its work hits upon broad environmental concerns, UCS also has an important program on global security, including missile defense, the comprehensive test ban, nuclear weapons, and global cooperation.

Publications: UCS produces a number of reports on security topics, all available from the Cambridge office for a fee. Executive summaries are available on-line.

The U.S.-China Policy Foundation
316 Pennsylvania Avenue, S.E.
Suite 201-202
Washington, DC 20003
(202) 547-8615
FAX: (202) 547-8853
Web site: http://www.uscpf.org

The U.S.-China Policy Foundation seeks to promote better understanding of the issues that both divide and unite the People's Republic of China, Taiwan, and the United States. It promotes both scholarly and public policy debate through seminars, conferences, print and electronic publications, and other networking fora to enhance the ties between these three societies. As a nonpartisan, nonadvocacy organization, the foundation uses scholarship as the basis for deepening these links. Additionally, it produces a weekly television program, *The China Forum,* where the most timely issues are discussed. The program is available on cable in selected television networks, mainly on the East Coast.

Publications: Both the *Washington Journal of Modern China,* a semiannual journal, and the *U.S.-China Policy Review* are published by the foundation to promote a better understanding of Sino-U.S. relations among policymakers and scholars in the People's Republic of China, Taiwan, and the United States.

Veterans of Foreign Wars
Headquarters
406 West 24th Street
Kansas City, MO 64111
(816) 756-3390
E-mail: info@vfw.org
Web site: http://www.vfw.org

Washington Office
200 Maryland Avenue, N.E.
Washington, DC 20002
(202) 543-2239
FAX: (202) 543-0961

The Veterans of Foreign Wars (VFW) is unique among the groups in this volume for its approach to protecting and preserving the memory and dignity of those who have served their country in conflict abroad. As the distinction grows between those who have served in the U.S. military and those who have not, the VFW points to the issues it believes are being forgotten—the need to protect democracy and the need to honor the sacrifices of the veteran, who in the post-Vietnam decades was increasingly taken for granted. The VFW holds a national meeting to commemorate the decisions that have called U.S. armed forces overseas, but most VFW activities take place in the smaller posts in towns across the country.

The VFW offers extensive educational activities to remind citizens of the sacrifices required in war and to remind children, in particular, of the successes that U.S. commitments have brought in World War II and other conflicts. Many other VFW projects aim to enhance the living conditions of aging veterans. The VFW itself is a not-for-profit organization.

Lobbying Affiliate: The Veterans of Foreign Wars Legislative Office in Washington, DC, is a lobbying arm of the VFW. The Action Corps undertakes grassroots lobbying in all sectors of the country and can be joined on-line at http://www.vfwdc.org/AC/1action.htm. In addition to concerns about veterans' rights, the VFW is highly committed to a strong U.S. defense posture.

Publications: The VFW Web site includes an extensive set of links and on-line materials regarding issues pertinent to its membership. Testimony by VFW leadership, press releases, and an independent budget analysis are also available on-line.

Educational Affiliate: The VFW has an educational arm, the

VFW Foundation. The foundation coordinates the various high school and elementary school activities of the VFW as well as more general public education in communities across the country.

War Resisters' League
339 Lafayette Street
New York, NY 10012
(212) 228-0450
FAX: (212) 228-6193
E-mail: wrl@warresisters.org
Web site: http://www.wrl.org

The War Resisters' League (WRL), established in response to the horrors of World War I, has argued since its founding in 1923 that world peace is necessary, and it has always accepted private citizens' donations to support its work toward this goal. The WRL seeks to promote anything that avoids conflict, including war-tax resistance and conscientious objection on the part of draft-age men. The league is part of a larger international organization by the same name, and it was particularly important as a pacifist organization during the turbulent 1960s and 1980s, when it worked around the world as well as in the United States. WRL work is largely done on university and college campuses across the country and in small chapters in many states.

Publications: The WRL produces a significant amount of pacifist literature, most notably the annual "Peace Calendar" and the *Nonviolent Activist* magazine. It also has a Web site exclusively for children, located at http://www.warresisters.org/Roots/roots.frames.html.

Washington Office on Latin America
1630 Connecticut Avenue, N.W., Suite 200
Washington, DC 20009
(202) 797-2171
FAX: (202) 797-2172
E-mail: wola@wola.org
Web site: http://www.wola.org

The Washington Office on Latin America (WOLA) began in 1975 to help formulate legislation on the U.S.–Latin American relationship that promotes, rather than hinders, human rights. WOLA, headquartered in the United States but with offices in Guatemala and El Salvador, works to educate the public and Congress and to enhance coalitions among interested parties in the region. WOLA is conducting major projects on Peru and Colombia as well as on empowering democracies, promoting equitable economic growth and development, and stabilizing societies; WOLA is one of the most thoughtful analytical organizations on these topics. It also works within the region to strengthen the position of NGOs that seek public policy changes. WOLA offers internships to interested college students.

Publications: WOLA publishes two newsletters on the region: *Enlace* and *CrossCurrents.* It also produces a range of reports on individual nations and on policy questions, such as public security and drug policy.

Women in International Security
Center for Peace and Security Studies
Walsh School of Foreign Service
Georgetown University
P.O. Box 571145
Washington, DC 20057-1145
(301) 405-7612
FAX: (301) 403-8107
E-mail: info@wiis.org
Web site: http://www.wiis.org

Women in International Security (WIIS) began in 1987 as a network for women seeking opportunities to enter the national security debate. Originally housed at the University of Maryland in College Park, WIIS moved in 2001 to the Walsh School at Georgetown University, giving it better access to the Washington community. In a field where men have dominated, the founders of WIIS sought to make available the sorts of opportunities and knowledge that could encourage younger women to bring their creativity into the arena.

With this goal in mind, WIIS has long emphasized education for women graduate students. It organizes an annual summer symposium (to which men are also invited) and also offers shorter activities, including half-day conferences, speeches, and seminars on specific security questions or techniques such as preparation for entering the job market. WIIS has affiliations with other public policy groups around the world and occasionally sponsors conferences and study tours outside of the United States, such as those to Ukraine or Russia.

Publication: WIIS promotes its members as speakers and experts in the security field through the *WIIS Media Guide,* which lists the expertise of each member.

Women's Action for New Directions
691 Massachusetts Avenue
Arlington, MA 02476
(781) 643-6740
FAX: (781) 643-6784
E-mail: info@wand.org
Web site: http://www.wand.org

Founded in 1980 by the Australian physician and activist Helen Caldicott, the Women's Survival Party became Women's Action for Nuclear Disarmament (WAND) in the 1980s and Women's Action for New Directions in the 1990s. It has a decidedly antinuclear and antimilitary bent and works to raise public consciousness about alternatives to military responses to national security issues. In 1996, the Women Take Action! Campaign encouraged one hundred thousand men and women in the United States to argue that too much of the federal budget goes to military spending.

Lobbying Affiliate: WAND has two lobbying affiliates. The Women's Legislator Lobby (WiLL) aims to bring elected women together with their grassroots supporters on relevant topics. WAND PAC is specifically dedicated to getting women with security concerns and antimilitarist visions elected to Congress and state legislatures.

Publications: WAND publishes fact sheets and quarterly bulletins on-line. The organization's Web site also includes an extensive set of links to related organizations.

World Policy Institute
New School University
66 Fifth Avenue, 9th floor
New York, NY 10011
(212) 229-5808
FAX: (212) 807-1153
E-mail: DoveR@newschool.edu
Web site: http://www.worldpolicy.org/wpi/index.html

An offshoot of the Institute for World Order, which was established in 1948, the World Policy Institute began work in 1982 and became part of the New School University in 1991. The institute's goal is to provide a forum for domestic and international discussion of public policy questions facing the global community, especially those resulting from the increased pressures of globalization. The institute tries to promote discussion among civic and business leaders, policymakers, and journalists, as well as academics. It accomplishes this through seminars on regional issues that span the globe, through a media center that publishes the work of experts affiliated with the institute in fourteen different subject areas, and through several distinct research projects, entitled Arms Trade, U.S. Cuba Education, the Eurasia Project, the UN Project, the Americas Project, Emerging Powers, and the U.S. and the World lecture series. The overall objective of reconsidering the U.S. relationship with the world is clearly covered by these efforts.

Publication: The *World Policy Journal* is a quarterly covering the institute's concerns. It often produces some of the most innovative policy options of any journal in the United States. Recent issues of the journal are available on-line.

Governmental Organizations

Agency for International Development
The Ronald Reagan Building
14th Street, N.W.
Washington, DC 20523-1000
(202) 712-4810
FAX: (202) 216-3524
E-mail: pinquiries@usaid.gov
Web site: http://www.usaid.gov

The Agency for International Development (USAID) dates to the Kennedy administration, when it was created to offer technical assistance to developing countries in the Third World. USAID was a direct response to the Cuban Revolution and to the economic dependency theory postulated by UN Conference on Trade and Development General Secretary Raúl Prebisch. It also was charged by some critics with being an instrument for spreading U.S. counterinsurgency activities during the height of the Cold War. With the end of that conflict, the agency's role has been scaled back, and it now focuses on technical and educational assistance in specific, targeted areas of nation-building and economic development, such as birth control, tax collection, disease prevention, and many of the other new security concerns.

Air War College
1 Chennault Circle
Maxwell AFB, AL 36112
(334) 953-6996
Web site: http://www.au.af.mil/au/awc/awchome.htm

The Air War College, the senior-most educational opportunity for students in Air Force Professional Military Education (PME), is one of the six Senior Service Schools. It offers an opportunity to study airpower issues at the highest level of analysis. The college encourages perspectives beyond those of the U.S. Air Force; it is open not only to Air Force officers of the rank of lieutenant colonel and colonel but also to civilians and a small number of officers from other services.

Army War College
Department of the Army
122 Forbes Avenue
Carlisle, PA 17013
E-mail: AWCC-DPA@awc.carlisle.army.mil
Web site: carlisle-www.army.mil

The Army War College, founded in 1901 in Washington, DC, is a Senior Service School, providing the highest level of education within the U.S. Army. Now located at Carlisle Barracks in south-central Pennsylvania, it is an active location for scholarship on issues facing the army in particular and on U.S. national security concerns generally. It includes the Center for Strategic Leadership, the Military History Institute, the Peacekeeping Institute, and the Army Physical Fitness Research Institute.

Asia Pacific Center for Security Studies
2058 Maluhia Road
Honolulu, HI 96815
(808) 971-8900
FAX: (808) 971-8999
E-mail: pao@apcss.org
Web site: http://www.apcss.org

The Asia Pacific Center for Security Studies (APCSS) began in 1995 as part of the Clinton administration outreach and nation-building effort around the world. With a focus on Asia, it emphasizes ties to the Pacific Command, also based in Honolulu. APCSS aims to educate officers and civilians from the Pacific-rim nations about the value of multilateral approaches to security in the post–Cold War environment.

The center hosts twelve-week courses for future regional leaders, both civilian and military, and a one-week intensive course for current leaders. The intent is to bring the widest array of individuals together to discuss common concerns and work at their most realistic solutions across this vast theater. The center also holds many conferences, some outside of the United States, which bring scholars and practitioners together in dialogue about evolving threats and cooperative activities. The center has a College of Security Studies and a Research Division, which bring scholars from the region and from the United States together with students and guest speakers.

Publications: On its Web site, the center publishes summaries of its conference reports, seminar reports, and an occasional paper series.

Center for Hemispheric Defense Studies
National Defense University
Washington, DC 20319
(202) 685-4670
FAX: (202) 685-4674
Web site: http://www.ndu.edu/chds/index.html

The Center for Hemispheric Defense Studies (CHDS) was created in 1997 to help the civilian and military leaders in the Western Hemisphere to resolve some of their enduring conflicts about civil-military relations while also learning the U.S. approach to budgeting, public administration, and other aspects of governance that have long been difficult to develop in some countries in the region. Students come to the center for a three-week intensive course on these questions. CHDS also offers seminars in other Western Hemisphere nations for those participants unable to come to the United States. CHDS occasionally holds more general conferences and broad gatherings to discuss issues of common concern.

Central Intelligence Agency
Office of Public Affairs
Washington, DC 20505

(703) 482-0623
FAX: (703) 482-1739
Web site: http://www.cia.gov

The Central Intelligence Agency (CIA) was created after the end of World War II with the Defense Reorganization Act of 1947, which consolidated the Department of War and Navy and Army Departments into a single defense organization. As its title suggests, the CIA was a repository and consolidation place for intelligence in the U.S. government, although subsequently the Congress has seen it necessary to create other intelligence organizations such as the Defense Intelligence Agency. The CIA has prominence, however, as the head of the agency is also the Director of Central Intelligence, who leads twelve other agencies in the U.S. intelligence community.

The CIA has a vast network of intelligence operations. Its work is broken into two major areas: operations and analysis. Within the agency, offices specialize in counterterrorism, counterproliferation, counternarcotics, military balances, and assessments of science and technology. While the agency is often accused of being overly active in U.S. foreign policy, the overwhelming majority of its work is in analysis rather than operations.

The CIA includes the Center for the Study of Intelligence, which hosts conferences and publishes historical studies on various intelligence topics, including its series *Studies in Intelligence.* The agency also publishes an array of other materials. Its annual *CIA World Factbook,* available on-line, on CD-ROM, or in print, is highly sought-after. It also translates foreign language broadcasts and sources through the Foreign Broadcast Information Service (FBIS).

Congressional Research Service
The Library of Congress
The Madison Building
Washington, DC 20540
(202) 707-5000
Web site: http://www.loc.gov/crsinfo

The Congressional Research Service (CRS) is a division of the Library of Congress to which the Congress and its staff turn when they have pressing questions about any public policy issue. The CRS is organized in six issue-based clusters, of which Foreign Affairs, Defense, and Trade is one significant group. The CRS staff have exceptional knowledge of their fields; often called upon to produce a report in a matter of hours, they do so with incredible competence and depth.

Publications: The CRS Reports are generally prepared only for members of Congress and their staff, but U.S. law does not prohibit their further distribution.

Defense Technical Information Center
8725 John Kingman Road, Suite 0944
Fort Belvoir, VA 22060-6218
(800) 225-3842
E-mail: bcporder@dtic.mil
Web site: http://www.dtic.mil

The Defense Technical Information Center (DTIC) collects and disseminates nonclassified technical information for the Department of Defense. DTIC focuses on collecting scientific and technical materials in a widely defined defense field. It produces studies, helps with searches for various topics, and serves as a central clearinghouse on defense technical matters.

Drug Enforcement Agency
2401 Jefferson Davis Highway
Alexandria, VA 22301
(800) 882-9539
Web site: http://www.dea.gov

The Drug Enforcement Agency (DEA) has the charge of enforcing the controlled substance laws of the United States. This is deemed a national security task because controlled substances increasingly include illegal drugs that are a threat to the nation's public health and safety. DEA carries out its activities by investigating the trafficking of controlled substances and the criminal networks engaged in promoting and selling such substances and by coordinating with the antidrug efforts of the United Nations and international law enforcement agencies. DEA has been an element of the government since its founding under the Department of Justice in 1973, but its roots are in the 1920s Prohibition period and it has since evolved through several agency titles for the purpose of refining its mission.

Federal Bureau of Investigation
J. Edgar Hoover Building
935 Pennsylvania Avenue, N.W.
Washington, DC 20535-0001
(202) 324-3000
Web site: http://www.fbi.gov

The Federal Bureau of Investigation (FBI) dates to the early 1900s, when it was a small office of federal agents charged with investigating crimes against federal laws (as opposed to state or local laws). Initially these were mostly banking and financial crimes, but during World War I the bureau's activities expanded to investigating espionage. From 1924 on under Director J. Edgar Hoover, the investigations focused on Prohibition violations and what are now referred to as civil rights issues in the South. With the federal government expansion under President Franklin D. Roosevelt (1933–1945), the bureau's work also expanded, although it still concentrated on federal crimes. Director Hoover was the most enduring power in the U.S. government until his death in 1972.

The government's ability to persecute minority views has always been challenged in the U.S. political system, and the FBI has often been at the center of such debate. During Hoover's directorship, the FBI attracted public controversy when it expanded its ability to monitor the public because of its perceived requirements to protect national security during the Cold War. Hoover's FBI engaged in domestic spying against what the director believed were unpatriotic elements of society, and subsequent directors have always faced the same questions, particularly as surveillance technology has become more advanced.

In the 1990s and particularly after 9/11, its focus has moved steadily to national security rather than merely law enforcement. The bureau has had to adjust to a rapidly changing international system, and must now also try to track various groups around the world threatening the United States. In autumn 2001, the bureau suffered frustration as it unsuccessfully attempted to apprehend the perpetrators of anthrax attacks along the east coast. In spring 2002, the FBI was accused of having missed obvious signs of the impending 9/11 terrorist attacks due to excessive bureaucracy; a charge the bureau denied. President Bush has suggested reforms to help the FBI prevent similar tragedies. In the midst of these challenges, it is clear that the FBI plays a crucial role in the government's efforts to promote national security through homeland defense.

The FBI is headquartered in Washington, DC, and has field offices across the United States and in key foreign countries (under the auspices of the U.S. Embassy). The FBI maintains lists of the criminals that the bureau most wants to capture, including the Ten Most Wanted and the Most Wanted Terrorists lists.

General Accounting Office (*See* Office of the Comptroller General)

Industrial College of the Armed Forces
Eisenhower Hall
Fort Lesley J. McNair
Washington, DC 20319
(202) 685-4333
FAX: (202) 685-4175
Web site: http://www.ndu.edu/icaf/main/index.htm

The Industrial College of the Armed Forces (ICAF) is one of two Senior Service Schools located at historic Fort Lesley J. McNair in southwest Washington, DC. Like the National War College (see p. 273), the Industrial College is responsible for educating U.S. military officers in the ranks of lieutenant colonel, commander, colonel, and captain as well as senior civilian government officials about national strategy and resourcing that strategy. The college's ten-month master's degree program provides students the opportunity to think about the challenges facing the nation while understanding the limitations on U.S. power projection.

Information Resource Management College
George C. Marshall Hall
Fort Lesley J. McNair
Washington, DC 20319
(202) 685-2080
E-mail: childr@ndu.edu
Web site: http://www.ndu.edu/irmc

The Information Resource Management College (IRMC) of the National Defense University (see p. 272) seeks to provide students with a thorough understanding of how information will shape the national security agenda in the coming decades. Its courses are short, from one day to several months in duration, and intensive. The college offers accredited programs for chief information officers and others, both in government and in the private sector.

Institute for National Strategic Studies
Fort Lesley J. McNair
Washington, DC 20319
(202) 685-3838
FAX: (202) 685-3972
E-mail: websterk@ndu.edu
Web site: http://www.ndu.edu/inss/insshp.html

The Institute for National Strategic Studies (INSS), which is part of the National Defense University (see p. 272), is often referred to as the "think tank for the Joint Chiefs of Staff." The institute is responsible for pursuing issues identified by the Joint Staff as most likely to pose a threat to the United States in the next generation. These issues may be topical or regional.

INSS has several sections, including the War Gaming and Simulation Center, which develops and executes war games for specific scenarios; the China Center, which evaluates the Chinese military; and the National Defense University Press, which publishes works on national security issues in several formats. INSS also holds a variety of conferences, seminars, and meetings on security questions, attended by leaders from the United States and other countries.

Publications: The best-known INSS publication is *Joint Force Quarterly,* established in 1992 as a forum for discussion of the joint mission facing the armed forces and other elements of the U.S. government. The institute also publishes the *McNair Papers,* periodic, short monographs on national security concerns; *Strategic Fora,* four-page assessments of current event issues; and conference reports. Its Web site makes conference papers available for years after the meetings are held.

Institute for Peace
1200 Seventeenth Street, N.W., Suite 200
Washington, DC 20036-3011
E-mail: requests@usip.org
Web site: http://www.usip.org

The U.S. Institute for Peace was created by Congress in 1984 to study peaceful approaches to resolving global conflict. The institute's board of directors is appointed by Congress and works through a variety of mechanisms to study the peaceful resolution of conflict. The institute publishes a variety of volumes on issues relating to peaceful conflict resolution and holds annual competitions for grants on designated topics to generate new research in the area.

Publications: The Institute for Peace publishes a wide range of monographs, reports, and studies. Many of them are also available on-line through the institute's Web site.

Joint Forces Staff College
7800 Hampton Boulevard
Norfolk, VA 23511
(757) 443-6212
FAX: (757) 443-6210
E-mail: fritzk@jfsc.ndu.edu
Web site: http://www.jfsc.ndu.edu/

The Joint Forces Staff College (JFSC) is the joint educational institution sponsored by the Joint Chiefs of Staff to prepare midgrade officers from all of the armed services and a small number of civilians to work for commanders in chief of the Unified Commands around the world. This program exposes students to joint doctrine and other required activities while also offering some regional analysis.

Marine Corps University
Quantico Marine Base
Quantico, VA
(703) 784-2105
Web site: http://www.mcu.usmc.mil/new_web_site/Information.htm

The Marine Corps University is the newest of the war colleges, also called Senior Service Schools. Located at the Marine headquarters in Quantico, Virginia, the Marine Corps University is a small facility that asks its students—officers of the rank of lieutenant colonel and colonel—to think at the strategic level. The program of study is extensive, covering Marine issues as well as national security concerns. The university also includes a Command and Staff College for lower-ranking officers.

George C. Marshall European Center for Security Studies
International Office
Director
Gernackerstrasse 2
82467 Garmisch-Partenkirchen, Germany
(49) 8821-750-793

U.S. Office
Director
Unit 24502 ECMC-PA
APO AE 09053
Web site: http://www.marshallcenter.org

The George C. Marshall European Center for Security Studies, established in 1992, aims to educate military leaders from the former Warsaw Bloc states about the restrictions, challenges, and opportunities of life in a democratic system. Officers and officials from across Eastern and Central Europe attend the center for a fixed period of time to study a variety of topics. The center's work, which falls within the jurisdiction of the U.S. European Command in Germany, is an example of the type of outreach and nation building that the Clinton administration felt was crucial after the Cold War ended.

The Marshall Center is composed of several distinct units that are becoming a major component of U.S. ties with militaries in the rest of the world. As foreign assistance (particularly for former Soviet block militaries) is drying up, the Marshall Center offers both education and outreach, seeking to alter the approach that militaries in the region have to one another as well as with their own societies. Like the Asia Pacific Center, the Center for Hemispheric Defense Studies, the Africa Center for Security Studies, and the Near East–South Asia Center, the Marshall Center is creating a broader definition of how security is approached around the world.

The Marshall Center includes the College of International and Security Studies, with senior level seminars for high-ranking officers and civilian officials to discuss various topics relevant across the region, such as leadership. The college also provides the base for European language studies for U.S. and NATO language specialists. The Marshall Center also maintains a Virtual College, which provides distance learning for those individuals unable to afford the time or cost of getting to Germany. This college is intended to provide education to far more students than the center can accommodate. Further, the Marshall Center holds almost two dozen major international conferences annually, to bring together civilian and military officials for the purpose of exploring various views on issues like corruption and terrorism. Finally, the Marshall Center offers a vast array of resources through its Web site.

National Defense University
Fort Lesley J. McNair
Washington, DC 20319
(202) 685-3938
FAX: (202) 685-3328
E-mail: PAO@ndu.edu
Web site: http://www.ndu.edu

In 1976 the National Defense University received its charter from Congress to serve as the umbrella organization for the National War College and the Industrial College of the Armed Forces (see p. 273 and p. 268, respectively), the two flagship schools focusing on the strategic level of analysis in national security. Headed by a three-star officer (lieutenant general or vice admiral rank) for a three-year term, the university now includes a much wider range of functions tied to national security strategy. Its primary campus is located at Fort Lesley J. McNair in southwest Washington, DC, but NDU also includes the Joint Forces Staff College, a school for midgrade officers in Norfolk, Virginia. The university lies directly within the chain of command that originates with the chairman of the Joint Chiefs of Staff and is tasked by the Joint Staff. Primarily a university, with the academic freedom and intellectual curiosity of a traditional educational institution, the National Defense University has a unique "not-for-attribution" policy that guarantees speakers and students the ability to speak their minds without fear of media attention or political reprisals.

Along with the two degree-granting institutions, the National Defense University has assumed a much broader role in the national security field than its title would imply. NDU also encompasses the Information Management College, the Institute for National Strategic Studies, the Joint Forces Staff College, the Center for Hemispheric Defense Studies, the Africa Center for Strategic Studies, the Near East–South Asia Center for Strategic Studies, and several other small components. The "regional" centers, established during the 1990s and paralleling the George

Marshall Center in Germany and the Asia Pacific Center for Security Studies, aim to enhance discussions of strategic issues while trumpeting the role of democracy in the future of these regions. Three of the new centers are under the National Defense University and make the NDU mission much different than it was a decade ago.

National Technical Information Service
5285 Port Royal Road
Springfield, VA 22161
(703) 605-6585
E-mail: webmaster@ntis.gov
Web site: http://www.ntis.gov

Part of the Department of Commerce, the National Technical Information Service (NTIS) produces information to enhance economic growth and job creation, both crucial to the protection of national security. The NTIS covers topics ranging from engineering to energy to communication. The reports it produces are intended to connect aspects of the government with public sectors more closely. The NTIS helps in the national security field by consolidating reports on a variety of technical subjects such as computers and information theory.

National War College
Fort Lesley J. McNair
Washington, DC 20319-5078
(202) 685-4343
FAX: (202) 685-4654
Web site: http://www.ndu.edu/nwc

Created out of the vision of Generals Eisenhower and Marshall at the end of World War II to ensure an interagency and interservice understanding of national security strategy, the National War College is one of two Senior Service Schools in the United States that focus exclusively on national security strategy questions. The college serves students from all the armed services at the ranks of colonel and lieutenant colonel (or, among Navy students, the ranks of captain and commander) and senior civilians from the national security communities of the U.S. government. The college prides itself not on teaching students what to think, but on letting students push beyond a "school solution" to the security issues facing the country in the next generation. The faculty also engages in research and outreach to a broad array of national and international organizations. Students earn a master's degree in national security studies upon completing the ten-month program.

Naval Post-Graduate School
1 University Circle
Monterey, CA 93943-5001
(831) 656-2441 or (831) 656-2442
Web site: http://www.nps.navy.mil

The Naval Post-Graduate School (NPS) is in the unique position of offering studies in business, operational research, international studies, and engineering and applied sciences at the graduate level to satisfy the U.S. Navy's requirements for qualified personnel in technical and social science fields. It is a fully accredited university, serving students from various civilian and military agencies as well as foreign countries. With two hundred faculty and several programs across its areas of concentration, NPS offers both resident and distance-learning opportunities for graduate work.

In the broadest sense of national security, meaning the development of officers and officials from the civilian sector, one could say that everything done at NPS is national security. It does have, however, a Department of National Security that offers many varied courses. Additionally, NPS is the home of the Civil-Military Center, which conducts International Military Education and Training (IMET) for different regional commands of the U.S. armed forces. Finally, NPS is a location for joint professional military education, as are the Senior Service Schools listed in this volume.

Naval War College
686 Cushing Road
Newport, RI 02841-1207
(401) 841-2135
E-mail: cce@nwc.navy.mil
Web site: http://www.nwc.navy.mil or cce.nwc.navy.mil

The Naval War College was established in 1884 as the center for study of strategy, tactics, operations, and the science of naval warfare. It educates U.S. Naval officers and other students in the national security field, including foreign officers, about the issues facing the navy as it contemplates an increasingly complex global arena. The college's role includes performing research on questions that will plague the service in the long term; indeed, it has always been a place for challenging conventional wisdom.

The Naval War College is probably best-known for a famous individual and a famous war game. Alfred Thayer Mahan, president of the Naval War College from 1882 to 1883 and again in 1886–1889, wrote a highly influential study called *The Influence of Seapower upon History, 1660–1873*. This history asked not only about the role of a navy in a country's defense, but also about power projection and the balance of various issues in the security calculation. During the interwar period, the Naval War College conducted a long series of war games on the possibility of Japan becoming a threat in Asia, thus providing invaluable planning for World War II as a result of War Game Orange.

Publication: The *Naval War College Review* quarterly addresses the broadest questions facing the country in an ever-changing world.

Near East–South Asia Center for Strategic Studies
National Defense University
U.S. Coast Guard (Transpoint) Building, Suite 4308
2100 2nd Street, S.W.
Washington, DC 20593-0001
E-mail: nesa-center@ndu.edu
Web site: http://www.ndu.edu/nesa/index.htm

The Near East–South Asia Center for Strategic Studies was one of five centers established in the 1990s to assist in both the transition from authoritarian to democratic regimes in the world as well as improving the quality of strategic thinking (the others being the Asia Pacific Center, the Center for Hemispheric Defense Studies, the Africa Center for Security Studies, and the George C. Marshall European Center for Security Studies). It concentrates on the area ranging from Morocco east to India. The center brings decision makers, both civilian and military, from the relevant states for short executive-level courses on issues relating to strategy. It also holds periodic conferences to address topics relevant to the region. Another significant mission of the center is to engage in discussions in the region to promote the broadening of thought necessary in the new international context.

Office of Homeland Security
The White House
1600 Pennsylvania Avenue, N.W.
Washington, DC 20500
(202) 456-1414
Web site: http://www.whitehouse.gov/homeland/

The Office of Homeland Security was created by President George W. Bush in October 2001, one month after the tragic attacks on the Pentagon and World Trade Center. Its purpose is to develop and coordinate a national strategy for preventing similar attacks on the United States in the future. The office was created by a presidential executive order, hence it functions at the highest levels of the government. Its first director, former Pennsylvania Governor Thomas Ridge, has been working to coordinate the many agencies and organizations within the U.S. federal and state governments that handle antiterrorism and other aspects of homeland security. The president's June 2002 proposal would, if ratified and funded by Congress, raise the office to Cabinet level and greatly broaden its member agencies to streamline the process of protecting the homeland.

Office of the Comptroller General
441 G Street, N.W.
Washington, DC 20548
(202) 512-4800
E-mail: webmaster@gao.gov
Web site: http://www.gao.gov

The Comptroller General is the head of a legislative-branch organization known as the U.S. General Accounting Office; it has eleven regional offices across the country, each roughly colocated with a major city or government facility such as an Air Force base. Founded as a result of the Budget Reorganization Act of 1921, the Office of the Comptroller General is responsible for investigating issues that concern use of U.S. government funds. A major task of the comptroller is to investigate aspects of the U.S. national security regime. The investigations are of two main types: oversight, or examining any general aspect of the overall program, and fiscal, or reconciling and accounting an individual program to evaluate whether it has overspent its allocation of funds. The comptroller does annual evaluations of some programs in the defense community (e.g., weapons systems and general procurement and acquisition) and looks at various overseas programs to evaluate their effectiveness (e.g., U.S. assistance to Colombia in narcotics interdiction or foreign aid to the former Soviet Republic of Armenia). Reports by the comptroller are intended to be strictly nonpartisan, but they are occasionally used by politicians and others with a clearly political intent.

Office of the U.S. Trade Representative
600 17th Street, N.W.
Washington, DC 20508
(888) 473-8787
E-mail: contactustr@ustr.gov
Web site: http://www.ustr.gov

As the importance of economics and trade in the national security arena has increased, so has the role of the Office of the U.S. Trade Representative. This office, created by law in 1963 and elevated to Cabinet rank in 1980, is now considered a major player as the United States formulates its relationships with both major and smaller countries around the world. The U.S. trade representative is responsible both for negotiating with foreign governments and for advising the president of his government's policy options in the trade area. The work of the Office of the U.S. Trade Representative is divided into various regions and issues around the world.

Web Addresses for Governmental Organizations

The United States and its government are complex organisms; the same can be said of the elements of government charged with national security. As noted elsewhere in this volume, national security can be loosely or narrowly defined, depending upon one's particular agenda. For those who prefer to approach the world from a more traditional view, national security is roughly equated to defense and the most basic elements of protection of society. This definition was particularly applicable as long as the primary threats to the nation appeared outside of the country. That posture is difficult to maintain after the events of September 11, 2001, when the United States itself was hit by terrorism.

It would be inaccurate, however, to say that the definition of national security was broadened overnight in September 2001.

National security has been changing as the world and the nation evolve. Even the concept of homeland security had been introduced well before the tragedy of 2001. Although one can argue about the failure to anticipate the attacks, people had already begun to ask questions about our fundamental assumptions regarding national safety long before the events proved those questions appropriate.

Given the breadth of concerns that national security includes, there are many government organizations with a role in national security, and not all of them are delineated in the previous section. The reason for that omission is that the national security role is not their primary requirement as a federal agency. In the case of agencies like the Homeland Security office or the Federal Bureau of Investigation, their pivotal positions in national security are obvious and have been laid out above. But a description of each and every office with a national security role is not practical, nor would it be particularly useful to the reader. Instead, a list of organizations of the federal government that involve national security, along with their Web site URLs, provides a starting point for investigation. Some of these offices have been listed earlier in the chapter, but this section provides a handy reference for finding government agencies.

The publications of two Cabinet offices require special note. First, the Department of State produces the *Country Background Notes* series on states around the world, available in print from a Federal Government Repository Library or on-line at http://www.state.gov/r/pa/ei/bgn/. The State Department also produces periodic reports on various topics or regions that are available on-line or in print. Second, the Defense Department produces a wide array of reports on topics crucial to this volume. These are available through any Federal Government Repository Library or on-line through DefenseLink at http://www.defense-link.mil/pubs/.

Africa Center for Security Studies,
     http://www.africacenter.org
Air Force, http://www.af.mil
Air Force Thunderbirds,
     http://www.airforce.com/thunderbirds
Army, http://www.army.mil
Army Golden Knights,
     http://www.usarec.army.mil/hq/goldenknights/

Asia Pacific Center for Security Studies, http://www.apcss.org
Blue Angels, http://www.blueangels.navy.mil
BosniaLink, http://www.dtic.mil/bosnia
Bureau of Export Administration, http://www.bxa.doc.gov
Centers for Disease Control, http://www.cdc.gov
Central Command, http://www.centcom.mil
Central Intelligence Agency, http://www.cia.gov
Congressional Budget Office, http://www.cbo.gov
Defense Information Systems Agency,
    http://www.itsi.disa.mil/
Defense Intelligence Agency, http://www.dia.mil/
Defense Logistic Agency, http://www.dla.mil
Defense Technical Information Center, http://www.dtic.mil
Department of Commerce, Home2.doc.gov
Department of Defense, http://www.defenselink.mil
Department of Energy, http://www.energy.gov
Department of Justice, http://www.usdoj.gov
Department of State, http://www.state.gov
Department of the Treasury, http://www.treasury.gov
Department of Transportation, http://www.dot.gov
Drug Enforcement Agency, http://www.dea.gov
European Command, http://www.eucom.mil
Federal Bureau of Investigation, http://www.fbi.gov
Federal Emergency Management Agency,
    http://www.fema.gov
Federal Energy Regulatory Commission,
    http://www.ferc.fed.us
Federal Maritime Commission, http://www.fmc.gov
Financial Crimes Enforcement Network,
    http://www.ustreas.gov/fincen
House Committee on Appropriations,
    http://www.house.gov/appropriations
House Committee on Armed Services,
    http://www.house.gov/hasc
House Committee on International Relations,
    http://www.house.gov/international_relations/
House Committee on Ways and Means,
    http://waysandmeans.house.gov
House Permanent Select Committee on Intelligence,
    http://Intelligence.house.gov
Immigration and Naturalization Service, http://www.ins.gov
International Trade Administration, http://www.ita.doc.gov

Joint Chiefs of Staff, http://www.dtic.mil/jcs/
Joint Forces Command, http://www.jfcom.mil
Leap Frogs,
　　http://www.sealchallenge.navy.mil/leapfrogs.htm
Los Alamos National Laboratory,
　　http://www.lanl.gov/worldview
Marine Corps, http://www.usmc.mil
Marshall Center (George C. Marshall European Center for
　　Security Studies), http://www.marshallcenter.org
Missile Defense Agency, http://www.acq.osd.mil/bmdo/
National Drug Intelligence Center,
　　http://www.usdoj.gov/ndic
National Guard, http://www.ngb.dtic.mil
National Reconnaissance Office, http://www.nro.gov
National Security Agency, http://www.nsa.gov
National Security Council, http://www.whitehouse.gov/nsc
National Technical Information Service, http://www.ntis.gov
Navy, http://www.navy.mil
Near East–South Asia Center for Security Studies,
　　http://www.ndu.edu/nesa
North American Aerospace Defense Command,
　　http://www.norad.mil
North Atlantic Treaty Organization, http://www.nato.int
Office of Homeland Security,
　　http://www.whitehouse.gov/homeland
Office of Management and Budget,
　　http://www.whitehouse.gov/omb
Office of National Drug Control Policy,
　　http://www.whitehousedrugpolicy.gov
Office of Nonproliferation and National Security,
　　http://www.energy.gov/security
Office of Secretary of Defense,
　　http://www.defenselink.mil/osd
Pacific Command, http://www.pacom.mil
Peace Corps, http://www.peacecorps.gov/index
Secret Service, http://www.ustreas.gov/usss
Senate Appropriations Committee, Appropriations.senate.gov
Senate Armed Services Committee,
　　http://www.senate.gov/~armed_services
Senate Foreign Relations Committee, Foreign.senate.gov
Senate Select Committee on Intelligence,
　　Intelligence.senate.gov

Southern Command, http://www.southcom.mil/home
Strategic Command, http://www.stratcom.mil
U.S. Agency for International Development,
     http://www.usaid.gov
U.S. Arms Control and Disarmament Agency,
     http://www.state.gov/www/global/arms/index.html
U.S. Coast Guard, http://www.uscg.mil
U.S. Customs Service, http://www.customs.ustreas.gov
U.S. Trade Representative, http://www.ustr.gov
Voice of America, http://www.voa.gov

7

Selected Print and Nonprint Resources

T he field of national security has changed dramatically in terms of the resources available to those tracking it. The World Wide Web and other nonprint media have opened an amazing number of outlets as well as alternative views on national security, particularly since the 1990s boom in personal computers and Internet access. Although this new abundance of information can be a tremendous aid for both the serious researcher and the casual surfer, it does make culling through resources for the reliable versus the prejudiced or factually incorrect quite time-consuming. Not all of these new outlets and alternate views are reliable or useful, and one must remember that there are no thoroughly impartial sources.

As the previous chapters have indicated, the focus of national security has also changed dramatically since the end of the Cold War, expanding to include many other threats and concerns than before. National security is such a broadly interpreted topic that many relevant resources might not be obvious at first glance. An example would be the Frontline biography entitled *John Paul II: The Millennial Pope.* This program focuses on the life and significance of John Paul II, not only as a spiritual leader, but as a key figure in the fight against Communism. These and other resources provide insights into U.S. national security concerns that might be overlooked by a more traditional perspective.

This chapter includes resources on today's many and varied national security issues. I have categorized them into three areas: (1) print resources, including weeklies and journals, reference books, monographs, and articles, (2) nonprint resources, including videos and the Internet, and (3) commercial media, including cable and network television, radio, newspapers, and wire services. This selective list of resources only hints at the vast material available in a variety of media on U.S. national security. Indeed, any bibliography on national security will almost certainly fall short of including all resources because new material is being produced hourly. The intent of this chapter is not to be comprehensive, but to give any student of national security in the United States some initial research avenues to pursue. For assistance in locating additional resources, consult a reference librarian.

Print Resources

I have divided print materials into five categories: weeklies and journals, reference books, monographs, articles, and series. Many journals are now available both in hard copy and on-line. Reference books on national security are easily found in libraries around the world, so I have mentioned only five here. Most of the resources in this section are monographs and significant articles on U.S. national security.

Weeklies and Journals

A large number of specialized weekly newspapers report on national security. The best known weekly in the world with a sophisticated emphasis on national security concerns is the *Economist*, published in London. Its analysis is succinct but relatively strong for the United States and other areas of the world. The *Wall Street Journal's Far Eastern Economic Affairs* is a weekly news source that reports on a wide range of Asian issues, from Pakistan to Japan. *Defense News* is a U.S. weekly publication focusing on issues relating to all of the defense industries, with special reports from various parts of the world.

A number of high-quality journals focus on national security. The oldest is the Council on Foreign Relations' *Foreign Affairs*, first published in 1922, and its more recent competitor, *Foreign Policy*, is from the Carnegie Endowment for International Peace. Both are bimonthly publications with an emphasis on the practitioner/scholar rather than purely on academics. The Nitze School for Advanced International Studies of Johns Hopkins University publishes the *SAIS Review*, a quarterly. Georgetown University began publishing the *National Security Studies Quarterly* in the 1990s. *Orbis*, another quarterly, is published by the Foreign Policy Research Institute in Philadelphia. The *Washington Quarterly* is published by MIT Press with a strong connection to the Center for Strategic and International Studies in Washington. The World Policy Institute in New York publishes the *World Policy Journal*. None of these journals are particularly theoretical, being much more policy-oriented in focus. *Diplomatic History*, the journal for the Society of Historians of American Foreign Relations, thoroughly treats all issues in the national security realm and has a mix of policy and scholarly articles.

The journals that provide a broader mix of policy and theory include *International Security*, published by the MIT Press, *World Policy*, and various regionally dedicated titles, including *Middle East Quarterly*, *Journal of Inter-American Studies and World Affairs*, *Asian Survey*, *China Quarterly*, *Pacific Affairs*, and *African Studies*. The flagship journal of the International Studies Association, *International Studies Quarterly*, is a highly quantitative, theoretical journal on international issues, some of which focus on national security. However, this is a highly specialized publication. The International Studies Association also began publishing the *Mershon Center Review* in the mid-1990s to consider issues related to the teaching of international studies along with policy questions in international affairs, many of which target U.S. national security issues. At the other end of the spectrum, *Current History* is a monthly publication that is valuable not only for its individual articles but also for its end-of-year assessments of U.S. strategy around the world. *Commentary*, a Jewish monthly, also includes a significant number of articles aimed at national security issues.

Other journals with materials relevant to national security are listed below. Some of these provide complementary material on-line; others require a subscription for both on-line and print materials. Some produce different on-line and print editions.

Access Asia Review, http://www.nbr.org/publications/
review/index.html
Aerospace Daily, http://www.aviationnow.com/
aviationnow/aerospacedaily_marketing_page.jsp
Air Force Magazine, http://www.afa.org/magazine/
aboutmag.asp

Air Force Speeches, http://www.af.mil/news/speech
Air University Review, http://www.airpower.maxwell.
    af.mil/airchronicles/aureview/index.html
Airpower Journal, http://www.airpower.maxwell.af.mil
American Diplomacy, http://www.unc.edu/depts/diplomat
Armed Forces & Society, search.epnet.com
Armed Forces Journal International, http://www.afji.com
Arms Sales Monitor, sun00781.dn.net/asmp/library/
    armsonitor.html
Army, http://www.ausa.org/armyzine
Asia-Pacific Defense FORUM, http://www.pacom.mil/
    forum/forum.htm
Bulletin of Atomic Scientists, http://www.thebulletin.org/
    issues/yearindex.html
Defense Aerospace News, http://www.defense-
    aerospace.com/
Defense Almanac, http://www.defenselink.mil/
    pubs/almanac
Defense Analysis, search.epnet.com
Defense Monitor, http://www.cdi.org/dm/
*DISAM Journal of International Security Assistance
    Management,* http://disam.osd.mil/Journal.htm
Fletcher Forum of World Affairs,
    fletcher.tufts.edu/forum/index.asp
Foreign Service Journal, http://www.afsa.org/
    fsj/index.html
Global Issues, usinfo.state.gov/journals/journals.htm
Intelligence Online, http://www.intelligenceonline.com/
Joint Force Quarterly, http://www.dtic.mil/doctrine/
    jel/jfq_pubs/index.htm or search.epnet.com
Military Review, search.epnet.com
Naval War College Review, http://www.nwc.navy.mil/
    press/Review/aboutNWCR.htm
Parameters, carlisle-www.army.mil/usawc/Parameters/
RAND Review, http://www.rand.org/publications/
    randreview
Surface Warfare, surface.nswc.navy.mil/
    magazine.ma_toc.html
Survival, www3.oup.co.uk/surviv/contents/

Reference Materials

Jentleson, Bruce, and Thomas Paterson, eds. *Encyclopedia of U.S. Foreign Relations.* 4 vols. London: Oxford University Press, 1997.

This encyclopedia is a thorough treatment of the national security and foreign affairs issues from 1945 to the mid-1990s.

Jordan, Amos, William Taylor, Michael Mazarr, and Sam Nunn. *American National Security.* 5th ed. Baltimore: Johns Hopkins University Press, 1998.

This reference book is useful for all interested in the basics of national security.

Judge, Edward, and John Langdon. *The Cold War: A History Through Documents.* New York: Prentice Hall, 1999.

This is a good introduction to the documents that provided the justification and evidence for the Cold War. It includes all of the basic U.S. citations from the period.

National Security Archive Collection. London: Chadwyck-Healey, various years.

This index provides a listing of all the materials that have been released in the United States under the Freedom of Information Act of 1974 and published by the National Security Archive (see chapter 6). The *Collection,* which is updated regularly, includes full publications details about all of the NSA materials. The Digital National Security Archive Collection is also available by subscription (nsarchive.chadwyck).

Shultz, Richard, Roy Godson, and George Quester, eds. *Security Studies in the Twenty-first Century.* New York: Brassey's, 1997.

A thorough treatment, this work is particularly strong in its explanation of the various scholarly approaches to national security and its descriptions of national security studies throughout the world.

Watson, Cynthia A. *U.S. National Security Policy Groups.* Westport, CT: Greenwood Books, 1990.

My previous book examines national security organizations, funding sources, products, and outreach efforts. Now dated because of its focus on the Cold War, it remains a useful volume for its detailed information on the policy groups across the range of U.S. society that were trying to influence national security issues at the end of the Cold War. Information on their orientation, influence methods, and funding levels is provided.

Monographs

Acheson, Dean. *Present at the Creation.* New York: Norton, 1969.

This is the memoir of Dean Acheson, one of the most important figures of the first half of the Cold War. Secretary of state during the last years of the Truman administration and the Korean War, Acheson was instrumental in determining the line the United States followed as the Cold War accelerated.

Alibek, Ken, and S. Handleman. *Biohazard: The Chilling True Story of the Largest Covert Biological Weapons Program in the World—Told from Inside by the Man Who Ran It.* New York: Delta, 2000.

This account, by the self-proclaimed leader of the Soviet Union's biological weapons program, is a frustrating and startling indication of the weapons development that was being carried out for use against the United States and other adversaries. It is a wake-up call.

Allison, Graham. *The Essence of Decision: Explaining the Cuban Missile Crisis.* Boston: Little, Brown, 1971.

This book is probably the most-cited study of decision making in the U.S. government. Centering on the 1962 Cuban Missile Crisis, it examines three different decision-making approaches and explains why each produces a different outcome.

Alperovitz, Gar. *Atomic Diplomacy: Hiroshima and Potsdam.* New York: Pluto Press, 1994.

This volume infuriates many people in the United States because of its assertions that Washington unilaterally initiated the nuclear competition between the United States and the Soviet Union. It is useful, however, because this view is far more commonly held outside of the United States than most people would like to acknowledge.

Ambrose, Stephen. *Nixon: The Triumph of a Politician, 1962–1972.* New York: Simon & Schuster, 1989.

This extraordinary assessment of U.S. President Richard Nixon during his time in the political "wilderness" explains how he emerged to be elected president in 1968. One of the premier biographers and popular historians of his era, Ambrose is solid in his analysis and documentation.

Ambrose, Stephen E., and Douglas G. Brinkley. *Rise to Globalism: American Foreign Policy since 1938.* 8th ed. New York: Penguin Books, 1997.

An excellent primer for anyone not familiar with the period immediately following World War II, this work is updated regularly to bring more current affairs to the reader's attention. Highly readable, this volume gives any reader, whether already familiar with U.S. national security concerns or new to the topic, a good direction to follow in looking at the U.S. leadership role in the global context.

Beckwith, Charlie, and Donald Knox. *Delta Force: The Army's Elite Counter-Terrorist Unit.* New York: Avon Books, 2000.

This is a study of the Delta Force, a secretive arm of the U.S. Army charged with some of the toughest U.S. missions, such as counterterrorism and peacekeeping in Somalia. It is interesting in part because the army continues to be most unwilling to discuss the Force's actions for fear of compromising its work and making its members vulnerable to attacks.

Bergen, Peter. *Holy War, Inc.: Inside the Secret World of Osama Bin Laden.* New York: Free Press, 2001.

This book was one of the first books about the shadowy and hateful world of Usama Bin Laden to appear after September 11, 2001. Bergen traces Bin Laden's history, including the apparent reasons for his strong antipathy toward the United States and his ability to move people to support his cause.

Beschloss, Michael, and Strobe Talbott. *At the Highest Levels: The Inside Story of the End of the Cold War.* Boston: Little, Brown, 1993.

This study, by two well-known analysts of national security, describes the debate within the U.S. and Soviet governments as the Cold War came to an end. The authors enjoyed access to the highest-level decision makers, and this work reveals their thorough understanding of the implications of various options that confronted the two countries in the late 1980s and early 1990s.

Bill, James. *The Eagle and the Lion: The Tragedy of American-Iranian Relations.* New Haven, CT: Yale University Press, 1988.

This study was one of the first to thoroughly treat the downward spiral of Washington's relationship with the shah of Iran and the animosity between the United States and the Islamic-fundamentalist regime that succeeded him. It is a careful examination of how a superpower's ties with a country can deteriorate when competing pressures make its ruler unwilling to bend to the popular will.

Bowden, Mark. *Blackhawk Down: A Story of Modern War.* New York: Signet, 2001.

Mark Bowden, a *Philadelphia Inquirer* journalist, gives a gripping description of the Somalia incident in 1993, when Army Special Forces troops were subject to Somali mob violence, leading to President Clinton's rushed decision to leave Somalia. It is a compelling lesson about future conflicts.

———. *Killing Pablo.* New York: Atlantic Monthly Press, 2001.

This is an account of the tracking and capture of the world's most famous *narcotraficante*, Pablo Escobar Gaviria, from the Medellín cartel. It's a cautionary tale about how tough the new national security threats can be when money is part of the equation.

Brands, H. W. *The Devil We Knew.* New York: Oxford University Press, 1993.

This is a fascinating study of the evolution of U.S. concerns about Communism and the need to create new policies in the years after World War II to prevent the Soviets from gaining ground around the world. It traces U.S. domestic history along with changes around the world between 1947 and the early 1990s.

Brodie, Bernard. *Strategy in the Missile Age.* Princeton, NJ: Princeton University Press, 1959.

This is a fundamental examination of the effects that missile technology and proliferation had on the international context and on decision making in the middle of the Cold War.

Brown, Harold. *Thinking about National Security: Defense and Foreign Policy in a Dangerous World.* Boulder: Westview Press, 1983.

This thoughtful assessment examines the new world that began to evolve after Ronald Reagan was elected president in 1980. Harold Brown, known as an intense thinker, carefully argues that the foreign and national security contexts were altered in the early 1980s and that the world thereafter faced a much more complicated global context. He penned this in the aftermath of the Iranian Revolution, at the beginning of the Persian Gulf War between Iran and Iraq, and soon after the Soviet Union began its intervention in Afghanistan.

Brzezinski, Zbigniew. *Power and Principle: Memoirs of the National Security Advisor, 1977–1981.* New York: Farrar, Straus, Giroux, 1983.

Many people accused Zbigniew Brzezinski of modeling his career after Henry Kissinger's since both were former European academics at Ivy League schools. Written after Brzezinski left the Carter administration, this work describes the problems facing all administrations as they work through the internal tensions inherent in decision making. Additionally, he explains the complexity of the problems that came together in 1980, contributing to Carter's reelection defeat, and describes them as a harbinger of a new world.

Buchanan, Patrick. *The Death of the West: How Dying Populations and Immigrant Invasions Imperil Our Country and Civilization.* New York: Dunne Books, 2001.

Probably the most controversial individual on the national political scene, Patrick Buchanan argues that the immigrants coming into the United States, along with the demographic reality of decreasing traditional population bases in the United States, make the country vulnerable to significant changes that will decrease its power.

Carter, Jimmy. *Keeping Faith: Memoirs of a President.* New York: Bantam, 1982.

This is the memoir of one of the more controversial presidents of the twentieth century, particularly in national security issues. Jimmy Carter's emphasis on human rights and a different approach to our adversaries became disastrous in 1979, when the Iranian hostage crisis and the Soviet invasion of Afghanistan proved decisive in his defeat for reelection.

Chace, James. *Acheson: The Secretary of State Who Created the American World.* New York: Simon & Schuster, 1998.

James Chace's work is a fascinating, detailed biography of one of the most effective shapers of the U.S. national security environment and the global scene after World War II. Dean Acheson is probably best known as the secretary of state who issued the "perimeter" speech in 1950 (see chapter 5), supposedly giving the North Koreans the green light to invade South Korea later that year. Chace's biography shows that Acheson's contributions were far greater than that.

Christopher, Warren. *In the Stream of History: Shaping Foreign Policy for a New Era.* Stanford, CA: Stanford University Press, 1998.

Warren Christopher's experience as Bill Clinton's first secretary of state illustrates the danger and strength of having a balanced, legal mind in that position. His memoir examines the problems that the Clinton administration never overcame as it sought to get its bearings in national security affairs. Christopher's tenure was marked by disappointments over Somalia, Haiti, and Bosnia, and his memoir indicates the complexity he and the administration were never able to address.

Clancy, Tom, Carl Steiner, and Tony Koltz. *Shadow Warriors: Inside Special Forces.* New York: Putnam Publishing Group, 2002.

This study of U.S. Special Forces not only outlines their contemporary activities but also provides some historical perspective on their role in the defense establishment.

Clark, Wesley. *Waging Modern War: Bosnia, Kosovo, and the Future of Combat.* New York: Public Affairs, 2001.

These memoirs of the U.S. general who served as supreme allied commander of Europe during the Kosovo campaign of 1999 are at least as revealing about the political dynamics in the United States during this period as about the waging of modern combat. Clark's disappointment in his political leaders is palpable and begs the question of how the United States will interact with allies as well as domestic groups in the future.

Clodfelter, Mark. *The Limits of Air Power: The American Bombing of North Vietnam.* New York: Free Press, 1989.

Written by an active duty U.S. Air Force officer, this study indicates that air power was far less successful at winning wars than the Air Force and the civilians seeking to avoid casualties were willing to admit. This volume discusses the strategic advantages and the challenges that air power actually brings in an era when there is increasing pressure on decision makers to limit casualties.

Cohen, Warren. *America in the Age of Soviet Power.* **Cambridge History of American Foreign Relations Series.** Cambridge: Cambridge University Press, 1993.

This is a crucial history of the United States in the years after World War II. Written by one of the most prominent Asian specialists, it presents a thorough and fascinating image of the period.

———. *America's Response to China.* New York: Columbia University Press, 1990.

The author gives a full treatment of the U.S.-Chinese relationship over the past three decades. The book gives various reasons for the policies of each power and outlines alternate approaches that could have been chosen.

Cole, Bernard D. *The Great Wall at Sea: China's Navy Enters the Twenty-first Century.* Annapolis, MD: Naval Institute Press, 2001.

The first serious treatment of China's navy in eighteen years, this work indicates that although the Chinese are modernizing, they are far behind the U.S. Navy. Cole argues that they appear to be preparing for a regional role rather than a global role.

Dam, Kenneth W. *The Rules of the Global Game.* Chicago: University of Chicago Press, 2001.

This book, by a Bush administration treasury official, indicates the new obstacles and opportunities involved in the evolving trade regime that has hurt the United States even while making it much more able to compete in some markets.

Emerson, Steve. *American Jihad: The Terrorists Living Among Us.* New York: Simon & Schuster, 2002.

Steve Emerson is a reporter who has become more interested in covering controversial issues relating to terrorism and proliferation and other nontraditional threats against the United States. This volume postulates that the terrorists threatening the United States have been among us for a long while as "sleeper cells" but are now becoming more awake.

Feaver, Peter, and Richard H. Kohn, eds. *Soldiers and Civilians: The Civil-Military Gap and American National Security.* Cambridge: MIT Press, 2001.

This study of the relationship between the military and the public at large is a follow-up of the discussions that have transpired since Kohn's 1993 article in *The National Interest,* which questioned whether the military had taken positions that were outside of the norm in the civil-military balance. Feaver and Kohn, a political scientist and a historian, respectively, may be the premier scholars in the field today.

Fitzgerald, Frances. *Way Out There in the Blue: Reagan, Star Wars, and the End of the Cold War.* New York: Simon & Schuster, 2000.

The daughter of one of the pioneers of the CIA, Frances

Fitzgerald writes poignantly of the contrasts between the hype of the Strategic Defense Initiative and the end of the Cold War, coming together in the person of President Reagan.

Flemming, Denna F. *The Cold War and Its Origins, 1917–1960.* 2 vols. Garden City, NY: Doubleday, 1961.

This volume is fairly nontraditional in tracing the beginning of the Cold War not to 1945 but to the creation of the Soviet Union in 1918. Not as well organized as it might be, the book does cover the period in a more comprehensive, critical light than most other histories.

Friedman, Thomas. *The Lexus and the Olive Tree.* New York: Anchor, 2000.

This is one of the most widely read books on the evolving impact of globalization on the international community and on national security. It shows how globalization is pulling some countries along while leaving others far behind.

———. *From Beirut to Jerusalem.* New York: Anchor Books, Doubleday, 1989.

This *New York Times* editorialist was the primary reporter in the Middle East in the 1980s. His views of the region and his understanding of how the United States affects the various states there are cutting, decisive, and thorough.

Gaddis, John Lewis. *Now We Know: Rethinking Cold War History.* Oxford: Oxford University Press, 1997.

The volume is an outgrowth of the Cold War History Project at the Smithsonian Institution, written by one of the most-respected U.S. scholars on strategy in this era. It unveils a number of policies undertaken by the Soviets, especially under Stalin, that confirmed our worst fears about Soviet behavior.

———. *Strategies of Containment: A Critical Appraisal of Postwar American National Security Policy.* New York: Oxford University Press, 1982.

This helpful study includes a framework for how to analyze the various strategies that successive U.S. administrations employed for dealing with the Soviet Union. It carefully examines the rationale behind the various policies and analyzes how each affected the successor administration. This thorough and analytical volume on the Cold War is especially appropriate for people who have not looked at the period in depth.

————. *The United States and the Origins of the Cold War, 1941–1947.* New York: Columbia University Press, 1972.

Gifted historian John Lewis Gaddis has written several books on the era immediately following the end of World War II and into the first moments of the Cold War. Among these is this book, which focuses on the initial years and how the views of the other side influenced, and even forced, U.S. behavior.

Garthoff, Raymond. *Détente and Confrontation: American-Soviet Relations from Nixon to Reagan.* Washington, DC: Brookings Institution, 1985.

This is an exceptional volume on the ebbs and flows of the U.S. ties with the Soviet Union, particularly during the détente period (1970–1977). Raymond Garthoff is a keen observer of the national security implications for both sides.

Gelb, Leslie, with Richard Betts. *The Irony of Vietnam: The System Worked.* Washington, DC: Brookings Institution, 1978.

This fine volume interprets the Vietnam War as a successful part of the grand scheme of our political and national security system. Leslie Gelb, president of the Council on Foreign Relations, and Richard Betts, a Columbia University professor, examine the evolution of the policy from a fresh point of view.

George, Alexander, and Richard Smoke. *Deterrence in American Foreign Policy: Theory and Practice.* New York: Columbia University Press, 1974.

This volume is important for its theoretical contribution to both deterrence and decision-making studies, concluding that deterrence is a fundamental part of U.S. strategy.

Gutman, Roy. *Banana Diplomacy: The Making of American Policy in Nicaragua, 1981–1987.* New York: Simon & Schuster, 1988.

Roy Gutman identifies the obvious and not-so-obvious reasons that the United States decided to take an aggressive counterrevolutionary position against Nicaragua's Sandinista government in the 1980s.

Halberstam, David. *The Best and the Brightest.* 20th Anniversary ed. New York: Random House, 2001.

This is a wonderfully written, fascinating study of the men who came to Washington, DC, under John F. Kennedy, examining the mistakes and assumptions they made and describing how they interacted. These were the men who advised the president to intensify the Vietnam conflict, with fateful consequences.

Halle, Louis. *The Cold War as History.* New York: Harper, Torch Books, 1967.

Thirty-five years later, this is still a remarkably strong and coherent analysis of the dilemmas of the years immediately after World War II, the origins of the Cold War, and the policy choices taken by the United States as it evaluated the new global context.

Halperin, Morton. *Bureaucratic Politics and Foreign Policy.* Washington, DC: Brookings Institution, 1971.

This examination of the effects that bureaucratic politics have on foreign policy decision making is written by one of those who learned the hard way in the Nixon administration. Halperin was a member of the staff that supported Special Assistant to the President for National Security Affairs Henry Kissinger, who thought Halperin was disloyal and had him bugged to see whether he was leaking information.

Harding, Harry. *A Fragile Partnership: The United States and China since 1972.* Washington, DC: Brookings Institution, 1992.

Although it is now somewhat dated, this book provides the best explanation of the difficulties and ties that keep the United States turning to China over the decades. It effectively outlines the benefits and dangers inherent in the relationship for both the United States and China.

Herring, George. *America's Longest War.* New York: McGraw Hill, 1986.

George Herring gives a long, detailed analysis of the evolution of the Vietnam War. This is a masterful study of a complicated period, with emphasis on the Johnson administration.

Hersh, Seymour. *The Price of Power: Kissinger in the White House.* New York: Summit Books, 1993.

This is a highly critical volume on Kissinger's role as special assistant to the president for national security affairs. Seymour Hersh's interpretations of Kissinger's actions are not charitable.

Holloway, David. *Stalin and the Bomb: The Soviet Union and Atomic Energy, 1939–1956.* New Haven, CT: Yale University Press, 1994.

This is the most detailed study in English on Stalin's decisions to develop nuclear weapons. It also includes a great deal of information on the various Soviet spies that were able to infiltrate U.S. and British nuclear establishments.

Holsti, Ole, and James Rosenau. *American Leadership in World Affairs: Vietnam and the Breakdown of Consensus.* Boston: Allen and Unwin, 1984.

This book covers an important period for the United States, when it saw major domestic discontent about national security decision making. Ole Holsti and James Rosenau are important senior scholars who bring a serious understanding to this complex topic.

Huntington, Samuel. *The Clash of Civilizations and the Remaking of the World Order.* New York: Simon and Schuster, 1996.

An outgrowth of a controversial *Foreign Affairs* article on Islam versus the West, this full-length volume explains why the United States and its traditional allies are likely to have problems in the future. Samuel Huntington asserts that there are basic differences between the United States and the Islamic world, and that these differences will lead to violent encounters that are only likely to increase in an era of globalization. Although frequently rejected by many who find the description too simplistic, the book has served as one of the most decisive arguments about the differences between the Judeo-Christian West and the other great civilizations of the world.

————. *The Soldier and the State.* Cambridge: The Belknap Press of Harvard University, 1957.

This is one of the first serious treatments of the question of civil-military affairs in the United States. Huntington advocated a professionalism in the military that has become the standard for many.

Immerman, Richard. *The CIA in Guatemala: The Foreign Policy of Intervention.* Austin: University of Texas Press, 1982.

This is an outstanding study of the CIA's role in the overthrow of Jacobo Arbenz Gúzman in Guatemala in 1954. Focusing on why the intervention occurred, it analyzes the trend toward intervention that characterized U.S. strategy during the Cold War.

Isaacson, Walter, and Evan Thomas. *The Wise Men: Six Friends and the World They Made.* New York: Simon & Schuster, 1986.

This is a most interesting view of six important figures in the earliest years after World War II—individuals from the northeast "establishment" who were crucial in getting the United States through the Cold War. These men—Dean Acheson, John McCloy, George Kennan, William Averill Harriman, Charles Bohlen, and Robert Lovett—were friends as well as influential policy drivers.

Janowitz, Morris. *The Professional Soldier.* New York: The Free Press, 1971.

Along with Huntington's *The Soldier and the State,* this is one of the standards on civil-military professionalism in the United States (the way that the military subordinates itself to civilian leadership in our political system). It is often consulted by strategists around the world who are trying to improve the civil-military relationship.

Johnson, Chalmers. *Blowback: The Costs and Consequences of American Empire.* New York: Owl Books, 2001.

Chalmers Johnson is a long-time critic of many of the U.S. actions in east Asia. Here he shows that there will be significant costs involved in maintaining a global empire, which he accuses the United States of doing in the post–Cold War world.

Kaplan, Robert. *The Coming Anarchy: Shattering the Dreams of the Post–Cold War.* New York: Vintage Books, 2001.

This book stemmed from an *Atlantic Monthly* article, which attracted much attention in the mid-1990s, about decaying states in west Africa and the possible ramifications for U.S. national security strategy. The book expands on the topic to include broader issues.

Karnow, Stanley. *Vietnam.* New York: Viking Books, 1997.

This huge volume, written for the general reader, considers the long history of Western involvement in Vietnam, culminating in the U.S. intervention lasting between 1954 and 1985. Stanley Karnow gives a wide-ranging view of the country and explains how the United States made mistakes in its involvement.

Katz, Milton. *Ban the Bomb.* Westport, CT: Greenwood Press, 1986.

This is a fine book that shows the growth of the Nuclear Freeze movement in the early 1980s. Crisply written, it illustrates the power of a grassroots movement when sufficiently galvanized.

Kennan, George. *Memoirs, 1925–1950.* Boston: Little, Brown, 1967.

This collection of the diplomat's thoughts during a crucial time in the growth of the U.S. role in world affairs is delightful to read. George Kennan's iconoclastic orientation, skillfully expressed, makes it a model for getting to the heart of the U.S. perspective on the international system. Not all readers will be satisfied with his assessment, but most will find Kennan's honesty refreshing.

Kissinger, Henry. *Diplomacy.* New York: Simon & Schuster, 1994.

This is a massive study on the history and applicability of diplomacy in an ever-changing post–Cold War world. Henry Kissinger's analytical skills are on stage as he makes this long and complicated history relatively accessible to the public as well as interested specialists.

———. *Years of Upheaval.* Boston: Little, Brown, 1982.

The second book in Kissinger's trilogy about his time with the Nixon White House, this volume covers the best period for him personally, documenting his evolution from being President

Nixon's special assistant for national security affairs to being secretary of state. For the United States, this was a period of incredible change, including the opening to China, the Antiballistic Missile and Strategic Arms Limitation Treaties signed with the Soviet Union (see chapter 5), the Yom Kippur War, and Nixon's resignation in 1974.

————. *White House Years.* Boston: Little, Brown, 1979.

The first of three volumes of memoirs about being President Richard Nixon's special assistant for national security affairs, Kissinger's book goes into detail about his time in office. It is easy to read, but much of it is a bit hard to accept because he wrote it as an exceptionally skilled bureaucrat, not a political novice coming from academics with no government experience.

————. *Nuclear Weapons and Foreign Policy.* New York: Norton, 1969.

This volume, written before Kissinger attained his fame as a master strategist under President Nixon, was one of the first to examine the question of limited nuclear war. It remains a classic.

Kornbluh, Peter, Malcolm Byrne, and Theodore Draper, eds. *The Iran-Contra Scandal: The Declassified History.* Washington, DC: The New Press, 1993.

This volume is a crucial compendium of the materials relating to the Iran-Contra affair. In an arrangement uncovered in 1986, the Reagan administration traded arms to Iran for hostages in the Middle East and partially funded the Nicaraguan antigovernment guerrillas known as contras, for counterrevolutionaries. This thorough review of the scandal is based on relevant documents, dating from the early 1980s.

LaFeber, Walter. *America, Russia, and the Cold War.* 7th ed. New York: Wiley, 1993.

This fascinating argument about the role that the United States played in initiating the Cold War is written by one of the most prominent historians of his generation. Walter LaFeber is highly critical of the U.S. view that the Soviets were the major cause of the tensions.

Lake, Anthony. *Six Nightmares: Real Threats in a Dangerous World and How America Can Meet Them.* Boston: Little, Brown, 2000.

Anthony Lake, who served as the special assistant to President Clinton for national security affairs, foretold in this book of the "asymmetrical" issues confronting U.S. strategists in the post–September 11 environment, including terrorism, weapons of mass destruction, and other means by which less traditionally powerful states try to have an impact on large, overwhelmingly powerful states like the United States.

Lieber, Robert, ed. *Eagle Rules? Foreign Policy and American Primacy in the Twenty-first Century.* Upper Saddle River, NJ: Prentice Hall Publishing, 2001.

This compilation of essays by several well-versed scholars focuses on themes relating to the U.S. world order. It is compelling and thought provoking as well as a good starting point for looking at the new global environment.

May, Ernest. *Lessons of the Past: The Use and Misuse of History in American Foreign Policy.* New York: Oxford University Press, 1973.

This volume identifies the possible dangers of using history to analyze U.S. foreign policy. Although here Ernest May concentrates on difficult issues of historical theory, his writing is accessible.

Mayers, David. *George Kennan and the Dilemmas of American Foreign Policy.* New York: Oxford University Press, 1988.

David Mayers of Boston University gives a thorough treatment of George Kennan's central role in the post–World War II decision-making arena. Kennan's contribution to the debate, which he won occasionally and lost often, is examined in detail.

McMaster, H. R. *Dereliction of Duty.* New York: Harper, 1997.

This highly acclaimed book studies the civilian and military unwillingness to exercise judgment in the early years of the Vietnam War. When he wrote it, McMaster was an active duty army officer, risking the condemnation of his peers as he elaborated on the military's failings as well as those of the civilian leadership. His work remains a cogent discussion today, when many in the military still feel the civilians alone were at fault for failure in Vietnam.

McNaugher, Thomas. *New Weapons, Old Politics: America's Military Procurement Mess.* Washington, DC: Brookings Institution, 1989.

This book handily explains why the United States appears so frustrated with the process of buying weapons systems. The factors behind this "mess" are domestic as well as international and do not appear likely to change any time in the near future.

Melanson, Richard. *American Foreign Policy since the Vietnam War: The Search for Consensus from Nixon to Clinton.* 3rd ed. Armonk, NY: M.E. Sharpe, 2000.

Here Richard Melanson details the various foreign policy positions taken in presidential administrations since the Nixon period. Nicely written, this book describes the continuities as well as divergences between administrations in a manner accessible to the casual questioner and the more advanced scholar.

Miller, Judith, Stephen Engleberg, and William Broad. *Germs: Bioweapons and America's Secret War.* New York: Simon & Schuster, 2001.

This volume discusses the burgeoning problem of biological agents in international conflict, which are especially threatening to the United States and its homeland because the weapons are small and easily delivered. This work is particularly relevant after the release of anthrax in the autumn of 2001, a crime that killed half a dozen people and still remains unsolved.

Muravchik, Joshua. *The Uncertain Crusade: Jimmy Carter and the Dilemmas of Human Rights.* Lanham, MD: University Press of America, 1986.

The Carter administration's avowed position on the need to delineate human rights responsibilities has been a source of debate in the United States for a quarter of a century. Joshua Muravchik makes clear the difficult choices this stance presented to the country as we sought to respond to states engaging in massive human rights abuses.

Newhouse, John. *Cold Dawn: The Story of SALT.* New York: Holt, Rinehart, and Winston, 1973.

This is an exceptionally interesting description of the process by which the Strategic Arms Limitation Treaty was negotiated, signed, and ratified in the early 1970s.

Nye, Joseph S., Jr. *The Paradox of American Power: Why the World's Only Superpower Can't Go It Alone.* New York: Oxford University Press, 2001.

This is one of a growing number of books criticizing the early months of the George W. Bush administration, joining the many critics who believe the United States is becoming too unilateral in its actions. Nye, a Harvard professor and former Department of Defense official in the Clinton administration, is concerned that this cannot be sustained as a viable policy.

Oye, Kenneth, Donald Rothchild, and Robert Lieber, eds. *Eagle Defiant: United States Foreign Policy in the 1980s.* Boston: Little, Brown, 1983.

This is one of a series of books used as undergraduate textbooks on U.S. foreign affairs. Its title illustrates the mood that was prevalent in the Reagan administration. The coeditors were able to attract a prestigious group of scholars to write the individual chapters.

———. *Eagle Entangled: U.S. Foreign Policy in a Complex World.* New York: Longman, 1979.

The first of a series of compilations used at U.S. universities and colleges, this book discusses the pessimism about the U.S. role in the world that prevailed during the end of the Carter administration.

Paterson, Thomas, ed. *Major Problems in American Foreign Policy.* Vol. 1, *Since 1914.* 3rd ed. Lexington: D.C. Heath, 1989.

This volume is a treasure trove of information on national security. Several of the essays, such as that by Barton Bernstein, are truly fundamental to understanding the nature of U.S. security concerns and national consensus after World War II. Many original documents are included in the volume along with these essays, offering readers the opportunity to probe in some depth into the issues facing the United States over the past five decades in a coherent, structured manner.

Paterson, Thomas, J. Garry Clifford, and Kenneth Hagan. *American Foreign Policy: A History.* Lexington, MA: D.C. Heath, 1977.

This is an outstanding history of U.S. foreign policy.

Peele, Gillian. *Revival and Reaction: The Right in Contemporary America.* Oxford: Clarendon Press, 1984.

Gillian Peele is a British historian who here documents the role of the Christian Right and conservatives in the development of foreign policy in the early 1980s. A most critical view of their influence and abilities, this volume is different from most U.S. studies of the conservative Right. Because Peele is an outside observer, not part of the U.S. political system, she is able to reveal the contradictions and incongruities of the Right's role in national security.

Phillips, Kevin. *The Emerging Republican Majority.* New Rochelle, NY: Arlington House, 1969.

This book is not exclusively about foreign affairs, but it merits inclusion in this chapter because it so presciently describes the political changes that transformed the United States in the late 1960s. It describes the power of the civil rights legislation of 1964–1965 to influence the U.S. political system and, by extension, national security affairs.

Pillar, Paul R., and Michael H. Armacost. *Terrorism and U.S. Foreign Policy.* Washington, DC: Brookings Institution, 2001.

This study considers the risks that the United States faces from a variety of terrorist agents. It illustrates how complex it is to trace the perpetrators and outlines the difficulties facing a democratic society as it seeks to balance defense against terrorist threats with basic societal desires and norms.

Powell, Colin. *My American Journey.* London: Hutchinson, 1995.

This autobiography was written before Colin Powell became secretary of state under George W. Bush. Candid, clear, and politically savvy, this volume reveals the real dynamics of politics in the U.S. national security establishment. Powell proved himself skillful both as a soldier and as a politician, rising to become the special assistant to the president for national security affairs and chairman of the Joint Chiefs during the era of the fall of the Berlin Wall.

Prados, John. *Presidents' Secret Wars.* New York: William Morrow, 1986.

This volume, written by an extremely well-respected independent historian, delineates the covert actions available to presidents in the aftermath of World War II.

Quandt, William. *Camp David: Politics and Peacemaking.* Washington, DC: Brookings Institution, 1986.

William Quandt, who was on the National Security Council during the Carter administration, here presents a superb description of the evolution of the Camp David process from a complete absence of communication between Israel and Egypt in the early 1970s to the signing of an agreement at the end of the decade.

Rhodes, Richard. *The Making of the Hydrogen Bomb.* New York: Simon & Schuster, 1995.

This volume presents a fascinating and detailed elucidation of the scientific history and the decision-making process that led to the hydrogen bomb and a greater human capability for destruction. Written in a highly readable style, this volume shows the national security pressures that were exerted on decision makers in Washington and abroad. It serves as a companion to Rhodes's earlier work, *The Making of the Atomic Bomb.*

———. *The Making of the Atomic Bomb.* New York: Simon & Schuster, 1986.

This is the single most lucid and accessible scientific, technical, and strategic assessment of how the atomic bomb altered the course of history and the U.S. national security establishment. A tour de force on a highly technical topic, Richard Rhodes's work makes it clear that the men making the decisions were mere mortals.

Richelson, Jeffrey. *The U.S. Intelligence Community.* Cambridge, MA: Harper & Row, 1989.

Over the years, Jeffrey Richelson has written extensively about intelligence, and this is probably his most comprehensive contribution to the field.

Sanders, Jerry. *Peddlers of Crisis: The Committee on the Present Danger.* Boston: South End Press, 1983.

In this book, Jerry Sanders presents a very different history of the early years of the Cold War than most other authors. He details the influence of the Committee on the Present Danger on U.S. policy toward the Soviet Union in the 1940s and 1950s.

Schoultz, Lars. *National Security and United States Policy toward Latin America.* Princeton, NJ: Princeton University Press, 1987.

Lars Schoultz, a major scholar in the field of Latin American studies, describes in this book how the United States has discovered threats in Latin America and responded with policies that then created long-term distrust between the region and the United States. More scholarly than popular in its approach, it is well worth reading to understand the cycle of "neglect" and "attention" that characterizes U.S.–Latin American relations.

Shultz, George. *Turmoil and Triumph: My Years as Secretary of State.* New York: Scribner's, 1993.

The memoirs by this former secretary of state are illuminating not only for its description of the wide range of issues he addressed in six years as secretary, but also for its examination of the bureaucratic and ideological battles fought within the administration. George Shultz's ability to demonstrate the pettiness of some of the arguments is most interesting.

Smith, Hedrick. *The Power Game: How Washington Works.* New York: Random House, 1988.

This book considers domestic politics as well as national security questions. It reminds the reader that national security concerns, while important, are frequently not treated any differently than a farm bill in Washington.

Talbott, Strobe. *End Game: The Inside Story of SALT II.* New York: Harper & Row, 1979.

In this volume Strobe Talbott details the long negotiations about the Strategic Arms Limitation Talks that lead to a treaty in the final full year of the Carter administration.

Taylor, Maxwell. *The Uncertain Trumpet.* New York: Harper, 1959.

This book by the man who went on to be chairman of the Joint Chiefs and a major figure in the development of John F. Kennedy's Vietnam policy illustrates the assumptions about Soviet expansionism that were prevalent among the military and civilian elite midway through the Cold War.

Timperlake, Edward, and William C. Triplett II. *Red Dragon Rising: Communist China's Military Threat to America.* Washington, DC: Regnery Publishers, 1999.

This volume is an alarmist's view of the rising Chinese threat against the world in general and against the United States in particular. Triplett and Timperlake take the most adverse possible view of Chinese actions and assume China will succeed and that the United States will fail.

Vise, David A. *The Bureau and the Mole: The Unmasking of Robert Philip Hanssen, the Most Dangerous Double Agent in FBI History.* New York: Atlantic Monthly Press, 2001.

Robert Hanssen's capture in 2001 was a shocking blow that started a year of bad news for the FBI, culminating in its inability to anticipate or prevent the terrorist attacks in September. David Vise goes into excruciating detail about what should have been seen but was ignored about Hanssen, allowing him to cause tremendous damage to counterespionage and the bureau over many years.

Walker, Martin. *The Cold War: A History.* New York: Holt, 1993.

As former Washington correspondent for the *Manchester Guardian*, Martin Walker has apt and cogent insights about the way the United States viewed its role in the international system during the Cold War. This book offers somewhat of a different twist on Cold War history, and many of Walker's observations will annoy those in the United States who fancy their motives to have been pure and without prejudice.

Waller, Douglas. *Congress and the Nuclear Freeze.* Amherst, MA: University of Massachusetts Press, 1987.

In the years since the Reagan administration, it is often hard to remember what a strong grassroots effort the Nuclear Freeze movement was. Douglas Waller reminds us how the concerns of average citizens resonated in Congress during a period of major foreign policy upheaval.

Waltz, Kenneth. *Man, State and War.* New York: Columbia University Press, 1969.

This book takes a political science approach to predict how international conflict is likely to transpire in the future. Written by one of the major figures in international relations theory, it remains a major influence on the theoretical side of national security studies forty years after it appeared.

Williams, William Appleman. *The Tragedy of American Diplomacy.* Cleveland: World Publishing Company, 1962.

One of the most critical historians of U.S. national security, William Williams undercuts ideas of U.S. altruism and casts stones at the idea that the United States had global interests entirely in mind as it reconstructed the post–World War II environment.

Wills, Garry. *Reagan's America: Innocents at Home.* Garden City, NY: Doubleday, 1987.

With his customary wit, Garry Wills slams the hypocrisy and naiveté with which the United States conducts its foreign engagements. Well written and stinging, this book gives a sense of how the United States focused on foreign affairs while choosing to look the other way about things at home during the 1980s.

Yergin, Daniel. *The Prize: The Epic Quest for Oil, Money and Power.* New York: Simon & Schuster, 1991.

Here Daniel Yergin presents a detailed history of the role that petroleum has played in world affairs and national security around the world. This book was the basis for a PBS video series in the early 1990s.

————. *Shattered Peace: The Origins of the Cold War and the National Security State.* Boston: Houghton, Mifflin, 1977.

This volume explains some of the fundamental shifts after World War II that initiated the Cold War and inspired an enhanced concern about national security that previously had been absent from the U.S. perspective.

Articles

Bell, Daniel. **"The End of American Exceptionalism."** *Public Interest,* vol. 41 (1975).

This article explains why the United States viewed itself as different from all other nations in the mid-1970s. The "end" that the title refers to has not arrived, but it is still a compelling article.

Betts, Richard K. **"Fixing Intelligence."** *Foreign Affairs,* vol. 81, no. 1 (January/February 2002).

One of the most enduring academic analysts of the intelligence community argues that there are some basic problems that will always confront the country, preventing perfect protection from both mistakes and the types of attacks that produce September 11 catastrophes.

Brownstein, Ron. **"The New Politics of National Security."** *Public Opinion,* vol. 11 (1988).

Ron Brownstein, a reporter for the *Los Angeles Times,* describes the variety of politics that were operative in national security circles in the late months of the Reagan administration.

Buruma, Ian, and Margalit Avisahi. **"Occidentalism."** *New York Review of Books,* vol. 49, no. 1 (January 17, 2002).

This article outlines the basic differences in approach between Western and Eastern philosophies, world views, and approaches to conflict. It is enlightening to contrast with the approach of the

United States to the conflict in Afghanistan with modern terrorism.

Carlson, Allan. **"Foreign Policy and 'the America Way': The Rise and Fall of the Post–World War II Consensus."** *This World,* vol. 5 (1983).

This article examines why U.S. bipartisan consensus died in the early 1980s as pressures on the foreign policy establishment became overwhelming. Some evidence actually supports Carlson's point that divisiveness in U.S. society goes back a decade earlier, but the clear-cut partisan positions on how to approach the world did seem set by the 1980s.

Deibel, Terry. **"Bush's Foreign Policy: Mastery and Inaction."** *Foreign Policy,* vol. 84 (1991).

Written by a professor at the National War College, this article does not join in the euphoric praise of President George H. W. Bush's handling of foreign affairs at the end of the Cold War.

Dworkin, Ronald. **"The Threat to Patriotism."** *New York Review of Books,* vol. 49, no. 3 (February 28, 2002).

Ronald Dworkin argues that the effect of September 11, 2001, was to erode protections of basic civil rights and civil liberties in the United States, with the potential for far more damage than anticipated. While some arguments against the military tribunals and other suspensions of traditional rights are weak, many opponents are correctly pointing to a tremendous problem.

Garrett, Laurie. **"The Nightmare of Bioterrorism."** *Foreign Affairs,* vol. 80, no. 1 (January/February 2001).

Here Laurie Garrett follows her earlier book on exotic diseases such as the Ebola virus with a strong assessment of the difficulties of preventing or controlling bioterrorism. This is a balanced and well-researched work in a field that had received little public attention until recently.

Gershman, Carl. **"The Rise and Fall of the New Foreign-Policy Establishment."** *Commentary,* vol. 24 (July 1980).

This article criticizes the changes that affected foreign policy decision makers at the beginning of the Reagan era.

Gill, Bates, and Michael O'Hanlon. **"China's Hollow Military."** *The National Interest,* no. 56 (summer 1999).

This provocative article argues that U.S. policymakers and analysts who view China as a major military threat considerably overestimate the capabilities of the People's Liberation Army. The article generated a response on China's role as a regional hegemon by two other prominent scholars in the field, former Ambassador James Lilley and Deputy Secretary of State Carl Ford (see p. 314).

Hillen, John. **"U.N. Collective Security: Chapter Six and a Half."** *Parameters,* vol. 24 (spring 1994).

John Hillen, a former Special Forces officer, was highly critical of the Clinton administration's willingness to engage in foreign intervention that, in his opinion, did not support U.S. national interests. This article points out problems with the idea of collective security.

Holsti, Ole. **"Widening Gap between the U.S. Military and Civilian Society? Some Evidence, 1976–1996."** *International Security,* vol. 23 (1998/1999).

Here Ole Holsti argues that the social changes that appear to be pulling civilian society and the armed forces apart are manifest in public opinion data.

Kennan, George (pseudonym Mr. X). **"The Sources of Soviet Conduct."** *Foreign Affairs,* vol. 25 (July 1947).

This article by George Kennan, a true classic, is most often labeled as the basis of the containment policy by which the United States dealt with the Soviet Union for forty years. Kennan later claimed that his notion of containment was vastly misunderstood, and that the containment policy itself was not his goal. The article remains an amazing commentary on the Stalinist state (see p. 144).

Kirkpatrick, Jeane. **"Dictatorships and Double Standards."** *Commentary,* November 1979.

This article was thought to express the rationale behind the Reagan administration's willingness to engage closely with brutal authoritarian governments, particularly in the Western

Hemisphere, in the early 1980s. Jeane Kirkpatrick distinguished between authoritarian states and totalitarian states, arguing that the United States had the opportunity to alter authoritarian states while totalitarian states were impossible to change.

Kohn, Richard. **"Out of Control: The Crisis in Civil-Military Relations."** *National Interest*, vol. 35 (spring 1994).

A highly controversial article by a former Historian of the Air Force and highly respected scholar, this piece notes that the armed forces in the United States, particularly under Chairman of the Joint Chiefs of Staff General Colin Powell, has become too powerful in the civil-military equation, largely because the civilian realm is too weak.

Krauthammer, Charles. **"The Unipolar Moment."** *Foreign Affairs: America and the World 1990/1991*, vol. 70, no. 1 (1991).

In this article, Charles Krauthammer argues that the United States alone had unparalleled power in the aftermath of the fall of the Soviet Union. His article has been cited frequently since the terrorist attacks of September 11, 2001, especially by those who no longer share this view of U.S. hegemony.

Lake, Anthony. **"Confronting Backlash States."** *Foreign Affairs*, vol. 73 (March/April 1994).

The Clinton administration was criticized for spending too much political and military capital on nonvital national interests, but early in the administration Anthony Lake made this compelling argument for the importance of these seemingly peripheral areas.

Layne, Christopher. **"Kant or Cant: The Myth of Democratic Peace."** *International Security*, vol. 19 (1994).

The basic assumption that democracies do not fight each other and are stabilizing forces in the world comes under sharp criticism in this piece. Christopher Layne has long been a critic of any foreign policy that extends beyond defense of the national interest in the most restricted sense of the term.

Lilley, James, and Carl Ford. **"China's Military: A Second Opinion."** *The National Interest*, no. 57 (fall 1999).

In this rejoinder to the Gill and O'Hanlon article published earlier in 1999 (see p. 312), former Ambassador James Lilley and Deputy Secretary of State Carl Ford question the measure being used to assess Chinese military power. Arguing that the accurate term of comparison is not the United States but other militaries in East Asia, they come to a different conclusion about the Chinese threat.

Mallaby, Sebastian. **"The Reluctant Imperialist."** *Foreign Affairs,* vol. 81, no. 2 (March/April 2002).

This article argues that the United States is taking on the role of world guardian and imperialist, albeit reluctantly. Mallaby believes that this trend will only continue, contrary to assertions by President Bush during his election campaign.

Mearsheimer, John. **"Why We Will Soon Miss the Cold War."** *Atlantic Monthly,* August 1990.

In an article that surprised many, this University of Chicago professor argued that the United States would soon miss the predictability and structure of the Cold War as the country tried to find a course in a post–Cold War world.

Pfaff, William. **"The Question of Hegemony."** *Foreign Affairs,* vol. 80, no. 1 (January/February 2001).

William Pfaff, a U.S. citizen living in Paris, criticizes the goal of hegemony as part of U.S. strategy in the world. Pfaff's views are frequently seen as a barometer of public opinion in Europe, which is dubious of the long-term benefits of U.S. policies.

Ricks, Thomas. **"The Widening Gap between the Military and Society."** *Atlantic Monthly,* July 1997.

Thomas Ricks's work is always skillful and thoughtful, and it always stretches the normal journalistic perspective. This article argues that there is indeed a growing civil-military gap in the United States that needs be addressed.

"The Tiananmen Papers." Introduction by Andrew J. Nathan. *Foreign Affairs,* vol. 80, no 1 (January/February 2001).

This article in the widely read journal *Foreign Affairs* remains controversial among China specialists but is believed to be an accurate portrayal of the debate within the Communist Party of China in 1989, when the leadership decided to send tanks into Tiananmen Square to end the student demonstration. The article, based on a longer book, indicates serious divisions within the leadership and portrays a party quite concerned about its ability to maintain power.

Tucker, Nancy. **"A Precarious Balance: Clinton and China."** *Current History,* vol. 97 (1998).

This article illustrates the problems that Washington faces as it tries to balance long-standing but conflicting commitments to various interests in the Sino-U.S. relationship. The United States is not merely worried about Taiwan's security or the possibility that it might declare its independence from the mainland; the United States also has growing economic interests, religious concerns, and human rights cautions about China, just as China is modernizing and seeking to take what it believes is its rightful role as a world power alongside the United States.

Wolf, Martin. **"Will the Nation-State Survive Globalization?"** *Foreign Affairs,* vol. 80, no. 1 (January/February 2001).

This article poses a pivotal question about whether the tide of globalization—that phenomenon of economic ties binding the world together in recently unimaginable ways—will overcome the utility of the nation-state.

Series

Country Handbooks of the World. Washington, DC: GPO, various years.

This series is published by the Federal Research Division of the Library of Congress. Written by Library of Congress or academic specialists, volumes in this series focus on individual countries that might not be familiar to U.S. readers or where U.S. forces might be sent. The series is intended to orient the newcomer to the issues and concerns relating to each country.

EIU Country Reports. London: *Economist,* various dates.

The Economist Intelligence Unit (EIU) publishes periodic assessments of political and economic conditions and projections for individual states. These reports are available both on-line and in print. The EIU has offices in London and New York and representatives in other cities around the world.

Foreign Relations of the United States. Produced by the Office of the Historian, United States State Department. Washington, DC: GPO, various years.

Published on an annual basis, the books in this series present a thorough presentation of major agreements, treaties, letters, transcripts, and other documents relevant to U.S. foreign affairs.

Major Problems in American Foreign Policy. Edited by Thomas G. Paterson. Lexington: D.C. Heath, various years.

The volumes in this series present a bountiful discussion of many issues facing national security strategists. I highly recommend the volumes not only for their source material but for their references.

Reilly, John. *American Public Opinion and U.S. Foreign Policy 1995.* Chicago: Chicago Council on Foreign Relations, 1995.
————. *American Public Opinion and U.S. Foreign Policy 1991.* Chicago: Chicago Council on Foreign Relations, 1991.
————. *American Public Opinion and U.S. Foreign Policy 1987.* Chicago: Chicago Council on Foreign Relations, 1987.
————. *American Public Opinion and U.S. Foreign Policy 1979.* Chicago: Chicago Council on Foreign Relations, 1979.
————. *American Public Opinion and U.S. Foreign Policy 1975.* Chicago: Chicago Council on Foreign Relations, 1975.

Every four years, the Chicago Council on Foreign Relations (see chapter 6) conducts polls to gain a sense of how the U.S. elite and the population at large view national security and foreign affairs. The questions are formulated and the answers are tabulated by some of the most sophisticated pollsters in the country.

Nonprint Resources

This section is divided into several categories: World Wide Web resources, including search engines and individual Web sites on national security issues; and video and DVD recordings. There are some obvious and unavoidable overlaps, such as television or radio sources that also maintain Web sites. Remember, except for the most casual inquiry, the Internet is only a basic starting point; anyone interested in solid research should consult a reference librarian.

The World Wide Web

A vast expanse of information about national security is available on the Web to both casual and serious researchers who are willing to sleuth a bit. One advantage to Web-based information is there is no limit to the amount of information a researcher might find at a single Web site. A single site might house an author's entire collection, citing links to other related sites. Or a Web site may consist of only a single article. For example, the U.S.-China Security Review Commission makes available files of its assessments on the bilateral economic and security relationship between the United States and China. These files can be found at the U.S.-China Security Review Commission Web site, http://www.uscc.gov/rese.htm.

Another advantage of the Web is that the author's ability to organize links to various topics is virtually unrestrained. A good site will present a wide array of information and will arrange links to this information to allow the easiest access to the user. However, the World Wide Web has significant redundancies, and each site is only as organized as the person who created it. Helpful sites are abundant, but so are disorganized and unreliable sites. The researcher must be able first to find the relevant sites, and then to assess their quality.

Search Engines

Probably the most basic way to start finding resources on the Web is by using on-line search engines, also called portals. A search engine is a system by which the researcher gains access to various entry points on the World Wide Web. These engines allow users to find specific information; the user initiates a search by typing in the name of a specific topic or keyword(s) (e.g., "national security"), and the search engine locates appropriate sites, sometimes by the thousands. In a sense, a search engine is like a card catalogue or a reference librarian in that it helps the researcher search an entire database. A variety of search engines are available, although no single one is likely to get each and every document or speech or reference on a topic, including national security. This is because there is no systematic way by which the Web accesses the materials; unfortunately, things are somewhat more haphazard than that.

Some search engines are by subscription only, such as FirstSearch, but many are free and open to everyone with Internet access. Of the free search engines, I recommend using Google (http://www.google.com) as an excellent method of finding national security items. Other popular general search engines include Yahoo! (http://www.yahoo.com) and Alta Vista (http://www.altavista.com).

Additionally, there are specialized search engines for specific fields of inquiry. The search engines most relevant to national security studies include http://www.FirstGov.org, which is a U.S. government–sponsored site for locating materials in the vast federal government; http://www.SearchGov.com, which accesses materials such as the *CIA Factbook* on-line; and http://www.SearchMil.com, which gets the researcher into a variety of Web sites on the military. Another search engine, http://www.refdesk.com, was recommended by Secretary of State Colin Powell in an interview soon after he took office. One of its major search categories is foreign and national security issues. Each of these search engines will take the inquirer to Web sites replete with national security issues.

Selected Web Sites on National Security Issues
Foreign Broadcast Information Service
fbiscsd@rccb.osis.gov

World News Connection
http://www.wnc.fedworld.gov

The Foreign Broadcast Information Service (FBIS) and the World News Connection (WNC) are among the most valuable sources of information on national security available anywhere in the world. The Central Intelligence Agency (CIA) translates newspaper articles and radio and television broadcasts from countries around the world into English. Those translations then appear in an on-line digest (prior to 1996 FBIS was a print service), which is available to federal government employees through the FBIS and in a slightly different format through the WNC, which can be purchased on a weekly, monthly, or annual basis. FBIS is available on CD-ROM as well.

Global Trends 2015: A Dialogue about the Future with Nongovernment Experts
http://www.cia.gov/cia/publications/globaltrends2015

This study by the Central Intelligence Agency uses non-CIA scholars and specialists to ponder the range of changes the world will face by 2015. It concludes that this will be a vastly more dangerous world, with many more possible enemies and linkages between them through technology, globalization, and improved communication.

National War College
http://www.ndu.edu/nwc/index.htm

A major source of information on-line is the National War College, with many links to national security–related Web sites. The War College site is updated regularly, and its links provide diverse and important ties to other places in the world. Additionally, many members of the college faculty have their own individual Web pages that include links to various locations on the World Wide Web, both in the U.S. government and in the private sector.

Radio Free Europe/Radio Liberty
http://www.rferl.org/

Radio Free Europe and Radio Liberty (RFE/RL) are services of the U.S. government that go back to the height of the Cold War. They highlight issues in Europe and the former Soviet Union, but their work extends elsewhere as well. For example, they broadcast programs to Iraq under the guise of trying to oust Saddam Hussein from office. RFE/RL offers on-line radio service at http://www.rferl.org/realaudio/.

STRATFOR (Strategic Forecasting)
http://www.stratfor.com

A daily or immediate message delivery system is becoming a more popular way to keep up-to-date in national security affairs. Although CNN or the *New York Times* provide the best-known message delivery services, there are others. One of the most frequently cited for its focus on international affairs is STRATFOR (Strategic Forecasting), based in Austin, Texas. A subscription service, STRATFOR also offers free reports and news briefs and alerts via e-mail.

University of Texas at Austin
http://libraryweb.utep.edu/

The library at the University of Texas at Austin has an extensive Web linkage system. A helpful beginning point for researching national security issues is the "History and Biography Websites" page, located at http://libraryweb.utep.edu/ref/histweb.html.

Wall Street Journal
http://www.wsj.com

The *Wall Street Journal* Web site has pages that focus on international issues in Europe, Asia, and Latin America.

Many serial publications now appear on-line. These may be produced by commercial concerns, not-for-profit organizations, or the government. For example, the Center for Defense Information, a not-for-profit organization, publishes electronic editions of its serial publication, *Weekly Defense Monitor,* available at http://www.cdi.org/weekly/. The easiest method for locating these resources is through a reference librarian, particularly at a Federal Repository Library. See the Print Resources section of this chapter for the Web addresses of many periodicals relevant to national security studies.

This is just a small sample of Web-based materials relevant to national security. The following is a list of other useful links. Although not exhaustive, it will certainly provide researchers in the field with a place to start.

- http://www.access.gpo.gov/su_docs/index.htmls offers free electronic access to federal government products on-line and is a crucial entry into the world of federal publications.
- http://www.lib.umich.edu/govdocs/fedlegis.html allows users to obtain reports from the Congressional Research Service, which works for Congress.
- http://www.defenselink.mil is a home page for Department of Defense (DOD) information.
- http://www.defenselink.mil/pubs/dod101/ is an introduction link for the DOD.

- http://www.defenselink.mil/pubs/almanac/ provides information and statistical information about the DOD.
- http://www.hqda.army.mil/library/DODAUTH.html lists National Defense Authorization Laws.
- http://www.hqda.army.mil/library/DODAPPR.html lists National Defense Appropriation Laws.
- fedlaw.gas.gov/legal22.htm is a site devoted to legal issues in the military.
- fedlaw.gsa.gov/fedfra20.htm is devoted to international and foreign affairs.
- fedlaw.gas.gov/fedfr22q.htm is on national security and intelligence.
- http://www.gao.gov provides access to General Accounting Office materials.
- www2.whitehouse.gov/WH/EOP/NSC/html/ documents/nssrpref-1299.html lists the National Security Strategy Reports required under the 1986 Goldwater Nichols Military Reform Act.
- http://speakout.com/ accesses U.S. think tanks.
- http://www.state.gov/www/regions_missions.html allows one to find Web sites for U.S. missions overseas.
- wps.cfc.dnd.ca/links/milorg/ is a Canadian site that provides details on the armed forces of the world.
- http://www.ndu.edu./library/library.html provides access to the National Defense University Library.

Most organizations, including those listed in chapter 6, have Web sites that give detailed information about themselves and frequently include links to other groups.

Videos and DVDs

Video Series

A wide array of video series focus on national security issues. The Corporation for Public Broadcasting (CPB) and its Public Broadcasting Service (PBS) produce videos for broadcasting on the network of PBS stations across the country. Their series have included *War and Peace in the Nuclear Age, The Prize, Frontline, Vietnam,* and others.

Frontline is a weekly series that covers an impressive range of issues. In January 2002, in the aftermath of September 11, *Frontline* was quick to craft an hour-long program focusing on terrorism. Similarly, it did a program entitled "Dangerous Strait" to document the problems confronting the United States and China as they work together with the issue of Taiwan dividing them. *Frontline* has covered drug trafficking, biochemical warfare, and many other issues relating to national security concerns. The listing of all *Frontline* programs is available at http://www.frontline.com. Further information on the Corporation for Public Broadcasting is available at http://www.pbs.org.

In 1997–1998, the Cable News Network produced a twenty-four part series called *The Cold War*, which makes available new details on the entire Cold War period through interviews and detailed analysis. The series, shown on the Cable News Network, is also available on video from Warner Home Video (COLD WAR, P.O. Box 2385, Maple Plain, MN 55592-2385; (800) 750-8585; On-line orders: http://www.cnn.com/SPECIALS/cold.war/home.video/index.html).

The Insight Media *World Civilization* series includes programs focusing on Asia, China, Japan, India, Asian religions, Islam, the U.S. government, and world history topics. Contact information for the organization is: 2162 Broadway, New York, NY 10024-0621; (212) 721-6316 or (800) 233-9910.

Of course, not all video series on U.S. national security come from the United States. The British Broadcasting Corporation (BBC) has created several excellent series, including the *World at War, War at Sea,* and others. Information on these and other videos is available at the BBC Web site, http://www.bbc.co.uk.

Individual Video/DVD Recordings

Individual visual recordings that are particularly useful for classroom or educational applications include C-SPAN materials, declassified materials, commercial network productions, and university productions. C-SPAN is a television network that frequently records major discussions on national security topics and makes the videos available for users across the country. C-SPAN videos include "The Role of the National Security Adviser." Productions from the University of Virginia include "Foreign Policy for a Global Age." An organization from Louisville, Kentucky, called Declassified Films produced "Nuclear Weapons of the United States Navy" and "Air Delivery of Nuclear Weapons." There are numerous producers of videos and DVDs, so the best way to locate them is with the help of a reference librarian who can demonstrate how to use FirstSearch (FirstSearch.com). FirstSearch will locate U.S. government videos as well as commercial videos, so it gives access to gems like "National Strategies and Capabilities for a Changing World," produced by the Office of the Deputy Chief of Staff for Operations and Plans of the Department of the Army.

The following list includes a few more of the many videos that deal effectively with national security issues.

"Ambush in Mogadishu"
Frontline
60 minutes, 1 cassette
$19.98
Public Broadcasting Service

This documentary on the problems faced by U.S. Special Forces in Mogadishu, Somalia, on October 3, 1993, causes the civilian and military viewer alike to note how conflict has changed. The complexities and advantages of modern technology did not save soldiers faced with an ambush in an urban setting in one of the poorest countries in the world. Additionally, it shows why seemingly "impartial" interventions are rarely seen that way by the people on the ground.

"Dangerous Straits"
60 minutes, 1 cassette
$19.98
Public Broadcasting Service

This study of the relationship across the Taiwan Strait, arguably the place where the United States is most likely to go to war to protect an ally, illustrates how frustrating complex policy can be. This study, conducted in the months before September 2001, showed the deterioration of Sino-U.S. relations and the role that Taiwan plays in the U.S. political scene.

"Dot.Con"
60 minutes, 1 cassette
$29.98
Public Broadcasting Service

This documentary describes the role of globalization in the international economy, with evidence that the "dot.com" phenomenon, the rise of high-tech Internet businesses, may have been more of a chimera than a hard and proven fact. It also illustrates how quickly this seeming success collapsed for many, with paper profits disappearing for all but the biggest stockholders.

"The Fifty Years War: Israel and the Arabs"
200 minutes, 2 DVD disks
$34.98
Public Broadcasting Service

This documentary focuses on the ups and downs, the sorrows and joys of the half century in which Arabs and Israelis have tried to coexist in the ancient land of Palestine. It is compelling and heartbreaking at the same time because neither side feels it is in the least wrong and, therefore, both remain unwilling to concede.

"Gunning for Saddam"
60 minutes, 1 cassette
$19.98
Public Broadcasting Service

Saddam Hussein was the target of U.S. forces trying to oust the Iraqis from Kuwait in the Persian Gulf War of 1991. President George H. W. Bush chose not to press into Baghdad but made it clear that he hoped Hussein would fall. Instead, more than a decade later, the Iraqi leader is still in power and the United States finds him more frustrating all the time. This study looks at U.S. efforts to achieve consensus about ousting him, a task that is increasingly difficult by all standards.

"In Search of Bin Laden"
60 minutes, 1 cassette
$14.95
Public Broadcasting Service

The wealthy son of a Saudi construction engineer, Usama Bin Laden has become the most wanted man in the world after he apparently masterminded the attacks on the United States in September 2001. This fascinating study outlines efforts by the international community to track him down, highlighting his ability to elude capture or surveillance. The video reveals the frustration of the United States in its inability to find him, despite high-tech surveillance and cash rewards to those who might turn him in.

"Inside the Terror Network"
60 minutes, 1 cassette
$19.98
Public Broadcasting Service

This impressive study of the links between terrorists explains the roots of terrorism and the motivations of the people involved. It explains that terrorists are no longer merely disgruntled with a particular ruler but rather are dissatisfied with a way of life and fascinated with the money that can finance virtually anything.

"The Prize: Oil, Money, and Power"
8 hours, 4 cassettes

"The Prize" is an excellent discussion of how petroleum became so important to the international economy as well as the United States. The video series is a marvelous adaptation of the Pulitzer Prize winning book by Daniel Yergin.

Commercial Media

Cable and Television

Although newspapers, journals, and monographs are the traditional mediums for discussing national security issues, the information available regularly through the ever-increasing access to radio and cable television is also important. Cable News Network (CNN), founded by media mogul Ted Turner in 1980, is a daily, constant source of material from around the world. CNN also has subsidiary networks, such as CNNFn for financial information, CNN Headline News for briefer accounts of major stories, and CNN in Spanish, manifesting CNN's commitment to Spanish-language viewers. The CNN main Web site (http://www. cnn.com) includes links to all of the CNN sites. The major competition to CNN from abroad is the British Broadcasting Corporation, which has extensive international service. Sky Television is another source of news with an international flavor.

The U.S. commercial television networks concentrate less on national security and foreign issues than they did during the Cold War, but they remain relevant. National security information is provided on news and information programs from the major commercial networks: the American Broadcasting Corporation

(ABC: http://abc.abcnews.go.com/), the National Broadcasting Corporation (NBC: http://www.nbc.com), the Columbia Broadcasting Service (CBS: http://www.cbs.com), and Fox Television (http://www.fox.com/home.htm). Fox is the newest national network, with a significant commitment to national security stories. As mentioned previously, the Corporation for Public Broadcasting (CPB: http://www.cpb.org/) produces many programs relevant to national security. The CPB and its flagship news production, *The NewsHour with Jim Lehrer*, get considerable information from foreign reporters, and they also maintain their own reporters. The *NewsHour* Web site is http://www.newshour.com.

A great number of television stations have appeared since the advent of cable and satellite television. Many, however, are outgrowths of the traditional networks. MSNBC, a joint effort by Microsoft and NBC, and CNBC (Cable NBC) are both headquartered in NBC. The effect is that the actual number of news sources is not nearly as large as it might seem from the number of individual news entities because the reporters tend to be shared—in this case, across the NBC family, and the independent news outlets are not that numerous. Also worth noting is the possibility of a "feedback loop" by which one outlet reports something and the item then appears on another outlet and is continually noted as something new when in fact it is merely repeated news.

Radio

The United States has major investments in Radio Free Europe/Radio Liberty, Voice of America, and Radio Libertad. Each of these is a public diplomacy arm of the U.S. government. Beginning in the 1940s, the United States felt that radio broadcasting was an effective way to influence the thought of average citizens in Communist areas of the world. The same commitment has been continued to non-Communist areas, such as Iraq under Saddam Hussein and other areas with governments identified as opponents of the United States.

Although not as commonly used in the United States as it was before the advent of television and other mediums, radio probably still remains the major source of national security news around the world. The United States has a plethora of news sources on radio, but relatively few of them specialize in national security concerns. The major news outlets on television, ABC,

CBS, CNN, NBC, and Fox, all have radio services, tied to their television sources. Additionally, National Public Radio and Public Radio International are two outlets with high interest in international affairs. Finally, the Mutual Broadcasting Network has been reporting on national security affairs for many years and is available in most places around the country.

BBC Radio (http://www.bbc.co.uk/radio/) is accessible in the United States, both on long- and short-wave bands. Similarly, the German broadcaster Deutsche Welle (http://dw-world.de/) is a major source of radio news around the world, with a strong concentration on issues in Europe. The Canadian Broadcasting Corporation (CBC: http://www.cbc.ca/radioone/) is a major source for information on international security around the world. If one speaks foreign languages, it is also worthwhile to investigate domestic radio programming, as radio programs in virtually every state around the world report on subjects of national and international concern. Occasionally broadcasters also offer programs in English, such as the Israeli *Kol Israel* (The Voice of Israel), and these often contain information on U.S. national security concerns. However, one must remember that the target audience speaks the language of the country, so English is generally less useful.

Newspapers and Wire Services

All of the major newspapers in the United States cover national security and international affairs. The *Washington Post, New York Times, Christian Science Monitor, Washington Times, Los Angeles Times, Wall Street Journal,* and *Chicago Tribune* all have well-staffed foreign bureaus. These papers occasionally get information from the Associated Press (United Press International, which was the other major international news bureau in the United States, went bankrupt in the 1990s). Reuters, a British news service, is also used by a variety of U.S. news sources.

U.S. newspapers and other media almost always publish Web editions as well as print editions. It would be impossible to list each one of these, but here is a list of some of the newspapers with useful Web sites that are relevant to national security:

> *Asahi Shimbun* (Japan), http://www.asahi.com
> *Chicago Tribune,* http://www.chicagotribune.com
> *Christian Science Monitor,* http://www.csmonitor.com

Deutsche Zeitung (Germany), http://www.sueddeutsche.de
Economist magazine, http://www.economist.com
Far Eastern Economic Review, http://www.feer.com
Financial Times (London), http://www.FT.com
Manchester Guardian and *Manchester Observer,*
    http://www.guardian.co.uk
Inside U.S. Trade, http://www.insidetrade.com
International Herald Tribune, http://www.iht.com
Japan Digest, http://www.japandigest.com
Le Monde (Paris), http://www.lemonde.fr
New York Times, http://www.nytimes.com
Nikkei (the Tokyo equivalent of the *Wall Street Journal*),
    http://www.nni.nikkei.co.jp
Oriental Economist, http://www.orientaleconomist.com/
Times (London), http://www.thetimes.co.uk
Wall Street Journal, http://online.wsj.com/
Washington Post, http://www.washingtonpost.com
Washington Times, http://www.washingtontimes.com
Yomiuri On-Line, http://www.yomiuri.co.jp/index-e.htm

Index

About the Author

Cynthia A. Watson is a professor of strategy and director of faculty development at the National War College in Washington, DC, where she has been on the faculty since 1992. Dr. Watson earned her M.A. in economic history/Latin American studies at the London School of Economics and her doctorate in government and international studies at the University of Notre Dame. She has also worked for the U.S. House of Representatives and the General Accounting Office as well as at Loyola University and Ithaca College. Dr. Watson is a member of the International Institute for Strategic Studies and a fellow of the Inter-University Seminar on Armed Forces and Society, and she serves on the editorial board of *Third World Quarterly*. Dr. Watson is also certified as fluent in Spanish for Recording for the Blind and Dyslexic, a national resource for people with reading disabilities.

Dr. Watson has written for two decades on political violence, civil-military relations, and national security issues in the United States, Asia, and Latin America. She is author of *U.S. National Security Policy Groups* (1990) and coeditor and contributor to *The Political Use of the Military* (1996). Dr. Watson is completing a book on the collapse of Colombia (expected to be published in late 2002) and is researching civil-military issues in the People's Liberation Army in China.